Wright, Thomas C.

Landowners and reform in Chile

DATE			

Landowners and Reform in Chile

THOMAS C. WRIGHT

Landowners and Reform in Chile

The Sociedad Nacional de Agricultura, 1919-40

UNIVERSITY OF ILLINOIS PRESS
Urbana Chicago London

Library of Congress Cataloging in Publication Data

Wright, Thomas C
Landowners and reform in Chile.

Bibliography: p.
Includes index.
1. Sociedad Nacional de Agricultura de Chile—History.
2. Agriculture and state—Chile—History. 3. Land reform—Chile—History. I. Title.
HD1878 1981.W74 333.3'1'83 80-29663
ISBN 0-252-00853-7

For my mother, and for a fellow historian—my father.

Contents

Tables

Acknowledgments

Many people in Chile and the United States aided me in the project which culminates in this book. The scholars associated with the former Instituto de Investigaciones de Historia Americana—particularly Eugenio Pereira Salas, Gustavo Beyhaut, and Alvaro Jara—were very accommodating and helpful. I wish to thank the staffs of the Biblioteca Nacional, the Biblioteca del Congreso, and the Sociedad Nacional de Agricultura for their generous aid. Dolores Martin and the *Handbook of Latin American Studies* staff facilitated the research during the final stages. I am also indebted to Carolyn Wright for her help and support. I am especially grateful to Arnold Bauer for his friendship and encouragement through the years.

Several colleagues and friends have read the manuscript. I thank Arnold Bauer, Joseph A. Fry, Paul Drake, John S. Wright, Ann Hagerman Johnson, and John Swetnam for their incisive comments and suggestions. Joyce Nelson contributed countless hours of typing. My colleague and wife, Dina Titus, critiqued the manuscript and helped in other ways too numerous to mention.

For financial aid that supported the research, I am grateful to the Latin American Teaching Fellowship program, the University of California-Universidad de Chile Convenio, and the University of Nevada, Las Vegas, research council. A generous grant from the University of Nevada, Las Vegas, helped underwrite the costs of publication.

Abbreviations

CAS	Consorcio Agrícola del Sur (Southern Agricultural Consortium)
CERA	Centro de Reforma Agraria (Agrarian Reform Center)
CONSEMACH	Confederación Nacional de Sindicatos de Empleadores Agrícolas de Chile (National Confederation of Agricultural Employers of Chile)
CORA	Corporación de la Reforma Agraria (Agrarian Reform Corporation)
CORFO	Corporación de Fomento (Chilean Development Corporation)
CTCh	Confederación de Trabajadores de Chile (Chilean Labor Confederation)
FOCh	Federación Obrera de Chile (Chilean Labor Federation)
FRAP	Frente de Acción Popular (Popular Action Front)
INDAP	Instituto de Desarrollo Agropecuario (Agricultural Development Institute)
PDC	Partido Demócrata Cristiano (Christian Democratic Party)
SNA	Sociedad Nacional de Agricultura (National Agricultural Society)
SNM	Sociedad Nacional de Minería (National Mining Society)
SOFOFA	Sociedad de Fomento Fabril (Society for Industrial Development)
UP	Unidad Popular (Popular Unity)

Introduction

The study of Latin American politics has undergone an important shift of emphasis over the past several decades in response to changing perceptions of reality. In the fifties and through much of the sixties, when the cold war and the Cuban Revolution raised the specter or the hope of radical revolution, it was common to approach the study of Latin American political systems with the assumption that important change had occurred and would continue, even accelerate, in the future. Political change was considered inevitable: one could simply wait for revolution to take place or, as envisioned in the Alliance for Progress, implement reform to preempt the revolutionaries. Political scientists and historians during this period investigated current and past patterns of political change, seeking to understand, to predict, or to control the process. The prevailing assumptions about change were reflected in book titles of the period: *Latin America: World in Revolution, Politics of Change in Latin America, Latin America: Evolution or Explosion?,* and *Latin America, the Eleventh Hour.*[1]

In a 1961 essay, Stanley Stein cautioned historians against underestimating the political resilience of Latin America's socioeconomic elites.[2] A series of developments since the mid-sixties has borne out this concern, shattered the assumptions on which most political research rested, and radically altered perceptions of Latin America's political reality. The Brazilian military coup of 1964, United States intervention in the Dominican Republic the following year, the death of Che Guevara in 1967, and the establishment of Brazilian-style military regimes throughout the southern cone have had profound implications for the direction of research on Latin American politics and political history. These events led to the discovery that the forces of conservatism had surprising residual vitality and strength, while the forces of reform and revolution, which had been considered the arbiters of the future, were often fragmented and ineffectual. Observers began to question the applicability of the Cuban model of revolution and became skeptical about the chances of the "democratic left," Alliance for Progress style of reform. Retreating from the assumption of inevitable change, analysts began to turn their attention to what Claudio Véliz identified as the "the principal contemporary problem of Latin America"—its "excessive stability."[3] Book titles again provide a key to the new approaches and concerns: *Obstacles to Change in Latin America, The Politics of Conformity in Latin America, The Unrevolutionary Society: The Power of Latin American Conservatism in a Changing World,* and *Latin America: The Politics of Immobility.*[4] Along with the revised perception of Latin American political reality came new conceptual and analytical tools and new emphases in research: populism, corporatism, dependency theory, nationalism, military institutions, and elite studies.

This book, a historical case study in the politics of resistance to reform, is offered in response to the need for understanding the vitality of conservatism in modern Latin America. While drawing on the relevant theoretical and interpretive works, it investigates the strategies and mechanics of opposition to reform and revolution in a specific context. It examines a segment of Latin American society—large-scale rural landowners—which has traditionally been viewed as synonymous with political conservatism; more concretely, it focuses on one of the oldest and most influential Latin American landowner associations, the Sociedad Nacional de Agricultura (SNA) of Chile. By tracing the beginnings of conflict between reform and resistance to change, this study examines the genesis of attitudes, strategies, and tactics that the elites have commonly employed in their struggle to retain traditional rights and privileges. Knowledge of the historical sources of conservative strength and patterns of elite resistance to reform will provide a useful perspective on the continuing tension between political change and continuity in contemporary Latin America. In addition, the application of decisional as well as structural analysis to the political actions and power of organized landowners should help to dissipate the thick fog of myth and folklore which shrouds Latin American landowners as political actors.[5]

Twentieth-century Chilean political history may be interpreted as periods of reform alternating with periods of stalemate or reaction. The present study is concerned with the first period of reform between 1919 and 1940. Beginning in 1919, adverse economic conditions elicited mass mobilization in Chilean cities which threatened the social and political fabric of the Parliamentary Republic (1891-1925). The election of populist Arturo Alessandri to the presidency in 1920 launched an era in which the middle and working classes grew in strength and militance and achieved a share of political power with the traditional oligarchy. By the early thirties, the party system and institutional structure that existed until the military coup of 1973 had taken shape. Although the reform impulse slowed in the mid-thirties, in 1938 the Popular Front of Communists, Socialists, and middle-class Radicals was elected to office. Ascension of this left-center coalition represented the culmination of an evolutionary process in which the political system had become increasingly democratic and competitive. By 1940, however, the dominant group of the Popular Front, the Radicals, took a more conservative direction, leading to the dissolution of the left-center coalition in January 1941. The Radical party's change, reflecting the attitudes of the middle classes, halted the leftward movement of the electorate, slowed reform, and laid the basis for a period of political stalemate between left and right lasting from 1940 to 1964.

Political reforms by the government of Carlos Ibáñez (1952-58), the Cuban Revolution, and the Alliance for Progress established the groundwork for a second wave of reform under the Frei and Allende governments (1964-70, 1970-73). During the period of revived and intensified reform, Chile was in the international spotlight—first as a showcase of moderate reform as prescribed by the Alliance for Progress, then as a unique experiment in the peaceful and democratic transition to socialism. Despite its more radical nature, the second period of reform differed from the first in degree rather than in kind. Even the years of Allende's Unidad Popular government can be seen as a logical outgrowth of Chile's historical pattern of socioeconomic and political development. From the perspective of landowners, the reform period of the sixties and seventies represented simply a resurrection of the issues debated, legislated, and tentatively resolved between 1919 and 1940. The twenties and thirties, in fact, witnessed a full-dress rehearsal for the drama of rural reform during the Frei and Allende years, with the protagonist of the later production—the campesino—still playing a supporting role. For rural society, the most important difference between the two reform periods was the outcome: at the cost of important concessions, the fundamental prerogatives of large landowners survived the first wave of reform; they were virtually eradicated in the second, before being restored under the military government.

Until recently, few studies had stressed the continuity between the two periods of reform insofar as landowners were affected.[6] Despite a plethora of evidence in congressional debates, newspapers, books, and university theses of the time, most studies of the first reform period ignored the challenge to landowners' interests, while others tacitly or explicitly agreed with Robert Kaufman's statement that between 1920 and 1940 the "new urban groups did not challenge the older elite's control over rural property and over peasants."[7] Perhaps the most fundamental reason for the oversight was that most of these studies focused on change rather than on resistance to reform. While rural issues were intensely debated and often legislated, the most visible changes occurred in the urban setting. Thus historians emphasized the growth of labor unions, radicalization of the working classes, emergence of the Marxist parties, establishment of the social welfare system, and the democratization of politics—all of which had their greatest impact in the cities.

When domestic and international developments rekindled interest in rural reform in the sixties, observers found a rural social structure and a land tenure pattern little changed from 1940 or 1918 or, in fundamental ways, even from 1850. From the perspective of a modern urban society, the most impressive feature of rural Chile was, in Arnold Bauer's term, its apparent "constancy."[8] The attack on landowners in the sixties, then, was understandably if erroneously seen as a new phenomenon rather than as a revival of the struggle of the twenties and thirties.

Another reason the first challenge to landowners has escaped more thorough examination is that Chile between 1919 and 1940 did not experience the degree of rural mobilization that characterized Mexico during its revolution, Colombia in the thirties, Bolivia in 1952, or much of Latin America, including Chile, in the sixties. In fact, as Brian Loveman has demonstrated, the common image of the Chilean campesino as passive and politically apathetic prior to the 1960s is completely unwarranted. It remains true, however, that a self-sustaining peasant movement, independent of urban-based parties and labor unions, simply did not develop; nor did a significant pattern of land invasions, violence, or guerrilla warfare. Chile in the twenties and thirties had no Emiliano Zapata, nor even a Francisco Julião. The leading advocate of the Chilean peasant was Emilio Zapata; unlike his Mexican counterpart and namesake, who shot landowners, the Chilean Zapata debated them in Congress. Summarizing the Chilean Zapata's approach, Loveman writes: "Not proletarian revolution but manipulation of the existing parliamentary and administrative apparatus served as a tool in challenging the traditional authority of rural proprietors."[9] The relative quiescence of rural Chile prior to the sixties, then, has been taken as evidence that landowners continued firmly in control and free from political challenge during those years.

The absence of a well-developed peasant movement, however, did not prevent the rise of serious threats to the rural elites. The first round of challenge to landowners' interests was essentially an intermittent, protracted struggle of the nonagricultural working and middle classes against the rights and prerogatives of rural proprietors, with elements of the peasantry as frequent participants. This type of urban-rural interclass conflict became commonplace throughout Latin America in the 1960s, when reformist and revolutionary groups stepped up their attack on anachronistic agrarian structures. In Chile, however, the urban working- and middle-class attack on landowners' privileges and authority began several decades earlier, as the result of a peculiar conjuncture that differentiated the

Chilean experience from the general patterns in Spanish South America.

One can distinguish two distinct models of political development and socioeconomic conflict which together determined the timing and intensity of urban attack on large landowners' interests. One pattern emerged in Argentina and Uruguay, where populist reform came early, giving the working and middle classes a potential opportunity to institute rural reform at the expense of the landowning elites. However, with the prosperity generated by agricultural export economies, the heavy concentration of population in the cities, and the relatively small rural population available for political recruitment, reformist groups in the Platine countries essentially left the countryside to the landowner, concentrating instead on strategies for enhancing their participation in the national wealth. Although the *latifundista* came under verbal attack, his basic interests were safe from serious threat because he presided over much more modern and dynamic rural structures than those of the other South American republics.

The Andean countries offer a different variant of urban-rural conflict. From the nineteenth century, large landowners had been identified in *indigenista* literature, political rhetoric, and to some degree in public opinion as useless, antisocial elements whose very existence was the root of most national problems. From the time of González Prada in Peru and Alcides Argüedas in Bolivia, the landowner, the hated *gamonal*, was widely denounced as a feudal exploiter of the peasantry, a bastion of political reaction, and, especially in those countries with mineral export economies, a parasite upon the national society. Moreover, his control over the rural masses denied reformist and revolutionary parties access to a potentially great source of political strength. In the countries where the landowner was singled out as the enemy of the people and the republic, however, the urban working- and middle-class parties remained too weak to constitute a political threat to landowners' interests or, in the case of Peru, were kept marginal to the exercise of effective political power. Thus where the indigenist literati and political reformers had marked the landowner's destruction as the sine qua non of national progress, political realities denied the opportunity for execution.

Since the Chilean experience combines elements of both the Platine and the Andean patterns, the Chilean landowner came under serious political attack earlier and more intensely than did his South American counterparts. As in the Andean countries, the landowner in Chile was commonly portrayed as an antisocial element and the core of the national oligarchy; and after the onset of Chile's nitrate export cycle in the 1880s, he was seen as a parasite rather than a contributor to economic progress. Although his image was better in degree than that of the Peruvian or Bolivian landlord

—Chile, for one thing, did not have indigenista novels to dramatize the latifundista's crimes against humanity—the Chilean landowner was subject to the political liabilities concomitant to a very negative image. As in Argentina and Uruguay, populist reform began early in Chile, giving the working and middle classes a share of national political power and consequently the opportunity to press for reforms designed to reduce the traditional prerogatives of landowners. The relatively great strength of the Marxist left in Chile, moreover, subjected the landowner to more consistent and intense pressure than existed elsewhere. Between 1919 and 1940, demands from the left coupled with pressure from the right for co-optation and concession put the Chilean landowner squarely on the firing line, decades before the rural revolution of the Frei and Allende years.

As they gained in power, the parties of the working and middle classes demanded that large landowners give up some of their traditional rights in the interest of national progress. They demanded agrarian reform as a means of destroying the economic base of landowners and the national oligarchy, as a method for increasing production, and as a way of achieving social justice. They promoted rural unions as an instrument for improving the lot of agricultural labor and as a device for freeing the peasantry from landowners' political control—thus for attacking the electoral strength of the rightist parties. Finally, working- and middle-class groups sought to counteract the impact of inflation by establishing controls over food prices. These desired reforms struck at the essence of the traditional rural order. Landowners for the first time had to fight to preserve their rights to own land without restrictions, to organize and utilize labor without interference from unions or the state, and to cultivate and market produce without restrictions or controls of any kind.

In response to these challenges of mass politics, landowners turned to the SNA to supplement the declining strength of the rightist parties. Prior to 1919, the SNA had been essentially a developmental association dedicated to improving Chilean agricultural practices through education and persuasion. From its founding in 1869 the Society had a political function, and by the turn of the century it had become the voice of Chile's large agricultural producers in the intersectoral competition over economic policy. But it was the advent of mass politics that caused the SNA's transformation into the powerful and sophisticated pressure group that became familiar to observers of Latin America in the 1960s. The nature of the challenge to landowners, the transformation of the SNA, and that institution's actions in defense of vested interests constitute the substance of this case study in the politics of resistance to reform.

Notes

1. In order cited: Carleton Beals, *Latin America: World in Revolution* (New York, 1963); Joseph Maier and Richard W. Weatherhead, eds., *Politics of Change in Latin America* (New York, 1964); Mildred Adams, ed., *Latin America: Evolution or Explosion?* (New York, 1963); and Gary MacEóin, *Latin America, the Eleventh Hour* (New York, 1962).

2. Stanley J. Stein, "The Tasks Ahead for Latin American Historians," *Hispanic American Historical Review*, 41 (1961), 424-33.

3. Claudio Véliz, ed., *Obstacles to Change in Latin America* (London, 1965), p. 1.

4. In order cited: Véliz, ed., *Obstacles to Change*; Véliz, ed., *The Politics of Conformity in Latin America* (New York, 1967); John Mander, *The Unrevolutionary Society: The Power of Latin American Conservatism in a Changing World* (New York, 1969); and Robert F. Adie and Guy E. Poitras, *Latin America: The Politics of Immobility* (Englewood Cliffs, N.J., 1974).

5. For a perceptive analysis of the problems of studying landowners as political actors in nineteenth-century Latin America, see Richard Graham, "Political Power and Landownership in Nineteenth Century Latin America," in Graham and Peter H. Smith, eds., *New Approaches to Latin American History* (Austin, Tex., 1974), pp. 112-36.

6. See esp. two studies on rural unionism and labor relations: Almino Affonso *et al., Movimiento campesino chileno* (Santiago, 1970); and Brian Loveman, *Struggle in the Countryside: Politics and Rural Labor in Chile, 1919-1973* (Bloomington, Ind., 1976).

7. Robert R. Kaufman, *The Politics of Land Reform in Chile, 1950-1970* (Cambridge, Mass., 1972), p. 9.

8. Arnold J. Bauer, "Chilean Rural Labor in the Nineteenth Century," *American Historical Review*, 76 (1971), 1060; see also Bauer's *Chilean Rural Society from the Spanish Conquest to 1930* (Cambridge, Eng., 1975).

9. Loveman, *Struggle in the Countryside*, p. 151.

Landowners and Reform in Chile

1

Landowners, Politics, and the SNA, 1869–1918

During the SNA's first fifty years of existence, its primary function had been to promote the modernization of agriculture. When Chilean landowners faced the new challenges of mass politics following World War I, they turned to that same institution for political defense of their interests. In order to be an effective pressure group, the SNA would undergo important modifications in its organization and activities. Nonetheless, the modern SNA that emerged as defender of landowners' prerogatives also exhibited a high degree of continuity in style, structure, and membership traits with the Society that had developed in the more tranquil years leading up to 1919. The following overview of the SNA's formative first half-century will provide background for the subsequent examination of landowners' response to the advent of reform.

Formation and Development of the SNA

From the Spanish conquest to the 1880s, when the opulent age of nitrates began, the primacy of agriculture within the Chilean economy was uncontested. The Spanish had found in the "*fértil provincia*" of Chile climates and soils highly compatible with their Mediterranean agricultural traditions. As Spanish settlement spread out from Santiago, the familiar Iberian staples—wheat, olives, vines, citrus, cattle—appeared from the edge of the northern desert to the Indian frontier along the Bío-Bío River to the south. Throughout the colonial period and most of the nineteenth century, these agricultural staples constituted the diet, engaged the labor, and directly or indirectly provided the income of most of the Chilean population.[1]

Along with their crops and animals, the Spanish brought to Chile their "seignorial vision" and gave it free rein in the construction of a rural society which endured well into the present century. As in much of colonial America, Chilean rural society developed around the institution of the hacienda. Wresting the land from the aboriginal population, the Spanish granted it in generous tracts to conquerors, royal officials, court favorites, influential merchants and military men, and the Church. These grants soon encompassed the best lands of the Central Valley stretching south from the capital and the transverse valleys to the north, creating a land tenure pattern characterized by a dichotomy of large, often sprawling and underutilized estates alongside a much larger number of subsistence smallholdings on marginal land bordering the haciendas. Although typically lacking in amenities and spurned as permanent residences by their urban-dwelling owners, these haciendas supplied both income and status for the colonial aristocracy. Some seventeen of the most valuable haciendas were entailed, all but one in the eighteenth century, and twelve of these *mayorazgos* became the basis for noble titles of Castille.[2]

With only half a dozen important towns throughout the length of colonial Chile, the hacienda became the dominant economic, social, and even political entity in the countryside. After initially employing the device of *encomienda* to secure Indian labor, the hacienda had shifted by the seventeenth century to a free labor system combining resident and seasonal workers drawn from the developing mestizo rural population. Resident workers, the *inquilinos*, offered their labor and that of their families in exchange for the use of small plots of hacienda land and other perquisites. *Peón* or seasonal labor was provided by the rural landless and by the owners of neighboring dwarf holdings. Thus, for the surrounding rural lower strata as well as for its own resident workers, the hacienda during the colonial period constituted the "*patria chica*"—and its owner or his delegate the representative of unappealable authority. The hacienda system fostered, in George McBride's phrase, a "master-man" relationship between patrón and worker that persisted with little change into the twentieth century.[3]

The minuscule urban population, Chile's isolation, and Spanish trade restrictions combined to limit the development of market agriculture during the colonial period. The hacienda thus strove for self-sufficiency first and produced secondarily for the small domestic market and the export trade in wheat, hides, and dried beef. In the three decades following independence, mineral discoveries in the Norte Chico and the Australian and California gold rushes provided important but ephemeral markets for Chilean wheat and flour. By the 1860s, when rails had begun to link the Central Valley with seaports and Europe had turned to large-scale importation of food staples, Chile began to participate in the transatlantic grain trade on a substantial scale. This export agriculture quickened the pace of Chilean economic activity and greatly enhanced the incomes of estate owners in the 1860s and '70s.[4]

In contrast to the cases of North America, Australia, and Argentina, in Chile exportation of grain was not accompanied by widespread modernization of agricultural practices. For a variety of cultural and practical reasons, Chilean landowners did not invest on a large scale in the mechanical reapers and threshers that by the 1850s dotted the wheat fields of the United States. Rather than buying expensive machinery, subject to breakdowns and difficult to maintain 8,000 miles from the factory, landowners in Chile turned to the resources at hand — abundant land and labor — to increase output and enhance their incomes. Fallow or grazing land within hacienda borders was put under cultivation, while the growing rural landless and smallholder population was recruited and more efficiently exploited to meet the surging demand for wheat. Thus while the wheat flowing to Europe from the plains of Kansas was mechanically cut and threshed, that from the Chilean Central Valley and coastal range was produced in the traditional way, from broadcast planting to floor threshing by horse hoof or sled. Chile, then, was only marginally affected by the "agricultural revolution" that began to transform agricultural practices in much of the world at mid-century.[5]

It was this persistence of traditional, increasingly obsolete practices in agriculture that the SNA was founded to combat. In 1869, the government of President Joaquín Pérez sponsored an agricultural exposition which featured some 500 pieces of imported machinery. This display fully dramatized the growing technological gap between Chile and the modernizing Northern Hemisphere and spurred the government and landowners to action. With government support and encouragement, a group of prominent landowners founded the Sociedad Nacional de Agricultura in October 1869, as a voluntary association dedicated to "the progress and development of agriculture."[6]

Although formally a new and distinct entity, the SNA had direct antecedents in the Sociedad Chilena de Agricultura, an organization that flourished between 1838 and 1849 and finally dissolved after a brief revival in the 1850s. Much of the new association's charter membership had belonged to the earlier society, and the SNA's initial goals, organization, and style were heavily influenced by the experience of the Sociedad Chilena de Agricultura.[7] This earlier society itself had been inspired by the Sociedades de Amigos del País (Societies of Friends of the Country), the economic societies of eighteenth- and early nineteenth-century Spain and America. Those typically Hispanic institutions of the Enlightenment were voluntary associations devoted to economic progress as well as centers for the social and intellectual interaction of the local elites, in the manner of the French salons.[8]

In the Enlightenment tradition of the economic societies, the Sociedad

Chilena de Agricultura became the focal point for a broad range of activities. Established at government initiative, it assumed a variety of advisory and administrative functions, including the founding and management of the government's embryonic agricultural services located in the Quinta Normal in Santiago. In exchange for these and other services to the government, the society received various minor subsidies. It also imported plants, animals, and machinery and disseminated practical advice and instruction through its journal. Among its varied activities it established the Sociedad de Beneficencia (a charitable society), gathered information and statistics on Chile, and served as a literary and debating society. Benjamín Vicuña Mackenna, president of the society in the 1850s, believed that a majority of its members were not practicing agriculturists at all but "enthusiastic youth disposed to take part in all public enterprises."[9] The society's journals, *El Agricultor* (1838-49) and *El Mensajero de la Agricultura* (1856-67), are encyclopedic documents which reflect the catholic interests and wide-ranging activities of the original agricultural society.

Despite the precedents set by the Sociedad Chilena, within a few years of its founding the SNA had narrowed its purview essentially to matters of applied agriculture. The minutes of directors' meetings, annual reports, and the monthly *Boletín* reflected the decline of interest in the broader concerns of the original society and the preponderant emphasis on the improvement of agricultural methods. There were two main reasons for the SNA's more practical orientation. First, growing awareness of the backwardness of Chilean agricultural practices led the SNA to concentrate its efforts on practical improvements. Increased travel to Europe, circulation of foreign agricultural journals, and the activities of the SNA itself put Chilean landowners into closer contact with the innovations currently revolutionizing agriculture in the North Atlantic world. The prevalence of traditional, inefficient practices was not only an embarrassment to progressive agriculturists but also a threat to Chilean grain exports—the mainstay of agricultural income in the Central Valley. Second, by the last third of the nineteenth century the civic and intellectual energies of the upper classes had numerous outlets, among them the university, a well-developed press, the Sociedad de Beneficencia, the Club de la Unión, and three ideologically distinct political parties. With these specialized institutions in existence, the elites no longer had to rely on the SNA to be the multifunctional organization that its predecessor had been.[10]

For its first fifty years, then, the SNA assiduously fostered the modernization and diversification of Chilean agriculture. It encouraged the use of machinery, planting of improved seeds and new crops, upgrading of cattle herds with selected breeding stock, and a host of other measures designed to supersede traditional practices and routines. This message was disseminated through the SNA's *Boletín*, a technical journal full of practical information on crops and animals, current prices, and agricultural practices in Europe and the United States. The SNA also sponsored annual livestock expositions and kept herd books to promote the genetic improvement of Chilean cattle. Its commercial department sold fertilizers and imported machinery at discounts to members, and its library collected foreign agricultural journals and other relevant publications. Although its efforts failed to induce modernization on a large scale, the SNA can take much credit for the relatively limited changes that did occur in Chilean agricultural practices.[11]

Men joined the Society for two main reasons—to support its mission of agricultural modernization and to receive the practical benefits of membership. With the growth of functionally specialized associations for the elites, there was little reason to join the SNA for social prestige, intellectual stimulation, or, at least until the turn of the century, political advantage. Those who joined, then, were in large measure drawn from an elite of progressive agriculturists who applied the modern techniques that the SNA advocated to their own landholdings, or *fundos*. It is impossible to evaluate the degree of SNA members' progressiveness vis-à-vis that of nonmember landowners. However, there is a strong correlation between Society membership lists and the names cited in histories of Chilean agriculture for their contributions to improving agricultural practices. Some of the best known innovators, including Rafael Larraín Moxó, Salvador Izquierdo, and Ramón Cruz Montt, served long periods on the Society's board of directors. Several members owned model fundos which were featured in the SNA *Boletín*.[12]

Despite the Society's repeated appeals to Chilean agriculturists, the vast majority of them remained outside its ranks. Even among the landowners and producers of substantial means, only a small minority joined the Society. The SNA *Boletín* attributed this indifference to the "absence of a spirit of association" and to a deeply ingrained hostility toward progress.[13] Thus membership increased much more slowly than the Society desired: from a charter membership of 147, the SNA had reached some 400 members by 1900 and fewer than 800 by 1918.[14]

From its founding, the SNA appealed primarily to large landowners, without explicitly attempting to exclude agriculturists of more modest means. The Society believed that its goal of modernizing agriculture could only be accomplished by the large operator: "The mission of the large property of Chile consists in popularizing new discoveries, as only it can undertake costly and difficult experiments for which a comfortable social position is necessary."[15] Eventually, the "superior influence" and example of large landholders might percolate down through the strata of rural society and affect the tradition-bound, impoverished smallholder. The SNA reinforced its preference for large landowners with a dues schedule which, though insignificant to the wealthy, completely precluded the masses of smallholders and agricultural workers from joining. Membership was further restricted by the requirement that any applicant be sponsored by a current Society member.[16]

To identify the landed base of the SNA, two sets of tax rolls were checked against the Society's membership lists. The categories of property employed here are adapted from the definitions that the SNA used to interpret the 1874 tax rolls. As the SNA recognized, given the great disparity in productive potential from region to region and between irrigated and nonirrigated land, assessed value provides a more accurate comparative measure of the worth of agricultural property than does surface area. Thus "large" properties are those with high assessed value, regardless of surface area. After 1874, the rural tax rolls were next published in 1908. Value categories for the 1908 rolls are based on the 1874 definition, adjusted for the increase in total assessed value of rural property in the country as reported for 1911—the nearest available approximation to 1908 (see Table 1).[17]

Table 1
Distribution of Rural Property by Assessed Value in Pesos, 1874 and 1911

Category	Value	Number of Holdings	Percent of Total Holdings
	1874		
Small	less than $100	43,008	71.68
Medium	$100-999	14,813	24.69
Large	$1000 and over	2,179	3.63
Total		60,000	100.00
	1911		
Small	less than $5000	78,894	74.52
Medium	$5000-49,999	22,911	21.64
Large	$50,000 and over	4,060	3.84
Total		105,865	100.00

Note: Rural properties in the Norte Grande—Tacna, Tarapacá, and Antofagasta—were subtracted from the national totals as reported in the 1911 *Anuario estadístico* because the tax rolls did not distinguish between agricultural and rural mining properties; many of the larger ones were actually mines. Also see n. 17.

SOURCE: *BSNA*, 6 (1875), 538-57; Ministerio de Hacienda, *Memoria* (1875), p. 67; Dirección General de Estadística, *Anuario estadístico de la Republica de Chile, año 1911*, 2, 108-9.

The tax rolls of 1874 and 1908 establish two important traits of the SNA membership during the Society's initial fifty years of existence. First, approximately half the members owned properties that the SNA considered large—those among the upper 4 percent of all Chilean rural holdings by value. These large landowners in the SNA owned an average of 1.8 highly assessed properties in 1874 and 1.6 in 1908 (see Table 2). Second, the tax rolls reveal a geographic concentration of membership in the central provinces stretching from some 200 kilometers south of Santiago to 150 kilometers north—the heartland of the colonial hacienda where many properties

Table 2
SNA Members as Large Landowners,[a] 1874 and 1908

	1874	*1908*
Total SNA membership	231	698
SNA large landowners:		
number	134	321
percent of total membership	58.0	46.0
Total large properties	2,197	4,060[b]
SNA-owned large properties:		
number	245	510
percent of total large properties	11.2	12.6

[a]See Table 1 for definition of large properties and large landowners. Membership totals include only individual members (four businesses held membership in 1908 and are excluded).

[b]This figure is from 1911, the nearest available to 1908.

SOURCE: *MSNA* (1873 and 1909); *Impuesto agrícola: rol de contribuyentes* (1874); *Indice de propietarios rurales i valor de la propiedad rural según los roles de avalúos comunales* (1908); Dirección General de Estadística, *Anuario estadístico de la República de Chile, año 1911*, 2, 108-9.

were large, partially irrigated, within reach of urban and export markets, and thus capable of generating substantial incomes. In part, this pattern simply reflects the concentration of valuable holdings in the central zone. In 1874 some 60.2 percent of all large rural properties were located in and between the provinces of Aconcagua and Curicó, and in 1908, despite the spread of large-scale agriculture to the former Araucanian territory south of the Bío-Bío and extensive grazing to Magallanes in the extreme south, over half of the country's large holdings were still located in the core area. However, an even greater proportion of SNA members' large holdings were located there—80.4 percent in 1874 and 77.6 percent in 1908.[18]

The SNA's pronounced regional character was the result of both social and geographic factors. The SNA had been founded in Santiago by men

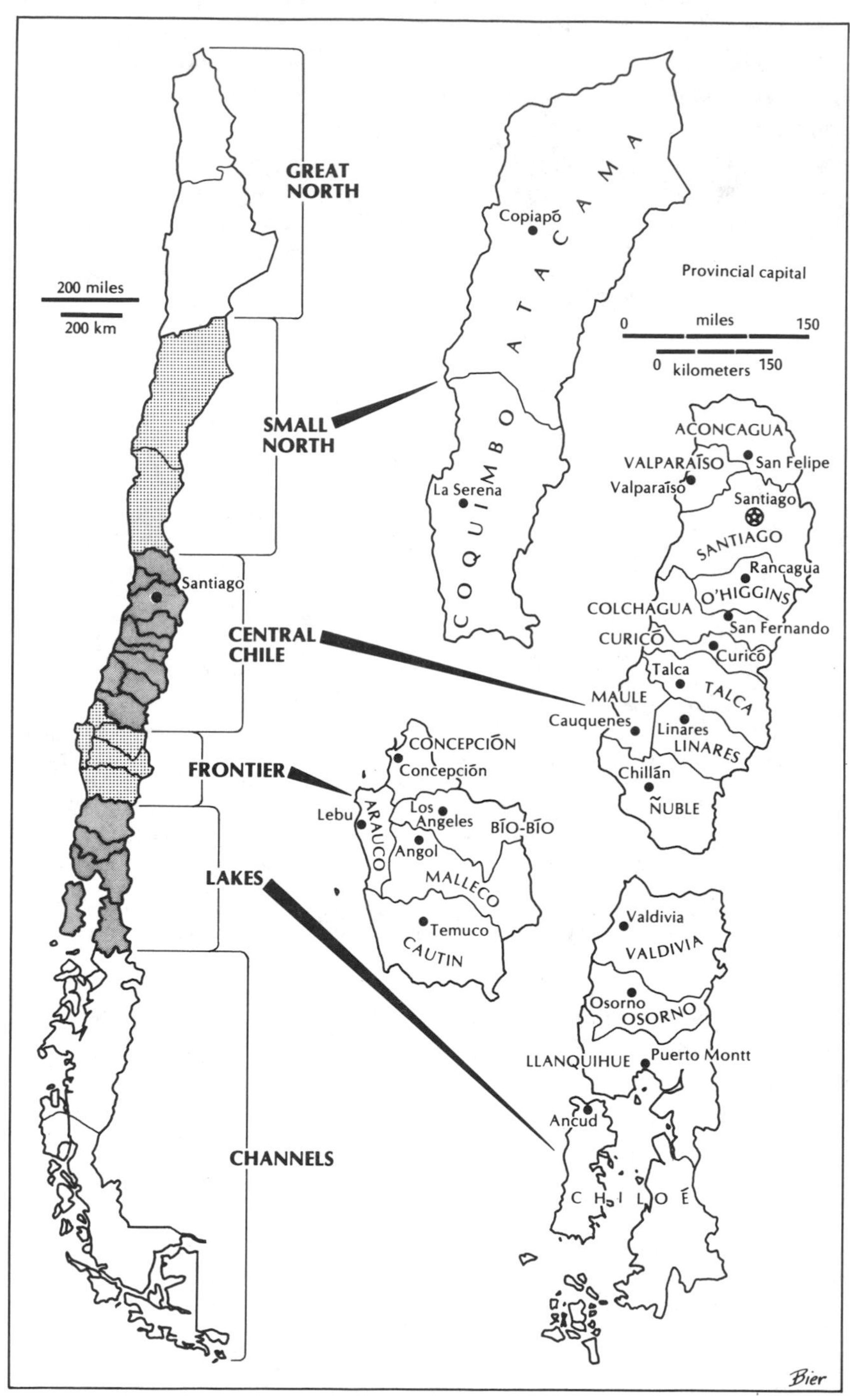

Agricultural Chile

who lived there and generally owned estates accessible from the capital. For large landowners who resided on their properties or in towns other than Santiago, social contacts with the capital's landholding elite were limited. In addition, agriculturists in Coquimbo or Valdivia could not easily participate in SNA activities or enjoy the practical benefits of membership, such as purchasing seeds and machinery or consulting in the Society's library. Moreover, while the SNA extended the offer of membership to all Chile's substantial landowners and producers, throughout its first half-century it took few concrete steps to recruit members in outlying areas. Landowners outside the core area surrounding the capital clearly recognized the regional character of the SNA, and beginning in the 1880s they established independent agricultural societies in several towns outside the Aconcagua-Curicó zone. Some of these, such as the societies founded in Talca and Chillán, failed to prosper, while those established in La Serena, Concepción, Temuco, and Osorno survived and functioned as the SNA's counterparts for the landowning elites of their own areas.[19]

Who were the SNA members not identifiable as owners of large rural holdings? The 1908 tax rolls were checked to a lower assessed value—$25,000—in seven sample departments to determine whether owners of more modest properties were joining the SNA in significant numbers. It was discovered that most SNA members who owned properties assessed between $25,000 and $50,000 also owned estates in the "large" category. Altogether only seven individuals were found to own these medium estates without concurrently owning large properties in the sample departments, where ninety-one SNA members held large estates. Nine more members were found in the department of Santiago among the middling proprietors.[20] Beyond that, it is likely that the SNA had acquired additional members who owned property valued under $50,000 in the Talca and Maule region when it absorbed the entire membership of the Sociedad Nacional de Viticultura in 1903.[21] However, most of the SNA's members who did not own large estates were not to be found among the relatively small stratum of medium landowners.

Renters and administrators of large holdings and relatives of landowners outnumbered the smaller proprietors. As noted above, those SNA members who did own large properties typically held more than one such estate. Moreover, as the 1908 tax rolls reveal, they very frequently owned properties of lower but still substantial assessed value, often widely spread throughout the country. Some of these multiple holdings were rented out—McBride estimated that by the 1920s a quarter of all large estates were rented—and most of the rest required the services of administrators.[22] Relatives were generally preferred as both renters and administrators, and family connections between landowning and nonowner SNA members can be established in some instances and inferred in a large number of cases. In 1908, for example, 147 (39 percent) of the members who did not own large property shared paternal surnames with members who did.[23] Still other nonlandowning members may have been owners or managers of agriculturally related businesses, such as import-export firms, agricultural supply houses, or commodity brokerages, who joined as individuals rather than in the company name. Despite the impossibility of precisely identifying all nonlandowning members, the evidence supports the thesis that many, probably most, of them were connected with the large estate by family ties, as renters or administrators, or in many cases by both blood and business ties.

As large landowners and men otherwise connected with the large estates in the central core of the country, many SNA members were also part of an interlocking national upper class that had crystallized by the turn of the century. Paul Reinsch, a North American political scientist who visited Chile in 1909, described this oligarchy as "an aristocracy of birth and wealth [which] has unquestioned control of social and political life. This society constitutes at the present time the only aristocracy in the world which still has full and acknowledged control of the economic, political and social forces of the state in which they live."[24] Alejandro Venegas's famous critique, *Sinceridad: Chile íntimo en 1910,* asserted that "there has come into being beside the Church and the State a third power which on many occasions dominates the other two: the power of the heads of the rich families."[25] The Chilean oligarchy by 1900 was a fluid, economically hybrid, but substantive entity divided by party affiliation, business interests, and philia for different European countries but united in fundamental values and in defense of its privileges.

Much research has been done in recent years on the question of linkages among the dominant sectors of the Chilean economy in the nineteenth and twentieth centuries, and most of it has supported Frederick Pike's contention that "by the turn of the century . . . urban and rural interests were crossed and crisscrossed to such a degree as to make the distinction often meaningless."[26] The investigations continue to identify individuals and families who owned land, manufacturing plants, import houses, urban real estate, bank and mining stocks, and who sat on boards of directors of varied enterprises.[27] Although absolute quantification is impossible, the mechanisms by which individuals and families combined landownership with other economic activities are clearly visible.

Arnold Bauer has cogently described the processes by which the colonial landholding aristocracy gradually assimilated the descendants of nineteenth-century immigrants who made their money in mining and commerce. Acquisition of landed estates was one of the principal means by which the nouveaux riches could "legitimize their claim to social status commensurate with their wealth," and the tax rolls reveal that as the century progressed the best estates increasingly changed hands and underwent subdivision to satisfy the land hunger of the upwardly mobile.[28] Diversification of individual and family portfolios also proceeded in the opposite direction as landowners invested in nonagricultural enterprises. After 1855, the Caja de Crédito Hipotecario provided cheap and abundant long-term mortgage credit on rural property. A depressed market for agriculture in the last quarter of the century and rapid growth of investment opportunities in finance, commerce, industry, and real estate provided the incentive for landowning families to establish linkages to other areas. This pattern reinforced the interlocking character of the sectoral economic elites.[29]

The SNA reflected the hybrid economic basis of the Chilean oligarchy. Its membership rolls included men for whom landownership was but an adjunct of a fortune based on mining, commerce, finance, or a profession. Along with a strong core of surnames from the colonial landholding "Castillian-Basque aristocracy"—the Larraín, Irarrázabal, García-Huidobro, Valdés, and Errázuriz—by the turn of the century the membership list included such names as Edwards, Cox, Ossa, Gallo, Cousiño, Charme, Subercaseaux, and others associated with banking, mining, or commerce. A list of Chile's millionaires published in 1882 contained sixty names, forty-eight of them men: of these, twelve belonged to the SNA, and seven of those were mentioned as having their primary interests outside of agriculture.[30] Several specific studies of intersectoral linkages have used SNA members as representatives of the landowning elites. One of these, for example, determined that of a total of 208 directors of the seventeen banks established in Chile through 1904, 73 were also SNA members.[31] Another study found that in a sample of 25,000 entries listing owners and shareholders of various business entities, landowners who belonged to the SNA demonstrated a higher incidence of linkage to nonagricultural enterprises than did nonmembers.[32] These kinds of evidence, while fragmentary and inconclusive, do establish that economic pluralism was the norm among large landowners, and that SNA-affiliated landowners were representative of that pattern.

SNA members, like other men of the oligarchy, tended to join the Club de la Unión in Santiago. Joining the Club de la Unión, like buying a rural estate, was a means for the newly rich to integrate with the established aristocracy. After its founding in 1864, the club quickly became the most prestigious social institution in Chile, and membership in that organization became the recognized symbol of social elite status at the national level. In two separate cross-checks of SNA and Club de la Unión membership lists, a majority of SNA members were found to belong to the prestigious social organization. In 1895, 137 of the SNA's 267 members (51.3 percent) belonged also to the club; by 1918, 431 of the Society's 782 members (55.1 percent) concurrently possessed the credentials of the national social elite.[33]

Members of the SNA revealed their elite status in the political realm also. Office-holding at the national level was, of course, a measure of one's political power. In Chile, especially during the Parliamentary Period (1891-1925), it was also an expression of an individual's or a family's economic and social status. Members of wealthy and prestigious families were accustomed to try their hand at politics, whether out of dedication to principle, a sense of civic duty, or as contemporary critics often lamented, as a means of self-gratification. Being elected senator or deputy in Congress, or being appointed cabinet minister, was the ambition of a large part of the national upper class. In three sample years between 1869 and 1900, 45.7 percent of current SNA members held national office at some time during their lives; in three other samples between 1900 and 1918 the rate of political participation declined to 22.7 percent. It should be noted that the decline in levels of participation after the turn of the century was an inevitable result of the SNA's growth; between 1873 and 1918 the Society tripled in membership, while the number of congressional seats expanded only from 117 to 155 and the ministries from five to six.[34]

The men of the SNA, then, not only commanded legions of humble workers on their estates; they also tapped the wealth of Chile's nitrate age through varied investments, occupied elegant townhouses in the fashionable districts of Santiago, moved in and out of national political office, and drank whisky and conversed in the friendly confines of the Club de la Unión. These traits of the oligarchy were even more prominent among the SNA's board of directors, a small group varying from seventeen to twenty-two, who exercised a practical monopoly of power within the Society. In 1895, 82.3 percent of the directors belonged to the Club de la Unión; and in 1918, 56.1 percent were political participants at the national level. While again it is impossible to quantify directors' nonagricultural investments, data on directors with a minimum of ten years' service indicate that there was a high incidence of intersectoral linkage.[35] The men who spoke for the SNA were a microcosm of the national establishment; they were the agrarian department of the Chilean oligarchy.

The SNA as a Political Institution

Although the SNA was primarily a developmental institution during its first half-century, prevented by its charter from engaging in "politics," it nonetheless was involved in the political process from the time of its founding. Its political role through the 1880s was shaped by the experience of the earlier agricultural society. This continuity was natural, in that the SNA was founded and initially led by veterans of the original society, while the structure and scope of government had changed little in the intervening years. The advisory and administrative functions of the earlier society were well suited to enhance the SNA's direct developmental efforts, and from the beginning it operated in a close, corporatist relationship with government that benefitted both parties. At minimal cost, the government harnessed the energies and talents of a public-spirited group which collectively formed a respectable, and moreover the only available, pool of expertise on agricultural matters. The SNA for its part was able to survive and pursue its mission, despite a small membership and limited finances, thanks to government subsidies and other aid.[36]

The SNA during its first twenty years functioned essentially as a voluntary, quasi-official ministry of agriculture. It advised on policy of all kinds affecting agriculture and acted in the public administration as the government's agent in a variety of programs and services. In return for its participation, the SNA received fees as well as subsidies to cover the costs of its office, staff, and the printing of its *Boletín*.

This corporatist arrangement was sanctioned by historical experience as well as by contemporary Chilean political culture, in which, beneath the trappings of liberal constitutionalism, the Hispanic patrimonial tradition was still very much alive. In the premodern Hispanic political culture, the blurring of lines between private and public domains and roles had been commonplace and normal. In Spain and colonial America, the state vested regulatory, administrative, and some judicial authority in corporate entities such as merchant and craft guilds, universities, and various units of the Church. These and other corporations represented the king's justice in their internal regulatory functions and concurrently served as advocates for their members' interests in conflicts with the king or other corporate groups.[37] The SNA's combination of private status with public powers exhibited the same corporatist spirit, but its public authority, entailing no judicial and limited administrative powers, was very circumscribed in comparison with historical cases. This modified Hispanic corporatist arrangement was well suited to the needs and political temperament of nineteenth-century Chile—so much so that the SNA charter served as a model for other economic associations established later in the century.[38]

Development and administration of government services were perhaps the SNA's most important functions during the two decades after its founding. From the outset it oversaw and expanded the small complex of experimental fields and related services founded by the original agricultural society in the Quinta Normal. In 1874 it established Chile's first professional school of agronomy, which had trained some two hundred agronomists by 1890. It also played a major role in founding and supervising practical schools of agriculture throughout the country. In these duties it was accountable to the Ministry of Hacienda (Finance), and as the government's agency for colonization in southern Chile it was responsible to the Ministry of Foreign Relations. The SNA also administered the patent office and accepted a wide range of specific and temporary assignments, such as evaluating rural smallholds in 1882 and organizing the Chilean displays in two international expositions. In 1883, at the government's request, the SNA founded both the Sociedad de Fomento Fabril (Society for Industrial Development, SOFOFA) and the Sociedad Nacional de Minería (SNM). In its administrative role, the SNA set policy and supervised budgets and operations within general guidelines given by the ministers. Public administration was the most consuming concern of the SNA council's biweekly meetings, and the ministerial archives contain voluminous correspondence attesting the Society's close attention to the smallest detail of its official duties.[39]

The SNA's direct participation in public administration lasted into the 1890s, when the agricultural services came under the jurisdiction of the new Department of Agriculture, an agency of the Ministry of Industry and Public Works. By this time, changing conditions had made the SNA's administrative role obsolete. Vastly increased revenues derived from the export tax on nitrates, combined with the availability of professional agronomists, allowed the government to expand the agricultural bureaucracy and bring it under direct control. After the 1890s, the SNA continued to serve government in a less direct advisory capacity and retained a portion of its subsidy.[40]

The SNA was not only an administrative arm of government but also a lobby for its members and agricultural producers in general. In its first two decades, however, promoting its constituents' interests required little effort, not because of the assumed vast power of landowners but because landowners had relatively little to ask. At the time of the SNA's founding, agriculturists enjoyed the fruits of strong export markets, cheap and docile labor, and abundant credit. Prior to the War of the Pacific, the policy interests of the main economic sectors—agriculture, mining, and commerce—were generally compatible.[41] The political system, dominated completely by the country's elites, provided no opportunity for the lower classes to challenge landowner prerogatives. Thus there were few instances of conflicting interests in which the SNA was used as a political tool of landowners and no overt use of pressure tactics.[42]

Most of the SNA's lobbying in early years was directly related to its mission of fostering agricultural development. It consistently called on government to expand agricultural education, improve technical and statistical services, and invest in transportation facilities. The only kind of measure it consistently advocated for the immediate economic benefit of landowners was the reduction of taxes, particularly the colonial *alcabala* or transfer tax on real property and the tobacco monopoly. This objective was finally accomplished after nitrate revenues made it feasible to reduce or eliminate most existing taxes on the wealthy.[43]

By the turn of the century, however, the SNA's role in the political system had undergone a subtle but significant transformation. It was still primarily an association of landowners concerned with the practical improvement of agriculture, but a majority within the governing council had adopted the view that the Society's mission could only be accomplished in a setting of favorable economic policy that would protect or increase profit margins in agriculture. In contrast to the SNA's transformation after 1919, when landowners faced the initial challenge of reform politics, there was no sharp break with established patterns and styles of political involvement. The difference was more of degree than of kind. With the reduction of its corporate ties to government, the Society was freer to function as an independent interest group. And after the late 1890s, the SNA lobbied more vigorously and consistently on a broader range of policy matters than it had previously, in a setting of intensified competition with other economic and social groups. The evolution of the SNA's political role was a response to the development of competing economic interests, the rise of protectionism, and the deterioration of market conditions for agriculture.

The development of competing economic interests was an outgrowth of Chile's victory over Peru and Bolivia in the War of the Pacific (1879–84). The war launched the fifty-year age of nitrates and set in motion forces which profoundly influenced the country's economic development, social structure, and ultimately its political evolution. Annexation of Tarapacá and Antofagasta ushered in an era of economic growth and diversification. Although in large measure a foreign enclave, the nitrate sector paid profits to Chilean investors and wages to a huge labor force, a heavy export tax to the government, and supported a variety of ancillary services and businesses. Growth of the nitrate economy thus fostered increased trade, production, consumption, and governmental activity.[44]

These developments in the economy inevitably had repercussions in matters of public policy. Whereas before the war only the SNA and the Cámara Central de Comercio (Central Chamber of Commerce, founded in 1858) had acted as sectoral lobbies, the founding of the SOFOFA and the SNM in 1883, reflecting Chile's recent economic diversification, brought new viewpoints to bear on policy formulation. Given the prosperity of the mining sector and the favorable framework of political economy within which it operated, the SNM advocated no substantive policy changes. The situation of the industrialists, however, was radically different. The numerous industries that had mushroomed in response to wartime demand faced collapse without tariff protection or subsidies after the war. The establishment of new industries, moreover, required protection against cheaper European and North American imports. Therefore from its founding the SOFOFA was the aggressive and persistent advocate of industrial protectionism in Chile.[45]

Intensive lobbying for industrial protection injected an element of competition over economic policy which had been largely absent before the war. The SOFOFA proposed tariffs on manufactures of all sorts including some, such as wire fencing, plows, and wine casks, which affected agriculture directly and others, such as railroad cars and cotton cloth, which bore indirectly upon costs and profits in agriculture. The rise of a vigorous industrial lobby thus posed the first potential threat of policy adverse to landowners.[46]

Concurrently with the development of competing economic interests, the prosperity of Central Valley agriculture declined over the last quarter of the nineteenth century. After 1850, landowners had geared production to the expanding world market for wheat to the point of extreme dependence on grain exports, and therefore were seriously affected by the world market price decline after 1875. In the more competitive market Chilean producers were at a distinct disadvantage compared to those in North America, Argentina, and other areas where modern technology and shorter distances to market combined to keep costs lower than in Chile. Despite healthy expansion of the domestic market after 1880, agriculturists complained with growing vehemence of shrinking income levels and began to demand protective tariffs and export and production subsidies for various crops. The SNA's abortive attempt in 1888 to obtain a tariff on imported livestock marked the beginning of agricultural protectionism as an issue in Chilean politics.[47]

Pressure mounted through the 1890s for agricultural interests to seek political solutions to their economic problems. The propaganda efforts of the SOFOFA and the general world trend toward higher tariffs had begun to make protectionism respectable in Chile. More important, conditions steadily worsened in the nineties as the decline of exports continued without, as yet, compensatory growth of internal demand. Further, an 1895 conversion law committing Chile to return to the gold standard jeopardized the prospects of agricultural recovery, given the role of currency devaluation in promoting exports. Bad harvests in 1894, 1895, and 1897 completed the gloomy picture of central zone agriculture in the nineties.

These conditions made protective tariffs and production subsidies to foster diversification increasingly popular notions in agricultural circles.[48]

The SNA responded to the crisis of the nineties by proposing and lobbying for various relief measures. However, its limited actions and conservative style failed to satisfy the more militant agriculturists, who formed a rival association, the Centro Industrial y Agrícola, in 1897. This organization, operating under the "protectionist flag," immediately began a vigorous lobbying campaign for protective tariffs and subsidies for agricultural products.[49] The growing pressure from agricultural groups was more than matched by the industrialists, who stood to lose the protection of devaluation following conversion of the currency. The informal alliance of industry and agriculture wielded sufficient power to give a moderate but definite protectionist orientation to the tariff reform law of 1897.[50] This modest shift toward systematic protectionism had an effect that transcended its immediate economic implications. It formally established that tariffs and other kinds of special interest economic policies were legitimate political exercises, and it erected the framework for future competition among economic sectors as well as between producers and consumers. This type of policy competition, however restrained, was ongoing and not susceptible to permanent solution, requiring a more active and permanent SNA involvement in the policy process.

By the late 1890s, in response to heightened competition over economic policy, declining agricultural profits, and pressure from landowners and the rival agricultural society, the SNA consciously undertook a more active lobbying role. An editorial in the July 1898 *Boletín* announced its intentions in typical understated fashion: "It is not only crops and their improvement, practical advice, and studies of technical matters that interest Chilean agriculturists today. . . . Legislation, administrative services, economic questions, social sciences today constitute numerous and serious problems intimately related to agricultural interests. . . . This Society cannot ignore the many bills presented in Congress, and debated and approved there, which injure delicate and valuable agricultural interests."[51]

The following year, on the occasion of a minor disagreement with the SNA, the minister of industry and public works challenged the Society's right to its role of independent advocate while continuing to receive a government subsidy. The SNA answered in a sharply worded public declaration of independence from the government which, together with the 1898 statement, announced a new departure for the Society: "We do not recall that heretofore such unconditional adherence has been demanded to whatever the authorities do. The Society of Agriculture is not subject to military discipline with respect to the government. It is a free association composed of free men who have banded together to work for the interests of their industry, an industry which has the right to make its voice, its complaints, and its petitions heard by all the public powers."[52]

By the turn of the century, the SNA and the other sectoral economic associations had acquired greater importance in the Chilean political system. In response to continuing economic diversification and increased policy competition, producers' and merchants' associations organized along regional and commodity lines—northern agriculturists, Talca merchants, nitrate miners, distillers—sprang up in the next few years to promote their specialized interests in the political arena. Thus, by the 1910s, Chile had an extensive and well-articulated network of entrepreneurial interest groups.[53]

The SNA's policy concerns were important but relatively simple. It sought to prevent enactment or execution of adverse measures, such as certain tariffs, railroad rate increases, or damaging commercial treaties, and to enhance landowners' welfare through policies such as selected tariffs, shipping subsidies, and government investment in agricultural services and irrigation projects. In pursuing its policy goals, the SNA had not only to compete with rival economic interests but also to contend with the inertia that characterized the parliamentary regime in economic matters. Thus its public statements frequently denounced the sterility of politics and advocated the adoption of prudent measures to develop agriculture and the economy as a whole.[54]

Despite its increased level of political activity, the SNA was not as visible in the political system as it would become after World War I. At most times the Society operated in a low-key manner suited to the genteel style of the period, without the use of high pressure tactics, and thus it seldom attracted public attention to its lobbying efforts.[55] One explanation of the SNA's moderate approach was the recovery of agricultural prosperity after 1900, which quickly ended the militancy that landowners had shown in the 1890s. Radical policy changes were thus no longer sought, and landowners' most pressing needs—roads, railroad spurs, and other public works—were addressed on a regional and local basis through the annual budgetary process in Congress.[56] Moreover, the SNA's approach was shaped by the multisectoral economic interests of its membership; in times of prosperity, the Society would hardly be inclined to press vigorously for the narrow interests of agriculture to the detriment of other economic sectors in which landowners commonly invested.

There were still other reasons why the SNA could operate unobtrusively but effectively. The years between the 1891 civil war and World War I were the halcyon days of the Chilean oligarchy—the era when it presided over a modernizing and burgeoning economy, a wealthy state, and a political system that protected its interests and privileges. Although the rise of a militant proletariat in the cities and the nitrate zone caused widespread concern about the "social question," oligarchic hegemony guaranteed the primacy of capital over labor and screened out demands for redistributive measures. Within this favorable context, there were additional factors that enhanced the SNA's position. Approximately half of all congressmen were themselves large landowners, and representatives of the rural districts constituted a large majority in Congress. At any time, moreover, approximately 20 percent of all senators and deputies were SNA members.[57] While these advantages did not ensure favorable legislative action on SNA proposals, the latent landowner veto power assured that nothing seriously detrimental to landowner interests would be tolerated. Given the prevailing prosperity, this was enough to satisfy landowners that the SNA was effectively protecting their interests.

The SNA's strengths allowed the organization to rely essentially on articulating the landowner viewpoint, in the *Boletín* and through formal communication with government entities. In addition, Society directors could pursue landowner policy concerns informally, through the multiple contacts offered by the intimate nature of aristocratic society. The casino at Viña del Mar, *tertulias* (social gatherings) at suburban fundos, the Club Hípico or the Club de la Unión, political party meetings, the halls of Congress, the stock exchange—all offered the SNA's leadership automatic and casual access to the upper levels of decision-making, in which they as individuals, moreover, played a central part.[58] The methods of political action that the SNA did not employ are equally telling about the Society's political role: it did not actively recruit members to enhance its power, hold mass meetings, use paid advertising, organize petition or telegram campaigns, or, with a single minor exception, become involved in electoral politics.

In sum, to conduct its business and satisfy its constituency within the framework of the Parliamentary Republic, the SNA had not yet resorted to the pressure tactics which are commonly identified with politically active interest groups. The advent of mass politics, however, would shortly alter landowners' casual approach to interest group politics.

Notes

1. Bauer, *Chilean Rural Society*, pp. 3-16. This includes bibliography on colonial agriculture and rural society.

2. Mario Góngora, *Encomenderos y estancieros* (Santiago, 1970); Bauer, *Chilean Rural Society*, pp. 16-21.

3. George M. McBride, *Chile: Land and Society* (Baltimore, 1936), pp. 3-14; Mario Góngora, *Orígen de los inquilinos de Chile central* (Santiago, 1960).

4. Sergio Sepúlveda, *El trigo chileno en el mercado mundial* (Santiago, 1956); Bauer, *Chilean Rural Society*, pp. 62-73.

5. Silvia Hernández, "Transformaciones tecnológicas en la agricultura de Chile central. Siglo xix," *Cuadernos del Centro de Estudios Socioeconómicos*, no. 3 (1966), 1-31; Bauer, *Chilean Rural Society*, pp. 101-6, 145-73.

6. From the SNA charter, in Sociedad Nacional de Agricultura, *Boletín* (hereafter cited as *BSNA*), 1 (1869-70), 4-5.

7. Gonzalo Izquierdo Fernández, *Un estudio de ideologías chilenas: la Sociedad de Agricultura en el siglo xix* (Santiago, 1968); Luis Correa Vergara, *Agricultura chilena* (Santiago, 1938), 1, 169-86; *El Campesino* (hereafter cited as *El C*), 70 (1938), edición extraordinaria (special pagination), has a full history of the institution and its predecessor. For seventy-five years the SNA considered itself a distinct entity, not a refounding of the earlier society, and this was reflected in the SNA's official letterhead stationery and other references. In 1934, Society director Luis Correa Vergara argued that the SNA was a revival of the Sociedad Chilena de Agricultura, and at that time of political stress, thirty more years of history and tradition apparently seemed worth claiming; the board of directors designated May 18, 1838, as the Society's date of founding, and its centennial was celebrated in 1938. *El C*, 66 (1934), 594.

8. Izquierdo, *Sociedad de Agricultura*. On the Sociedades de Amigos del País, see R. J. Shafer, *The Economic Societies in the Spanish World (1763-1821)* (Syracuse, N.Y., 1958).

9. *El Mensajero de la Agricultura*, 1 (1856), 77, quoted in Izquierdo, *Sociedad de Agricultura*, p. 27.

10. *Ibid.*, pp. 161-62. The *BSNA* continued to examine social and other nontechnical issues throughout the 1870s, under the editorship of Julio Menadier. On the state of Chilean agriculture in the nineteenth century, see Bauer, *Chilean Rural Society*, pp. 62-116.

11. Teodoro Schneider, *La agricultura en Chile en los últimos cincuenta años* (Santiago, 1904), pp. 165-213; Correa Vergara, *Agricultura chilena*, 1, 169-226; Bauer, *Chilean Rural Society*, pp. 101-6.

12. Schneider, *La agricultura en Chile*; Correa Vergara, *Agricultura chilena*.

13. E.g., *BSNA*, 1 (1869-70), 451-52; *ibid.*, 4 (1872-73), 30; *ibid.*, 31 (1900), 817; *ibid.*, 40 (1909), 8.

14. Membership rosters are from Sociedad Nacional de Agricultura, *Memoria* (hereafter cited as *MSNA*), years indicated. See Table 5.

15. *BSNA*, 3 (1871-72), 216.

16. *Ibid.*, 1 (1869-70), 6-7.

17. The tax rolls can be used with confidence for identifying individual landowners, but not for examining the agrarian property structure in accurate detail. See the discussion of tax rolls as sources in Arnold Bauer and Ann Hagerman Johnson, "Land and Labour in Rural Chile, 1850-1935," in Kenneth Duncan and Ian Rutledge, eds., *Land and Labour in Latin America: Essays on the Development of Agrarian Capitalism in the Nineteenth and Twentieth Centuries* (Cambridge, Eng., 1977), pp. 98-99. The assessment of 1874 was denounced for alleged political and personal favoritism and caused a major scandal; the 1908 list was a compilation of municipal assessments not based on nationally uniform criteria. It is impossible to establish the number of minifundia with any accuracy. Properties that yielded less than 100 pesos were neither taxed nor counted in 1874, and although taxable in 1908 they apparently were assessed only where there was some hope of collecting the

tax. The numbers of small holdings for both years are my rough estimates. The 1874 figure is based on the SNA's estimate, in Ministerio de Hacienda, *Memoria . . . 1875* (Santiago, 1875), p. 67; on the estimate in Martín Drouilly and Pedro Lucio Cuadra, *Ensayo sobre el estado económico de la agricultura en Chile* (Santiago, 1878); and on an 1881 survey of small holdings cited in Bauer and Johnson, "Land and Labour." The figure for 1908 is double that reported in the 1911 *Anuario estadístico* but may still be a conservative estimate.

Note that the system of evaluation changed between 1874 and 1908. In 1874, the old tithe system of assumed income was still in use, while by 1908 a value was assigned to the property per se.

18. *MSNA* (1873 and 1909); *Impuesto agrícola: rol de contribuyentes* (Santiago, 1874); *Indice de propietarios rurales i valor de la propiedad rural según los roles de avalúos comunales* (Santiago, 1908).

19. Schneider, *La agricultura en Chile*, pp. 196-200. See ch. 3, under "Unification," on the SNA's later relations with the regional societies.

20. *Indice de propietarios rurales; MSNA* (1909).

21. Ministerio de Industria y Obras Públicas, *Asociación de Viticultores* (Santiago, 1895). This association's annual *memorias* appeared in the same ministry's annual *memorias*.

22. McBride, *Land and Society*, pp. 141-44.

23. The biographical dictionaries establish family connections between landowning and nonowner SNA members in a few cases. In 1908, for example, only one of three Huneeus SNA members owned land, but all were related; three of five members of the Matte family on the SNA rolls owned land; one of the two Montt Montt brothers owned land; likewise with the Pacheco Zegers brothers; Ismael Tocornal owned land, but his son Domingo, also a SNA member, did not. The preceding, in order cited, are from Virgilio Figueroa, *Diccionario histórico y biográfico de Chile*, 5 vols. (Santiago, 1925-31), 3, 487-93; 4, 221-22; 4, 228; 4, 316; and 5, 894.

24. Paul S. Reinsch, "Parliamentary Government in Chile," *American Political Science Review*, 3 (1909), 508.

25. Alejandro Venegas (pseud., Dr. Julio Valdés Cange), *Sinceridad: Chile íntimo en 1910* (Santiago, 1910), p. 21.

26. Frederick B. Pike, *Chile and the United States, 1880-1962* (Notre Dame, Ind., 1965), p. 121.

27. See the ambitious study by Maurice Zeitlin and Richard Earl Ratcliff, "Research Methods for the Analysis of the Internal Structure of Dominant Classes: The Case of Landlords and Capitalists in Chile," *Latin American Research Review*, 10 (1975), 5-61. Henry Kirsch, *Industrial Development in a Traditional Society: The Conflict between Entrepreneurship and Modernization in Chile* (Gainesville, Fla., 1977), pp. 66-77, examines the sectoral linkages with special reference to industry, and Diana Balmori and Robert Oppenheimer investigate the same processes comparatively in "Family Clusters: Generational Nucleation in Nineteenth-Century Argentina and Chile," *Comparative Studies in Society and History*, 21 (1979), 231-61.

28. Bauer, *Chilean Rural Society*, p. 180; also pp. 174-203 for a discussion of the social role of landownership.

29. *Ibid.*, pp. 87-101, 174-203.

30. *El Mercurio* (Valparaíso), Apr. 26, 1882, p. 2.

31. Armand Mattelart, Carmen Castillo, and Leonardo Castillo, *La ideología de*

la dominación en una sociedad dependiente. La respuesta ideológica de la clase dominante chilena al reformismo (Buenos Aires, 1970), pp. 80-83.

32. Myriam Waiser P., Carlos Muñoz L., and Eduardo Irazabal L., "La clase hacendada en Chile durante el siglo xix" (Memoria de Prueba, Universidad de Chile, 1967), p. 96.

33. Appendix 2. See Guillermo Edwards Matte, *El Club de la Unión en sus ochenta años, 1864-1944* (Santiago, 1944); Reinsch, Parliamentary Government"; and Gertrude M. Yeager, "The Club de la Unión and Kinship: Social Aspects of Political Obstructionism in the Chilean Senate, 1920-1924," *The Americas*, 35 (1979), 539-72.

34. Appendix 1. For data on Congress and presidential cabinets, see Luis Valencia Avaria, *Anales de la República*, 2 vols. (Santiago, 1951).

35. See Appendixes 3, 4, and 5. Genaro Arriagada, *La oligarquía patronal chilena* (Santiago, 1970), establishes the pattern of oligarchic control within the SNA and other sectoral economic associations at a later period.

36. *BSNA*, 3 (1871-72), 63-64; *ibid.*, 7 (1876-77), 46-48; *El C*, 66 (1934), 531-45; Correa Vergara, *Agricultura chilena*, 1, 169-226, 291-346.

37. Stanley J. and Barbara H. Stein, *The Colonial Heritage of Latin America* (New York, 1970), pp. 158ff., discusses the "corporate spirit" as a colonial survival in the nineteenth century. See also: Magali Sarfatti, *Spanish Bureaucratic-Patrimonialism in America* (Berkeley, Cal., 1966); and John L. Phelan, *The Kingdom of Quito in the Seventeenth Century: Bureaucratic Politics in the Spanish Empire* (Madison, Wis., 1967).

38. *Lei de presupuestos de entradas y gastos ordinarios de la administración pública de Chile para el año 1896* (Santiago, 1896), pp. 19-21, lists five subsidized economic associations, three of them agricultural.

39. Correa Vergara, *Agricultura chilena*, 1, 291-346. See also the annual *MSNA* and monthly *BSNA*. Official correspondence is located in Archivo Nacional (hereafter cited as *AN*), Ministerio de Hacienda, vols. 894, 956, 1004, 1135, 1228, 1333, 1431, 1546, 1730; and Ministerio de Relaciones Exteriores, Culto y Colonización, vol. 204.

40. Government income is recorded in *Resúmen de la hacienda pública de Chile desde 1833 hasta 1914* (London, 1914). Expansion of the bureaucracy is described in Germán Urzúa Valenzuela and Anamaría García Barzelatto, *Diagnóstico de la burocracia chilena (1818-1969)* (Santiago, 1971). As late as 1897 the relationship between the government and the SNA was not clearly defined or understood. In that year the minister of Industria y Obras Públicas ordered the Society's possessions inventoried along with government property "*por considerarlos bienes fiscales*"; the Society protested energetically. *BSNA*, 28 (1897), 619.

41. Bauer, *Chilean Rural Society*, esp. chs. 3, 4, and 6. Claudio Véliz, "La mesa de tres patas," *Desarrollo Económico*, 3 (1963), 231-48, whose thesis about the compatibility of the main sectoral interests is valid up to the 1890s.

42. This point has been disputed in the literature. Izquierdo, *Sociedad de Agricultura*, asserts that the SNA "did not become the head of a pressure group" (p. 164); Waiser *et al.*, "Clase hacendada," pp. 58-66, 92-95, argue the opposite case, unconvincingly.

43. Daniel Martner, *Historia de Chile: historia económica* (Santiago, 1929), 1, 344-45; *Revista Económica*, año II (1888), 228-30; on taxation changes, Alberto Edwards, "Nuestro régimen tributario en los últimos 40 años," *Revista Chilena*, año I (1917), 337-56, cited in Arturo Valenzuela, *Political Brokers in Chile: Local Government in a Centralized Polity* (Durham, N.C., 1977), pp. 197-98.

44. On economic development following the War of the Pacific, see: Martner, *Historia económica*, 1, 412ff.; Kirsch, *Industrial Development*; Marcello Carmagnani, *Sviluppo industriale e sottosviluppo economico: il caso cileno (1860-1920)* (Turin, 1971); Carlos Hurtado Ruiz-Tagle, *Concentración de población y desarrollo económico: el caso chileno* (Santiago, 1966); Aníbal Pinto Santa Cruz, *Chile, un caso de desarrollo frustrado* (Santiago, 1962) pp. 44-105; Julio César Jobet, *Ensayo crítico del desarrollo económico-social de Chile* (Santiago, 1955), pp. 63-156.

45. Kirsch, *Industrial Development*, chs. 1 and 2, examines the early postwar growth of industry and critiques the literature on that subject. On contemporary tariff policy, see William F. Sater, "Economic Nationalism and Tax Reform in Late Nineteenth-Century Chile," *The Americas*, 33 (1976), 311-35.

46. See the SOFOFA's monthly *Boletín* and annual *Memoria*, 1883-1900; Pedro Luis González, *50 años de labor de la Sociedad de Fomento Fabril* (Santiago, 1933); Juan Eduardo Vargas Cariola, "La Sociedad de Fomento Fabril, 1883-1928," *Historia*, 13 (1976), 5-53.

47. See ch. 5, under "Cattle Tax." Sepúlveda, *El trigo chileno*, and Bauer, *Chilean Rural Society*, pp. 62-73, trace the growth and decline of wheat exports. On protectionism, see Thomas C. Wright, "Agriculture and Protectionism in Chile, 1880-1930," *Journal of Latin American Studies*, 7, no. 1 (May 1975), 45-58.

48. *BSNA*, 25-28 (1894-97); Wright, "Agriculture and Protectionism," pp. 51-52.

49. Centro Industrial y Agrícola, *Revista*, 2 (1900), 1; *ibid.*, p. 211.

50. Ricardo Anguita, *Leyes promulgadas en Chile desde 1810 hasta el primero de junio de 1913*, 5 vols. (Santiago, 1912-13), 3, 400-407; Wright, "Agriculture and Protectionism," pp. 52-53.

51. *BSNA*, 29 (1898), 1-2.

52. *Ibid.*, 30 (1899), 387-88.

53. See ch. 4, under "Corporate Representation," on the future growth of these economic associations. Constantine Menges, "Public Policy and Organized Business in Chile: A Preliminary Analysis," *Journal of International Affairs*, 20 (1966), 343-65, examines the business interest group network in the 1960s.

54. E.g., *BSNA*, 36 (1905), 702-3; *ibid.*, 39 (1908), 662-64; *ibid.*, 43 (1912), 534-35. On government during the Parliamentary Period, see: Manuel Rivas Vicuña, *Historia política y parlamentaria de Chile*, 3 vols. (Santiago, 1964); Julio Heise González, *Historia de Chile: el Período Parlamentario, 1861-1925* (Santiago, 1974); Jordan M. Young, "Chilean Parliamentary Government, 1891-1924" (unpublished dissertation in political science, Princeton University, 1953); and Karen L. Remmer, "The Timing, Pace and Sequence of Political Change in Chile: 1891-1925," *Hispanic American Historical Review*, 57 (1977), 205-30.

55. The SNA's and other interest groups' lobbying was so unobtrusive that Paul Reinsch felt that politics in Chile was unaffected by the intrusion of "vast material interests clamoring for attention." Reinsch, "Parliamentary Government," p. 507.

56. For a summary of the SNA's political activities, see *BSNA*, 53 (1922), 625-44. Agricultural prices rose some 200 percent between 1895-99 and 1914-18. Dirección General de Estadística, *Sinópsis estadístico de Chile, año 1918* (Santiago, 1919), p. 118; and *Sinópsis estadístico de Chile, año 1925* (Santiago, 1926), p. 117. Rural property values also rose greatly: Santiago Marín Vicuña, *La valorización territorial de la república* (Santiago, 1918), p. 14. For growth of the domestic market, see Wright, "Agriculture and Protectionism," p. 49. On the politics of the budget during the Parliamentary Period, Rivas Vicuña, *Historia política y parlamentaria*, 1, 74-75; and Valenzuela, *Political Brokers*, pp. 196-97.

57. Appendix 6; also Bauer, *Chilean Rural Society*, pp. 214–17.

58. Julio Subercaseaux Browne, *Reminiscencias* (Santiago, 1976), provides a contemporary's insights into the workings of aristocratic life; and Luis Barros Lezaeta and Ximena Vergara Johnson, *El modo de ser aristocrático: el caso de la oligarquía chilena hacia 1900* (Santiago, 1978) analyzes upper-class attitudes using literary sources.

2

Landowners and the Onset of Reform

The tranquility of the Parliamentary Republic was rudely shattered in 1919 when a massive economic crisis precipitated mass mobilization on a scale unprecedented in Chile. The election of Arturo Alessandri to the presidency in 1920—"the revolt of the electorate," in Alberto Edwards's evocative phrase—jeopardized the system that had made life comfortable and secure for the Chilean oligarchy.[1] Over the next twenty years many things changed: political participation increased, politics was realigned on a class basis, the state assumed social welfare and development functions, and old rights and privileges were challenged. By 1938 the political system had evolved to the point where Chile could elect a Popular Front government of Marxist and reformist parties. When the Popular Front collapsed in the first days of 1941, Chile had not become a mass democracy with full participation—far from it, in fact. But its political system was competitive, representatives of the working class shared power with those of the middle and upper classes, and the social and economic elites were on the defensive. As an integral part of the old privileged order, large landowners found themselves severely challenged by the advent of mass politics between 1919 and 1940.

Landowners and the Forces of Reform

The developments which most seriously threatened the interests of Chilean landowners after 1919 were the emergence of strong ideological and programmatic challenges and the steady growth of political forces of the left and center. With the exception of the increasingly moderate Democratic party, there had been no significant organized opposition to the oligarchic consensus before 1920. Then the decade of the twenties witnessed the breakdown of traditional political alliances based on personal, electoral, and religious factors and the reorientation of political groups along social and economic lines. Participation increased concurrently, and the working and middle sectors readily found leaders and organizations responsive to their class interests. By the early thirties the new configuration of Chilean politics had crystallized along class lines, and henceforth individuals, parties, and coalitions invariably were identified as being of the left, center, or right.[2]

The political forces most hostile to landowner interests, of course, were those of the new Marxist left. The main Marxist groups were the Communist party, founded in 1921 from the core of the Socialist Workers' party, and the Socialist party of Chile, established in 1933 as an amalgamation of six factions. Both parties were subject to periodic schism and spent as much energy fighting dissident factions and each other as they did in attacking the right. Nonetheless, increased industrialization and urbanization, pronounced economic fluctuations, and an ambience of relative political freedom gave impetus to the impressive growth of the left. By 1940 the two main Marxist parties commanded nearly a quarter of the country's electorate. Beyond its electoral strength, the left had developed an important power base in organized labor. The Chilean Confederation of Labor (CTCh) had some 150,000 members in key economic sectors by 1940, and the left also controlled a large extralegal or free union movement.[3]

Equally significant was the emergence of the Radical party as a distinctly middle-class entity with separate identity and objectives from both right and left. From its founding in 1868, the Radical party had been a heterogeneous aggregate of northern mining, frontier and southern agricultural, and urban middle sector interests; and through the Parliamentary Period it had differed from the Liberals and Conservatives mainly in its strident secularism and advocacy of state education. By the twenties and thirties, however, its ideology and platform had begun to reflect the growing influence of the disaffected urban middle class, while upper-class elements continued to be strongly represented in the party's leadership. The Radicals stood for industrialization, expansion of state services, and controlled social change within the framework of democratic institutions. The 1931 convention adopted as the party's goal a vaguely defined socialism, and during most of the thirties the Radicals pursued their reformist line in tacit or explicit alliance with the Marxist parties.

The right by the 1930s had been reduced primarily to the historic Conservative and Liberal parties. The traditional rivals found that the rise of threats to vested interests gave them much common ground, and although they often supported different presidential and congressional candidates they agreed on fundamentals. They stood for capitalism and private property and rejected the notion of class conflict, insisting instead that the nation's progress depended on harmonious class relations, order, and work. In short, the Liberals and Conservatives espoused the views and policies best calculated to preserve as much as possible of the old order and the prerogatives of the upper classes. Although its electoral strength was in decline after 1919, the right retained some important advantages over the competition. It controlled most of the country's press and had the money to engage on a large scale in the common practice of buying votes. The right's greatest strength was the continuing ability of landowners in the central provinces to deliver the votes of their workers and other dependents to Conservative or Liberal candidates, thus assuring heavy rightist representation from the rural core of the country.[4]

The changing composition of Congress provides one measure of the challenge to vested interests. Once the preserve of the aristocratic and the monied, the setting of genteel gamesmanship and polished but hollow discourse, the chambers of Congress by the thirties rang with vehement denunciations of the "feudal oligarchy." Despite the previously mentioned electoral advantages of the right and the additional benefit it derived from Chile's proportional system of elections, the left had become a sizeable congressional bloc by 1940, and the center had experienced considerable growth since 1919. The Conservative and Liberal parties lost their absolute majorities in both chambers of Congress for the first time in the 1932 elections, when their combined vote for deputies dipped to a mere 34.5 percent of total votes cast nationally; the right regained only a bare majority

Table 3
Left, Center, and Right Blocs in Congress, 1918-41[a]

Congress	Deputies, Percent				Senators, Percent			
	L	C	R	I&U[b]	L	C	R	I&U
32nd, 1918-21	5.1	25.4	66.1	3.4	5.4	13.5	73.0	8.1
33rd, 1921 24	9.3	34.8	55.9	0.0	8.1	16.2	75.7	0.0
34th, 1924	10.2	32.2	55.1	2.5	10.8	27.0	54.1	8.1
35th, 1926-30	15.1	28.8	52.3	3.8	6.7	31.1	57.8	4.4
37th, 1933-37[c]	19.0	31.7	45.8	3.5	24.4	37.8	37.8	0.0
38th, 1937-41	21.8	30.6	47.6	0.0	13.3	35.6	51.1	0.0

[a]The blocs consisted of the following parties (factions are subsumed under the parent party unless they belonged to a separate bloc). Right: Conservative, Liberal, Agrarian; Center: Radical, Falange Nacional, Nazi, Social Republicano, Demócrata (beginning with 37th Congress); Left: Demócrata (through 35th Congress), Democrático, Communist, Socialist, Radical Socialist.

[b]Independents and those whose party affiliation is unknown.

[c]Composition of the 36th Congress—the Thermal Congress—was arranged by Ibáñez and the major right and center parties. Since it did not reveal electoral strength of contending political groups, its composition is not given here.

SOURCE: *El Mercurio* (Santiago), Mar.-Apr. 1918, 1921, 1924, 1926, 1933; John Reese Stevenson, *The Chilean Popular Front*, pp. 96-97; Dirección General de Estadística, *Sinópsis geográfico y estadístico de Chile, año 1933*, pp. 34-35.

in the Senate in 1937.[5] By the thirties, then, the Conservatives and Liberals were forced to seek electoral and tactical alliances with moderate groups in order to retain a conditional and highly tentative veto power in Congress. Table 3 illustrates the changing composition of Congress in the twenties and thirties.

Presidential elections offer another indication of the decline of the traditional right in Chilean politics. After adoption of the 1925 constitution, the parliamentary system was replaced by a system of presidential supremacy which greatly enhanced the executive's role in policy-making.[6] The proportional voting system which favored the right in congressional elections did not apply to presidential contests, which thus more accurately reflected the attitude of the electorate. After 1915 the rightist parties were unable to elect a presidential candidate of their own, without coalition support, until the narrow victory of Jorge Alessandri in 1958. So, while most presidents between 1920 and 1940 were sympathetic to the right and were themselves essentially conservative, they governed under the constraints imposed by coalition politics and the prospects of future alliances, as well as by the composition of Congress. Therefore even with allies in the presidency, vested interests could no longer be served with sovereign disregard for the political and social consequences of government actions. (Table 4 lists the main presidential administrations between 1920 and 1940.)

Table 4
Presidential Administrations, 1920-41

President	Dates
Arturo Alessandri Palma	12/23/20 - 9/9/24
Four military juntas	9/9/24 - 3/20/25
Arturo Alessandri Palma	3/20/25 - 10/1/25
Vice-presidency of Luis Barros Borgoño	10/1/25 - 12/23/25
Emiliano Figueroa Larraín	12/23/25 - 4/7/27
Vice-presidency of Carlos Ibáñez del Campo	4/7/27 - 7/21/27
Carlos Ibáñez del Campo	7/21/27 - 7/26/31
Four civilian caretaker governments	7/26/31 - 12/4/31
Juan Esteban Montero Rodríguez	12/4/31 - 6/4/32
Socialist Republic (five civilian/military governments)	6/4/32 - 9/13/32
Two caretaker governments	9/13/32 - 12/24/32
Arturo Alessandri Palma	12/24/32 - 12/24/38
Pedro Aguirre Cerda	12/24/38 - 11/10/41

SOURCE: Luis Valencia Avaria, *Anales de la República*, 1, 393-445.

The ascendant parties of left and center had ideological, strategic, and practical reasons for attacking landowners' basic interests and prerogatives. To the Marxists, as well as the majority of Radicals, Chilean rural society was a feudal anachronism whose existence was inadmissible in a democracy and inconsistent with their respective visions of the ideal society. Modification or destruction of the rural social order was strategically necessary to end landowners' monopolization of the rural vote, the cornerstone of the right's electoral strength. At the practical level, the left and center could expect to gain the electoral support of the rural masses by improving their condition and liberating them from landowners' dominance and the allegiance of the urban poor by pursuing price controls to moderate the virtually constant inflation of foodstuffs. For these reasons, the left supported with conviction, and the center with some reservations, policies which landowners opposed—agrarian reform, the application of labor and social welfare legislation to agricultural workers, and controls on agricultural prices.

As if these were not reasons enough for challenging landowners' interests, there was still another important motive: attacking landowners was good politics and an easy and sure way of gaining favor with the urban lower and middle classes. Long before the advent of mass politics, the Chilean landowner had acquired a thoroughly negative image which made him the target of popular frustration and wrath. The landowner was widely held to be the villain of Chilean history, the people's enemy, an intractable obstacle to progress. A broad segment of the urban population held the landowner responsible for virtually every social, economic, or political problem facing the country. The intensity of the attack on landowners, then, was at least partially caused by the image they projected, its wide diffusion, and its political exploitability.

The Villain Landowner

Without the benefit of public opinion survey data, there is no accurate way to gauge how widely the negative image of landowners was held or the extent to which it influenced political decisions. Nonetheless, the instruments through which the image was disseminated are clearly visible: the daily press, political party tracts, novels, critiques, essays, congressional debates, political speeches—these and other vehicles of communication were available to spread the landowner stereotype. By the twenties and thirties, as a result of the growth of literacy, urbanization, radio broadcasting, and the rise of leftist groups which consciously propagated the image, a fairly broad segment of the urban population had undoubtedly been so familiarized with the main traits of the villain landowner that image and reality were indistinguishable. The most convincing evidence of the pervasiveness of the landowner stereotype is found in the frequent statements by landowner spokesmen in Congress, the press, the SNA's journal, and elsewhere, recognizing its currency and denying its validity. The following analysis of the composite landowner image will describe its development since the 1880s and demonstrate that the political left, while using and embellishing the image of landowners, certainly did not invent it.

The first discernible element of the stereotype was a by-product of the wheat export boom, the "golden age" of Chilean agriculture between approximately 1850 and 1875. The substantial profits accruing from wheat, combined with an abundance of cheap mortgage credit, put lavish use of money within reach of a large number of agriculturists, and the infusion of new money from mining and urban enterprises sustained the appearance of great prosperity among landowners well past the turn of the century. The years between the 1860s and the 1900s were the era when the rustic fundo house was remodeled in Second Empire or Georgian style and surrounded by landscaped parks—the period of the lavish town house in Santiago's finest neighborhoods, the European holidays, the imported fashions and carriages.[7] The change between 1850 and the turn of the century is depicted in fiction by the striking contrast between the austerity of Blest Gana's *Martín Rivas* and the opulence of the *belle époque* in Orrego Luco's *Casa Grande*. The ostentatious patterns of consumption widely practiced by landowners of this period gave rise to the image of a "*clase derrochadora*," a squandering class.[8]

Depiction of landowners as a "squandering class" began with contemporary descriptions and criticism and persisted through 1940 and beyond. In 1889, the economist Marcial González published an influential essay entitled "Our Enemy: Luxury," which denounced the squandering ways of rich landowners.[9] The "derrochadora" stereotype was well enough established by 1900 for a writer in an agricultural journal to ask cynically whether the poverty of Chile could be attributed to "the squandering of the money received to cultivate the land . . . on sterile luxuries, on gambling, on stupid financial combinations?"[10] A 1901 article in the SNA *Boletín* affirmed that landowners spent much of their mortgage credit on "furniture and wallpaper, theatre and carriages."[11] An agronomist writing in 1939 confirmed the durability of this element of the image: "It is commonly affirmed that agriculturists swim in abundance and that they rapidly accumulate fortunes."[12] The SNA and individual landowners persistently denied the image of great wealth and prodigality after the rise of mass politics made it a political liability. For example, SNA director Luis Correa Vergara stated in a 1929 speech: "The populace judges agriculturists in general by the rare cases seen in the cities boasting pompous ostentation, but those lucky ones are relatively few."[13]

Following the "clase derrochadora" image, there appeared the related but distinct stereotype of the landowner as "*papelero*"—the proponent and beneficiary of the fiduciary regime which continually expanded the money supply and contributed to inflation and devaluation of the Chilean currency after 1880.[14] This provided an explanation of how landowners achieved their ostentatious life-style: credit costs were lowered through inflation, while export earnings were converted to ever increasing amounts of pesos as a function of devaluation. The landowner's wealth, then, was illicit—the result not of work but of manipulation. The "papelero" stereotype seems to have been publicized originally by economist Roberto Espinoza around the turn of the century and was further elaborated and popularized by Agustín Ross Edwards, who wrote in 1910 that landowners "are accomplishing their purpose, insofar as reducing their own debts is concerned, by the gradual and persistent depreciation of paper money."[15]

Since it was fashionable to attribute most of the country's ills to the paper money regime, landowners as politically powerful "papeleros" were seen as responsible for the ruin of the currency, the general economic decline of the fin de siècle, and for the devastating impact of inflation on the working classes. Alejandro Venegas expressed the common view of the ruinous effects of paper money in his influential *Sinceridad: Chile íntimo en 1910*: "The paper money regime is the cause of all the perturbations which our country is suffering in the economic, political, administrative, and social realms."[16] In an attempt at refutation through irony, the SNA *Boletín* in 1914 articulated the supposed landowner culpability in the fiduciary regime: "All agriculturists are papeleros; to their influence and their insatiable and egotistical appetite for lucre are due the successive emissions of paper, the constant depreciation of the currency, and the consequent difficulties of everyone who lives on wages, a salary, or a fixed income."[17]

Contemporaneous with the public debate over paper money was the struggle over the so-called "cattle tax."[18] Landowners' advocacy of tariff protection for livestock, which was commonly expected to accelerate the already serious rate of inflation in the 1880s, provided further evidence of their alleged sovereign disregard for the general welfare and their exclusive concern with profits. This issue helped generalize the "papelero" image to portray the landowner as "exploiter of the people"—referring at this time to the urban consumer of scant or modest means. When first debated in 1888, the cattle tax proposal was labeled by Agustín Ross as a tax to be levied by the rich on the poor and by Democratic party spokesman Malaquías Concha as "legal hunger decreed by the representatives of the people, . . . tantamount to the deportation of our working classes to foreign shores."[19] Enactment of the cattle tax in 1897 and the subsequent struggle for its repeal brought forth stronger emotions and language; and the bloody Red Week of 1905, in which hundreds of people were killed protesting the tariff, could only have etched the negative image more deeply in the popular consciousness. In the aftermath of the Red Week, *El Mercurio* printed a volunteered letter claiming that "one can only consider those who daily fill their coffers fuller from abuse of the people's hunger as iniquitous exploiters."[20] Openly admitting the currency of that view, the SNA editorially denied that landowners were guilty of "exploitation of the poor by the rich, immoral speculation with the hunger of the needy, plundering of the worker."[21]

The "exploiter of the people" image was sustained by constant food price inflation and outlived the more topical paper money and cattle tax issues to become a permanent and central component of the composite stereotype. The frequent denials of evil intent by landowner spokesmen suggest that this was considered a serious liability. For example, in 1920 the SNA claimed that landowners had been viciously maligned by students from the school of agronomy, who entered a float in the spring festival which portrayed landowners as "despoilers of the people."[22] In a 1925 speech, a member of one of the southern agricultural societies carefully pointed out that his association did not intend "to speculate with the funds of the state or the hunger of the people."[23] And in 1938, Deputy Manuel Bart Herrera of the Agrarian party denounced the "manifest hostility continually expressed by some sectors of the Chamber of Deputies against the agricultural industry, which they accuse of only trying to enrich itself at the expense of the people's misery."[24]

Contributing to the persistence of the anti-people image was the rise of another component of the stereotype—that of the "retrograde agriculturist." The SNA itself, in its capacity as a development institution, had been primarily responsible for fostering consciousness of the technological backwardness of Chilean agriculture, and *El Mercurio* in 1908 drew what was undoubtedly a very common portrait of the landowner: "The Chilean hacendado suffers one of the common national defects: he is somewhat vain and indolent at the same time. The indolence and pride of the Chilean agriculturist consist in his belief that he has at his fingertips the most effective system for the cultivation and prosperity of his lands, taking instructions from no one."[25] Venegas claimed that "of the 10,000 owners of fundos of over 1,000 hectares in Chile, perhaps there are not 50 who have any knowledge of agricultural science, and perhaps not 10 who have systematically studied agronomy."[26] The result, he felt, was that Chilean practices had not evolved beyond those of Egypt in 4,000 B.C.[27] In 1922 a critic claimed in Congress that landowners "do not know presently how to improve the yields of their fields and have not been able to develop their industry."[28]

The retrograde image became a political liability after 1919 because landowners were seen as failing the country and the people by causing food price inflation and the widespread malnutrition that was first discovered in the twenties and avidly debated in the thirties.[29] Thus the SNA began to change its emphasis, blaming the continuing technological backwardness on labor problems or low profit margins and no longer on landowners' resistance to modernization: "It is the common opinion that the Chilean agriculturist rejects the use of machinery out of ignorance, traditionalist spirit, or simple indifference toward progress. In such a view there is much injustice."[30]

Another component of the image was the depiction of the landowner as feudal lord, as absolute master over his workers. Like most other elements of the total portrait, this one had roots in the nineteenth century, when foreign travelers and Chileans alike occasionally commented on the condition of the inquilino or the peón. After 1900, increasing attention focused on working conditions and social relations in agriculture, and the outbreak of rural strikes after 1919 and the subsequent national debate over agricultural unions intensified the scrutiny. The result was dissemination and widespread acceptance of the view of the landowner as tyrant and unconscionable exploiter of the worker, a feudal lord in a legally democratic society.[31]

One of the most influential statements of this image was the work of Tancredo Pinochet LeBrun, published in 1916. He concluded that "the Chilean inquilino is a beast of burden, an animal, not a conscious citizen of a democratic republic."[32] Statements of this kind readily slipped into the lexicon of the left and surfaced repeatedly. Two examples will illustrate the typical political usage of the image: the Radical daily *La Hora* excoriated landowners in 1939 for "the situation of misery and exploitation in which they maintain their peasantry"; and the Socialist deputies in 1940 prefaced a bill with the statement that landowners "live by the exploitation and enslavement" of their workers.[33] Frequent rebuttals were forthcoming from landowner spokesmen, such as the lament by Deputy Alfredo Cerda Jaraquemada in Congress that "continually in the press, in Congress, and in different circles" landowners were portrayed "exploiting their inquilinos, whom they pay miserable salaries besides providing as housing only indecent pigsties."[34] The SNA launched a major public relations campaign in 1936 to offset the feudal exploiter image.[35]

There was yet another facet of the landowner stereotype which became more explicit and pronounced in the 1930s as standard leftist rhetoric. This was the notion that landowners as a group constituted the core of the "oligarchy," that they ran the country as they saw fit. The view of landowner omnipotence was not new to the period of mass politics; it was implicit in the "papelero" and "exploiter of the people" images as the explanation of how landowners could foist their nefarious schemes upon an unwilling country. Alejandro Venegas was explicit in blaming paper money on landowner hegemony: "The rich agriculturist[s], the hacendado[s] . . . dominated in the government" where they "have been legislating for their exclusive benefit."[36] But in the context of mass politics the image of landowner omnipotence was a serious liability in that any blow against that caste was, ipso facto, a blow for progress and democracy. George McBride's statement that the landowner ran the country as if it were a great hacienda was echoed frequently.[37] The Communist party, for example, pronounced that "the enemy of the proletariat and of all the people is the oligarchy, represented primarily by landowners of the feudal type. These latifundistas . . . have dominated our country during its entire existence."[38] The SNA itself logically became the instrument of the oligarchy, as revealed in the Communist daily, *El Siglo*: "Landowners, from the SNA, continue to dominate the country."[39] Deputy Bart Herrera felt compelled to deny the notion, "diffused with excessive ease, that the agriculturist class has governed at the expense of the country."[40]

Occasional statements of the entire composite image of the landowner must have found their way into print, but it is difficult to find any one that is entirely satisfactory as a synthesis. The following three passages taken together, however, reconstruct most of the stereotype. In a pamphlet on railroads published in 1931, L. Aníbal Lagos maintained that the landowner class "wasted the abundant sums taken from credit institutions in permanent orgies, with criminal neglect of scientific cultivation of the land . . . and wanted to maintain the population in permanent and painful agony."[41] Francisco Antonio Encina, essayist, historian, and SNA director, wrote in 1919 that the landowner "is seen as the genuine representative of the detested oligarchy. He is the retrograde who keeps the rural population vegetating in abjection. His ineptitude keeps our fields from producing. His avarice is the determining cause of the high cost of our agricultural production."[42] And from the SNA itself, a 1925 circular to its members warned that "the dominant currents of opinion" considered landowners "a special caste among social classes, . . . the nucleus of the oligarchy, despoiler of the proletariat, and cause of the greatest ills which have befallen the Republic."[43]

While the influence of the negative popular view of the landowner eludes accurate measurement, the SNA's and individual landowners' insistence on denying or correcting it indicates that they considered it a liability. As early as 1911, the SNA editorially lamented that through constant repetition negative images were becoming "incontrovertible aphorisms . . . axioms among the populace" that produced "an instinctive bad will, a kind of unconscious hatred toward agriculture."[44] In a 1939 editorial, *El*

Campesino attributed the villain landowner image to a "clever campaign designed to estrange the agriculturist from the popular masses, because they [leftists] wanted the latter to see in the former their worst enemy, dressed in the clothing of the 'hated landowner' that tendentious novels depict."[45] And Agrarian Deputy Bart Herrera summarized the result of the negative image: landowners "have lived surrounded always by an atmosphere of hostility, of hate, of misunderstanding."[46]

Developments of the 1960s in Chile also shed some light on attitudes toward landowners and on how the SNA interpreted the consequences of the negative image. In 1966 the Society commissioned a public opinion survey in various cities to determine the image of agriculture, i.e., of landowners. The survey found that over 60 percent of the public held strongly negative views and that over 90 percent favored agrarian reform of some type.[47] Paraphrasing SNA statements of an earlier era, a Society spokesman blamed the negative attitude on "false images, based on isolated cases, which were disseminated through intelligent and very tenacious propaganda."[48] The SNA drew a direct relationship between this image and landowners' political liabilities: "Public opinion is unjustifiably prejudiced against the man of the country. This has led successive governments to punish [landowners] mercilessly."[49]

The political implications of the Chilean landowner's negative image might usefully be contrasted with the political advantage enjoyed by the North American farmer as the result of his very different image. Drawing extensively on the work of Henry Nash Smith, Richard Hofstadter traced the development of the image projected by the farmer and examined the political implications of that image. He found that the widely disseminated and internalized vision of the "yeoman farmer," which depicted the tiller of the soil as repository of all the peculiarly North American virtues, by the late nineteenth century had long outlived the rather scanty amount of reality on which it was originally based. Moreover, this anachronistic image, which he called the "agrarian myth," gave the farmer great political advantage long after his majority status within the national electorate had been lost.[50] Without overstating the comparability of the United States and Chilean contexts, one could suggest that by contrast with the "agrarian myth" which Hofstadter found to enhance the farmer's political power, the "villain landowner" image must certainly have exacerbated the liabilities of Chilean landowners in an increasingly competitive political system.

Landowners and the Right

The growth of left and moderate power in Congress, the left's control of organized labor, adverse legislation, prejudicial administrative rulings, and direct action in the countryside began to erode landowners' prerogatives and autonomy soon after 1919, and the degree of challenge continued to grow throughout the next two decades. Landowners nonetheless enjoyed a significant degree of protection against the more extreme proposals offered by the Marxist parties. Besides the support of Conservatives and Liberals, landowners generally could count also on the influence and the votes of the small Agrarian party after 1931, and of the reduced but still powerful conservative wing of the Radical party. Thus even when the right lost control of Congress in 1932, landowners could rely on the support of the Agrarians and conservative Radicals to help prevent enactment of truly costly reform.[51]

While the right and its agrarian-based allies thus offered protection against the more extreme designs of the Marxist parties, they also demanded that landowners make certain concessions to the left. Although many remained intransigent, by the 1930s a majority within the rightist political establishment had adopted what might be called a "national upper-class strategy" for dealing with mass politics. Expedient and flexible, this strategy was based on recognition of a need to make some concessions in pursuit of the larger goal of preserving and strengthening the hierarchical structure of society and the privileges of rank and wealth. Within the right there was considerable latitude in defining the terms of this national upper-class strategy. Some offered concessions only in times of crisis, as a means of surviving immediate threats; others called on vested interests to make real sacrifices in pursuit of genuine social reform, in order to broaden the base of the population having a stake in the system. Between the two extremes were those who favored remedial action on particularly exploitable issues that made the right vulnerable to leftist propaganda and those willing to adopt reform as a condition of electoral or congressional alliances with moderate groups.

In all cases, the common denominator was flexibility; in certain circumstances, token or real sacrifices had to be made in order to preserve the broader interests of the national upper class. The strategy was characterized by the "insider" approach—the tendency to cooperate in legislation and administration of reform, in the hope of moderating or blunting threatening proposals. Cooperation, rather than obstruction, aimed at avoiding dangerous impasses which might have invited revolution or military intervention. This progressive, insider approach to reform became the hallmark of the Chilean upper classes. From the 1930s to the 1970s, they generally refrained from obstructing reform up to the point of crisis, contributing instead to stability and the gradual evolution of the political system by offering the timely concession to relieve pressure. Chile's unusual record of stability and constitutional government in the twentieth century owed much to the right's flexibility.[52]

The right's response to mass politics affected landowners' interests more directly than did the left's reform attempts, because the right had more power to force concessions. In the overall strategy of the right, the economic and proprietary prerogatives of landowners were seen as part of the capital available for investment in preemptive reform or in forestalling dangerous mass mobilization. Landowners were particularly vulnerable to the rightist strategy for two basic reasons: the negative image and, to a large extent, the reality of rural conditions made them a political embarrassment to the right; and since landownership was so widely diffused within the national upper class, landowners' vulnerability to the left jeopardized the long-term welfare of the entire national upper class. Thus the right's actions vis-à-vis landowners' interests were attempts at internal regulation designed to make the rural sector less of a political liability to the oligarchy. If the condition of inquilino housing was politically embarrassing, regulatory legislation should be enacted; if mounting urban tensions could be defused by freezing or rolling back the price of bread, wheat growers would have to share the cost; if the social order could be reinforced by the creation of family farms, rightist politicians might modify landowners' property rights. In the context of the national upper-class strategy, then, landowners were called upon to contribute to the preservation of the general class interest by sacrificing, temporarily or permanently, some of their traditional rights and immunities.

The right's flexible approach to mass politics need not be attributed to any special sense of responsibility or political acumen. The progressive strategy was learned behavior, adopted reluctantly and gradually after a series of lessons indicated that neither outright repression of the masses nor obstruction of reform would work. The response of governments of the Parliamentary Period to the rise of a combative organized proletariat in the nitrate mines and the cities is well known and anything but benign: the bloody repressions of Valparaíso in 1903, Santiago in 1905, and Iquique in 1907 were the oligarchy's initial answer to the challenge of the masses. These violent episodes admittedly stirred the consciences of the upper classes and sparked the great debate over the "social question"; but it took challenges that could not be met by force or obstruction to gradually win over the conservative political establishment to the strategy of flexibility toward reform.

The masses' ability to challenge and elicit concessions from the oligarchy was the result of a long period of growth, organization, and radicalization.[53] The economic forces at work since the War of the Pacific created the modern Chilean proletariat in the nitrate mines, on the docks and the railroads, in industry, and in a variety of trades in the burgeoning cities. From the 1880s the working class exhibited a strong tendency toward organization and militance, particularly in the harsh conditions of the nitrate zone. By the turn of the century there were between 20,000 and 30,000 organized workers, and some 65,000 a decade later. As the labor movement grew, the predominant organizational form, the mutual aid society, was superseded by the sui generis resistance societies and *mancomunidades*—curious but revolutionary derivatives of socialist, anarchist, and trade union principles—which flourished in the north under the leadership of Luis Emilio Recabarren. The national Chilean Federation of Labor (FOCh) was founded in 1909, and Recabarren launched the avowedly revolutionary Socialist Labor party three years later. Despite the government's heavy-handedness with labor disputes, a total of some 150,000 workers participated in nearly 300 strikes between 1911 and 1920.[54]

Paralleling the development of the proletariat, substantial urban middle sectors had emerged by the 1910s. The process by which the middle sectors acquired political consciousness and dissident attitudes is not easily discernible since it lacked both the structure and the violence that characterized the working-class struggle. One important factor was the increasing "proletarianization" of the middle classes in the early twentieth century. The spread of free public education in cities and towns turned working-class children into aspiring middle-class adults faster than the economy could absorb them in suitable white-collar jobs.[55] Inflation also constantly threatened the middle classes' standard of living. These and other factors gradually eroded the middle sectors' traditional allegiance to the parties of the oligarchy, and the onset of economic crisis in 1918 persuaded large elements of the middle class to cast their lot at least temporarily with the working class in pursuit of reform.

This severe economic crisis which wracked Chile following World War I produced the first serious challenge to oligarchic hegemony. The end of wartime demand and the development of synthetic nitrates severely depressed the Chilean nitrate industry beginning in 1918. The majority of the nitrate labor force was out of work by 1919, and heavy unemployment rapidly spread throughout the economy and the country as a result of the close dependence of government revenue, the import trade, and agriculture on nitrate production.[56] Accompanying and exacerbating the rise of unemployment was a serious inflationary spiral produced largely by the sudden reorientation of world production and trade from wartime to peacetime patterns.[57] Thus the entire wage-earning and salaried segment of the Chilean population was affected by heightened inflation, while hundreds of thousands simultaneously lost their sources of income. The government's inability or unwillingness to alleviate the double crisis provoked widespread mobilization of the working and middle classes, who staged a series of massive demonstrations throughout the country in 1918 and 1919.

Following one, *El Mercurio* of Santiago editorialized: "Yesterday will be remembered a long time because it witnessed the largest of the popular manifestations which have taken place here, and whose significant intention signals, without any doubt, the point of departure of a new age in Chile, in which the people will participate more directly in running the national government, indicating by themselves what are their aspirations and ideals."[58]

The postwar mobilization was so massive and so generalized, as *El Mercurio* suggested, that it could not be resolved by force alone. When the initial demands for relief measures gave way in 1919 to a program for basic social and political reform, the ruling oligarchy split over strategy. The division over how to deal with the masses was the primary issue of the 1920 presidential campaign and the dominant question in national politics for the next several years. The majority of the upper-class political establishment offered cosmetic solutions but opposed real reforms, while the minority, led by Arturo Alessandri, opted to pacify the masses by concessions designed to counteract their growing alienation and radicalism. The populist approach prevailed in 1920, but intransigents dominated Congress throughout Alessandri's term. Despite mounting popular pressure, Alessandri's main prescription for the restoration of social peace, a package of labor laws, was blocked until 1924.[59]

The military intervention of 1924 proved an important learning experience for the Chilean upper classes. After resisting reform for three years, the rightist congressional majority saw its power suddenly and dramatically eclipsed by military coup in the gravest institutional crisis since the civil war of 1891. Unlike the traditional Latin American military coup, this was a blow for change. The officers forced Congress at bayonet point to enact the Alessandri program, virtually unchanged from the original proposals of 1921.[60] There were two related lessons inherent in the military intervention and its ramifications: first, that the upper classes could no longer count on the armed forces to do their bidding, and therefore that the traditional resort to repression was not a reliable option; and second, that uncompromising resistance to change entailed the risk of losing all input into the final legislative solution. Reflecting on the lessons of 1924, SNA president Jaime Larraín García-Moreno wrote a dozen years afterward: "The experiences have been hard and we have learned from them. We recall that obstinate campaign against the labor laws, begun in 1921, which paralyzed their study for almost three years. What good did it do? Only to make their passage the result of imposition and precipitation."[61]

Events following the 1924 coup suggest that the experience elicited some behavior modification within the conservative political establishment. When Alessandri returned in 1925 to finish his interrupted presidency, his main project was enactment of a new constitution to replace the Portalian document of 1833. His proposal sought to facilitate further reform by replacing the parliamentary regime which had stifled change for thirty-four years with a presidential system designed to be more effective and more responsive to the mood of the electorate. Moreover, it would legitimize the 1924 labor laws and future social reforms by explicitly declaring the state's social responsibilities and establishing a social interpretation of property rights. Rather than openly opposing or rejecting Alessandri's initiatives, which many privately viewed as dangerous, the rightist forces collaborated in the formulation and ratification of the new constitution, attempting to moderate it in the process.[62] During the subsequent brief administration of Emiliano Figueroa Larraín, the conservative elements in government began drafting a variety of mild reform measures designed to undercut the demands of the emergent left.[63] In general, following 1924 the stubborn obstructionism of the rightist majority began to give way to a more pragmatic insider approach to reform.

The position of the right during the Ibáñez years is more difficult to gauge because the general climate of repression discouraged open dissent. Despite serious reservations and subsequent disclaimers, however, the rightist parties in their majority cooperated actively or passively with Ibáñez in implementing the Alessandri reforms and legislating the constitutional mandates for state involvement in social relations and the economy. Under Ibáñez the first labor code was promulgated, the social security system established, and the tax structure reformed. The state assumed a major role in economic development for the first time and a greater degree of control over all aspects of the economy; a Ministry of Development was established to promote and guide economic growth and diversification; and the nitrate industry was nationalized. Demonstrating both a more tolerant view of reform and recognition of the benefits of controlled change, much of the right either condoned or promoted the establishment of the Chilean welfare and developmentalist state under Ibáñez.[64]

A series of developments clustering between 1930 and 1932 induced a profound sense of crisis in the Chilean upper classes and further demonstrated the need for flexibility in mass politics. The world depression had a severe impact on Chile, affecting it more adversely than any other Latin American country. A combined civilian and military movement overthrew the weakened Ibáñez government in 1931, leaving the country in open social and political ferment. Emerging strengthened from the underground, the Communists and Socialists found fertile ground for their political activities; and a 1931 naval revolt with revolutionary overtones provided additional evidence of threats to upper-class interests. Then elements of the military, supported by diverse leftist groups, seized power in

June 1932 and proclaimed the Socialist Republic. Although the officers quickly ousted the junta's more radical elements, the hundred-day existence of a self-proclaimed socialist regime supported by the military demonstrated the vulnerability of the system and the reality of the revolutionary threat, while confirming the unreliability of the armed forces. Finally, after the return of constitutional government, two elections in 1932 revealed a pronounced leftward shift in Chilean voting patterns: Alessandri, running as a center-left candidate, easily defeated two rightists and two leftists in his bid for a second presidential term; and the right lost control of Congress in the same year.[65]

The scores of books, pamphlets, and journalistic pieces written in response to these developments took stock of the situation and offered solutions to the systemic crisis.[66] There were two fundamental problems facing the upper classes. First, the behavior of the military in 1932 reaffirmed that the upper classes could not rely on the option of force to protect themselves against reform or revolution. Second, the dramatic decline of the right's electoral strength and the loss of its congressional majority indicated that its ability to obstruct reform legislation was weakened or lost. These two developments—the loss of its legislative veto power and the military's reassertion of political independence—made the flexible insider approach, embraced by a growing segment after 1924, virtually mandatory for the right in the 1930s. As Conservative party leader Rafael Luis Gumucio put it in 1933:

> The sad truth is that we do not have . . . recourse to a movement of popular opinion. This is the painful reality: we are absolutely impotent to impede any legislative attack that might be mounted against us. In order to obstruct or postpone, we must live [by] negotiating, making combinations, ceding constantly in order to save the basics, tolerating inconveniences, resisting impulses, subduing . . . impetuous urges of those who do not recognize the bitter reality. We need to realize such distressing labor because to give battle today, without the forces to conquer, would be reprehensible madness.[67]

As Gumucio's statement revealed, the right faced a very difficult challenge in the early thirties. On the one hand, based on the recognition that the right in Chile simply could not count on the military to protect its interests, it had to strengthen the fabric of civilian rule. To that end the right formed the Milicia Republicana, a paramilitary white guard with some 50,000 members throughout the country, as a counterweight to the military and a warning against further interventions. In following years, the right also assiduously wooed the military leadership in an attempt to disassociate it from possible sympathy with the left.[68] On the other hand, lacking recourse to military action, the right had to devise strategies for defending vested interests within the framework of constitutional government and mass politics. As mentioned earlier, the right still enjoyed the advantage of a captive rural vote and of various residual powers, and it also benefitted from the rise of corporatism; but as the electoral disasters of 1932 demonstrated, the right also needed to appeal to a broader spectrum of voters and thereby become more competitive in the political marketplace. The debate within the right, then, focused in the early thirties on whether and how much preemptive reform was necessary or advisable to slow the erosion of the upper classes' moral authority and to enhance the right's political appeal.

Three distinct strategies, each embellished with the appropriate ideological trappings and suffused with corporatist tendencies, emerged from the crisis. A minority within the right, particularly a faction of the Conservative party, opted to reemphasize laissez-faire capitalism and social Darwinism, buttressing their position with liberal economic doctrine and pre-Rerum Novarum Catholic social philosophy. A small group turned to the combination of authoritarianism and reform offered by fascism and joined or supported the Chilean National Socialist party. Yet another approach was given its ideological superstructure by the proto-Christian Democrats, first within the youth sector of the Conservative party and after 1937 in the Falange Nacional. This strategy emphasized the Christian duty of the monied to alleviate the masses' suffering through material improvements and Christian persuasion.[69] While it is impossible to gauge the extent to which the preemptive approach was accepted, it certainly spread well beyond the small core of partisan Nazis and Christian Democrats and found advocates among most major sectors of the right.

The second Alessandri government illustrates the ascendancy of the national upper-class strategy for dealing with mass politics. This assertion contrasts with the prevalent interpretation of the second Alessandri government, typified by Frederick Pike's claim that "by the end of his administration in 1938, Alessandri had managed to return Chile to essentially the same groups that had governed before 1920."[70] While Pike's statement is technically correct, it projects a distorted image of the second Alessandri administration by failing to take into account the evolution of the right's views on reform. Whereas Alessandri's populism was opposed by a majority of the right in 1920 and supported by most of the left, by the early thirties most of the right—often begrudgingly—had embraced Alessandri's watered-down populism, and most of the left, now more sophisticated and radical, rejected it. Thus within two years of electing him, most of the left and center parties judged him too conservative—and too heavy-handed with leftist opposition—and abandoned him. Recognizing an opportunity to regain power and influence, the rightist parties and independents stepped into the void and worked with Alessandri from 1934 through

1938.[71] The resurgence of the right under Alessandri, however, while immunizing vested interests against radical measures, made them more vulnerable to the upper-class strategy of preemptive reform.

The basic thrust of Alessandri's strategy was to strengthen the social and political fabric by a policy of concession. Through a variety of moderate reforms he sought to preempt the left, modify or eliminate situations and institutions that made the right vulnerable, and win the loyalty of broader segments of society to the system. In short, his strategy in the thirties was essentially what it was in the twenties, except that his collaborators during most of the second administration were from the opposite end of the political spectrum. It is usually recalled that Alessandri had his Gustavo Ross, the archconservative architect of the regime's fiscal policy, in the Ministry of Finance; it is seldom noted in the literature that Alessandri established the Ministry of Public Health and Social Welfare and installed the socially progressive Conservative Eduardo Cruz-Coke as minister. Cruz-Coke brought into the ministry the core of the future Christian Democratic party, who constantly exposed the unpleasant facts of Chilean life in the ministry's monthly *Acción Social* and needled the establishment for reform.[72] Landowners certainly felt threatened under Alessandri by the right's progressive strategy, which included government-sponsored legislation on agrarian reform, price controls, and working conditions and wages in agriculture.

Within the context of the competitive mass politics of the thirties, then, landowners were called upon to sacrifice some profits and some proprietary rights as their share of the overall cost of preserving the fundamental privileges of the upper classes. As was demonstrated during the Popular Front government, however, the rightist progressive strategy involved guarantees as well as threats to landowners' interests. The key to the right's remaining electoral strength was landowner hegemony over agrarian society with the concomitant rightist control of the rural vote. Thus not only landowners but the entire right bloc adamantly protected the landowner prerogatives upon which the right's electoral strength rested. With the upsurge of leftist power in the Popular Front, the left mobilized all its resources to crack landowners' dominance of the countryside through accelerated agrarian reform and rural unionization and thus to break the right's monopoly over the rural vote. At that critical juncture in modern Chilean history, the rightist strategy worked to landowners' advantage and aided in the preservation of their most crucial prerogatives.[73] Having weathered the storm of the Popular Front, landowners were able to take advantage of the political deadlock which ensued between right and left to enjoy the status quo for another twenty years, before the buildup of pressure for reform finally forced the right to compromise on fundamental rural issues.

Mass Politics and the SNA

The advent of mass politics in Chile and its implications for landowners had a profound and lasting impact on the SNA. With their interests under attack and their conventional sources of political power on the wane, landowners turned increasingly to their voluntary association for defense, and after 1919 the SNA's political role clearly superseded developmental activities as the organization's primary raison d'être. The minutes of directors' meetings vividly reflect the change; only during periods of unusually slack political activity were large segments of meetings given over to debating the virtues of different breeds of milk cows or strains of alfalfa. These concerns were usually left to the Society's growing bureaucracy and its specialized sections, and the council's time was devoted predominantly to setting guidelines for political action or financing the Society and its activities. Nor can the dramatic growth of SNA membership after 1919 be attributed to a sudden burst of interest in scientific agriculture. An SNA advertisement of 1938 left no doubt as to the priority of reasons for joining the institution: "Contribute to the defense of your interests and to the progress of the agricultural industry.[74]

The SNA by no means abandoned its developmental and educational endeavors after the political role became paramount. It continued to lobby for the same kinds of developmental measures that it had pursued before 1919, from agricultural schools to protective tariffs. Indeed its annual livestock exposition expanded and in the twenties the SNA established its own biological station and experimental farm and multiplied its commercial transactions.[75] However, the developmentalist state that emerged in the twenties and expanded in the thirties greatly overshadowed these SNA activities. The Ministries of Agriculture, Development, and Commerce, the Agricultural Export Board, the Agricultural Credit Board, and the Chilean Development Corporation played large roles in fostering agricultural development, independently of the SNA and on a much larger scale than the voluntary association could hope to achieve. Measured by its impact on Chilean landowners, then, the Society's role in political defense far outweighed its continuing and significant contributions as an agency of agricultural development.

As it assumed a more active and prominent political role the SNA came to be identified as an enemy of progress, an obstacle to change, or, as *El Siglo* put it, "a cell of conspirators and enemies of the Chilean people."[76] This contrasted sharply with the Society's image in the nineteenth century, when it was recognized as an instrument of change, a modernizing elite of progressive agriculturists. The Society's own image had become somewhat tarnished by the development of the villain landowner stereotype. But after the advent of mass politics, the surviving progressive image was rapidly eclipsed by a reactionary one as the SNA became the visible defender of obsolete institutions and anachronistic privilege. The newsworthy and emotional issues were precisely those on which the SNA had to take unpopular positions, while its lobbying for expansion of agricultural extension services and its record-setting sales of hybrid seed understandably passed unnoticed by the multitudes.

In order to meet its heightened political responsibilities in the era of mass politics, the SNA necessarily underwent important changes in structure and function. Between 1919 and 1940 the Society evolved from a small elite into a large and powerful pressure group. By the latter date, it had emerged as essentially the same SNA that was introduced to the world in the 1960s as a protagonist in the fight over agrarian reform.

Notes

1. Alberto Edwards Vives, *La fronda aristocrática*, 6th ed. (Santiago, 1966), pp. 197-202.

2. The following selection of works provides a variety of interpretations of the 1920s and '30s: John J. Johnson, *Political Change in Latin America: The Emergence of the Middle Sectors* (Stanford, Cal., 1958), pp. 66-93; Edwards, *Fronda aristocrática*, pp. 197-266; Pike, *Chile and the United States*, pp. 170-213; John Reese Stevenson, *The Chilean Popular Front* (Philadelphia, 1942); Julio Heise González, *La constitución de 1925 y las nuevas tendencias político-sociales* (Santiago, 1951); Jobet, *Ensayo crítico*, pp. 156-238; Fernando Pinto Lagarrigue, *Crónica política del siglo xx. Desde Errázuriz Echaurren hasta Alessandri Palma* (Santiago, 1972); and Ricardo Donoso, *Alessandri, agitador y demoledor* (Mexico City, 1952).

3. The following studies examine the political party system, They may be consulted for bibliography on individual parties: René León Echaíz, *Evolución histórica de los partidos políticos chilenos*, 2nd ed. (Buenos Aires, 1971); Alberto Edwards Vives and Eduardo Frei Montalva, *Historia de los partidos políticos chilenos* (Santiago, 1949); Sergio Guilisasti Tagle, *Partidos políticos chilenos*, 2nd ed. (Santiago, 1964); and Germán Urzúa Valenzuela, *Los partidos políticos chilenos* (Santiago, 1968). Lía Cortés and Jordi Fuentes, *Diccionario político de Chile (1810-1966)* (Santiago, 1967), contains solid outline histories of all important parties. On the labor movement during this period, see: Hernán Ramírez Necochea, *Historia del movimiento obrero en Chile. Antecedentes, siglo xix* (Santiago, 1956); Alan Angell, *Politics and the Labour Movement in Chile* (London, 1972), pp. 11-41; Jorge Barría Serón, *El movimiento obrero en Chile* (Santiago, 1971); Moisés Poblete Troncoso, *La organización sindical en Chile* (Santiago, 1926); and Tulio Lagos Valenzuela, *Bosquejo histórico del movimiento obrero en Chile* (Santiago, 1941).

4. Julio Heise González, "El caciquismo político en el Período Parlamentario (1891-1925)," in Neville Blanc Renard, ed., *Homenaje al Profesor Guillermo Feliú Cruz* (Santiago, 1973), pp. 537-75; Rivas Vicuña, *Historia política y parlamentaria*, 1, 168-73.

5. Paul W. Drake, *Socialism and Populism in Chile, 1932-52*, (Urbana, Ill., 1978), pp. 99-164, provides a cogent analysis of voting trends in the early thirties.

6. Some recent studies question the degree to which the new constitution actually strengthened the presidency: Jorge Tapia-Videla, "The Chilean Presidency in a Developmental Perspective," *Journal of Inter-American Studies and World Affairs*, 19 (1977), 451-81; and Crescente Donoso Letelier, "Notas sobre el orígen, acatamiento y desgaste del régimen presidencial, 1925-1973," *Historia*, 13 (1976), 271-352.

7. Bauer, *Chilean Rural Society*, esp. chs. 3, 7, and 8.

8. Alberto Blest Gana, *Martín Rivas*, 8th ed. (Santiago, 1961); Luis Orrego Luco, *Casa Grande*, 3rd ed. (Santiago, 1934).

9. Marcial González, "Nuestro enemigo el lujo," *Estudios Económicos* (Santiago, 1889), pp. 429-62.

10. Octavio Astorquiza, "Necesidades de nuestra agricultura," *Revista del Centro Industrial y Agrícola*, 2 (1900), 15.

11. *BSNA*, 32 (1901), 11-12.

12. Oscar Garrido Lozier, in *El Mercurio*, May 1, 1939, p. 36. Unless otherwise noted, references to *El Mercurio* are to the Santiago paper. For other statements of the same image, see Pedro Aguirre Cerda, *El problema agrario* (Paris, 1929), pp. 264-65; and Adolfo Matthei, *Política agraria chilena* (Padre Las Casas, Chile, 1935), p. 58.

13. *Boletín de la Asociación del Trabajo*, año V, no. 49 (Dec. 1929), 5.

14. On Chilean paper money, devaluation, and inflation, see Frank W. Fetter, *Monetary Inflation in Chile* (Princeton, N.J., 1931); see also ch. 5, n. 1. The tendency to blame landowners for devaluation persists even in relatively recent literature, but a detailed study of the economic interests of members of Congress and ministers of finance who determined fiscal policy after 1878 has not been done. The SNA as an institution consistently denounced the paper money regime and advocated strengthening the currency.

15. Agustín Ross Edwards, *Chile, 1851-1910: sesenta años de cuestiones monetarias y financieras y de problemas bancarios* (Valparaíso, 1910), p. 139. Ross drew extensively on Roberto Espinoza's works, the most influential of which was *Cuestiones financieras de Chile* (Santiago, 1909).

16. Venegas, *Sinceridad*, p. 13.

17. *BSNA*, 45 (1914), 513.

18. See ch. 5, under "Cattle Tax."

19. Agustín Ross Edwards, *El impuesto al ganado arjentino: folleto de actualidad* (Valparaíso, 1888), p. 60; *Representación del pueblo de Santiago al Congreso de la República con motivo del proyecto de impuesto al ganado arjentino* (Santiago, 1888), p. 10.

20. Heriberto Covarrubias P., in *El Mercurio*, Nov. 4, 1905, pp. 7-8.

21. *BSNA*, 36 (1905), 849.

22. Minutes, Oct. 18, 1920, in *El Agricultor*, 51 (1920), 231. Minutes of SNA council meetings are also available in the SNA's archive. The originals sometimes provide additional detail but little more of substance during the twenties and thirties. By the 1940s, the minutes published in *El Campesino* became little more than general outlines of the meetings' proceedings. Note that the SNA *Boletín* appeared as *El Agricultor* from 1917 to 1922 and in 1933 assumed its present title, *El Campesino*.

23. Juan de la C. Araneda, in SNA, *Congreso Regional Agrario de Concepción* (Santiago, 1925), p. 73.

24. *El Mercurio*, Aug. 17, 1938, p. 16.
25. Quoted in *BSNA*, 39 (1908), 670.
26. Venegas, *Sinceridad*, p. 15.
27. *Ibid.*, p. 18.
28. *El Mercurio* (Antofagasta), July 4, 1922, p. 6.
29. See ch. 5, under "Postwar Crisis" and "Second Alessandri Administration."
30. *BSNA*, 60 (1928), 789.
31. See ch. 7, under "Intellectual Background." As noted in ch. 1, the inquilino was a service tenant who resided on the large estate. The peón was a seasonal worker from outside the estate.
32. Tancredo Pinochet LeBrun, *Inquilinos en el fundo de Su Excelencia* (Santiago, 1916), p. 10.
33. *La Hora*, Apr. 28, 1939, p. 3; Congreso Nacional, Cámara de Diputados, *Sesiones ordinarias en 1940*, p. 2124.
34. Cámara de Diputados, *Sesiones ordinarias en 1938*, p. 2041.
35. See ch. 4, pp. 80-81, and ch. 7, pp. 156-58.
36. Venegas, *Sinceridad*, pp. 4, 14.
37. McBride, *Land and Society*, p. 202, actually quotes the nineteenth-century historian and agriculturist Benjamín Vicuña Mackenna, but McBride's book helped reinforce the landowner hegemony thesis. A more recent statement of the same is Federico Gil, *The Political System of Chile* (Boston, 1966), p. 59.
38. Juan Chacón Corona, *El problema agrario y el Partido Comunista. Informe ante el XI Congreso Nacional del Partido Comunista de Chile, 1939* (Santiago, 1940), p. 32.
39. *El Siglo*, Sept. 30, 1940, p. 7.
40. Cámara de Diputados, *Sesiones ordinarias en 1938*, p. 2186.
41. L. Aníbal Lagos, *Los ferrocarriles transandinos como instrumentos de confraternidad y expansión económica internacional* (Santiago, 1931), p. 10.
42. *El Mercurio*, Sept. 24, 1919, p. 5.
43. *BSNA*, 56 (1925), 303.
44. *Ibid.*, 42 (1911), 329-30.
45. *El C*, 71 (1939), 635.
46. Cámara de Diputados, *Sesiones ordinarias en 1938*, p. 2187.
47. Centro de Estudios Socio-Económicos, "Estudio: imágen de la agricultura en Chile," loose leaf, 3 vols. (Santiago, 1966).
48. "Comisión de Agricultura," *Convención Nacional de la Producción y del Comercio 1967-1968* (Santiago, 1968), pp. 2, 377.
49. *El C*, 100 (Jan. 1969), 14. Jacques Chonchol cites the negative image of landowners as a contributing factor to the enactment of agrarian reform: "Poder y reforma agraria en la experiencia chilena," *Cuadernos de la Realidad Nacional* (June 1970), pp. 50-87.
50. Henry Nash Smith, *Virgin Land: The American West as Symbol and Myth* (New York, 1950); Richard Hofstadter, *The Age of Reform: From Bryan to F.D.R.* (New York, 1956).
51. Two sections of ch. 7 analyze the Radicals' attitudes toward rural reform: "Rural Labor under the Popular Front," and "Landowners, Communists, and National Politics."
52. Drake, *Socialism and Populism*, pp. 113-15, deals thoughtfully with the reasons for and manifestations of the right's greater flexibility in politics, particularly in the 1931-33 period. See also Drake's "The Political Responses of the Chilean Upper Class to the Great Depression and the Threat of Socialism, 1931-33," in

Frederic Cople Jaher, ed., *The Rich, the Well Born, and the Powerful* (Urbana, Ill., 1973), pp. 304-37; also Mattelart *et al.*, *Ideología de la dominación.*

53. In addition to works cited in ch. 2, n. 3, see: Guillermo Kaempffer Villagrán, *Así sucedió 1850-1925. Sangrientos episodios de la lucha obrera en Chile* (Santiago, n.d.); Patricio Manns, *Las grandes masacres* (Santiago, 1972); Jorge Barría Serón, "Los movimientos sociales de principios del siglo xx" (Memoria de Prueba, Universidad de Chile, 1953); and James O. Morris, *Elites, Intellectuals and Consensus: A Study of the Social Question and the Industrial Relations System in Chile* (Ithaca, N.Y., 1966), pp. 78-118.

54. *Boletín de la Oficina del Trabajo*, año XIV, no. 22 (1924), 222-23. The FOCh was suppressed in the late 1920s, and after a period of labor disunity, the CTCh was founded in 1936.

55. Edwards, *Fronda aristocrática*, pp. 186-90; César A. de León, "Las capas medias en la sociedad chilena del siglo xix," *Anales de la Universidad de Chile*, año CXII (1964), 51-95; Heise González, *La constitución de 1925*, pp. 150-68; Arturo Olavarría Bravo, *La cuestión social en Chile* (Santiago, 1923), pp. 105-35.

56. On the nitrate crisis, see: Martner, *Historia económica*, 1, 627; *Boletín de la Oficina del Trabajo*, año XII, no. 18 (1922), 235; Leo Stanton Rowe, *The Early Effects of the European War on Chile* (New York, 1918); and Ricardo Couyoumdjian, "El mercado del salitre durante la primera guerra mundial y la postguerra, 1914-1921. Notas para su estudio," *Historia*, 12 (1974-75), 13-55.

57. See Table 12.

58. *El Mercurio*, Aug. 30, 1919, p. 3.

59. On the opposition to Alessandri's labor bills, see Morris, *Elites*, pp. 119-240, and Yeager, "Club de la Unión." On Alessandri's political career, including both his presidencies, see: Arturo Alessandri Palma, *Recuerdos de gobierno*, 3 vols. (Santiago, 1967); Donoso, *Alessandri*; and Robert J. Alexander, *Arturo Alessandri: A Biography*, 2 vols. (Ann Arbor, Mich., 1977).

60. Frederick M. Nunn, *Chilean Politics, 1920-1931: The Honorable Mission of the Armed Forces* (Albuquerque, N.M., 1970); Nunn, *The Military in Chilean History. Essays on Civil-Military Relations, 1810-1973* (Albuquerque, N.M., 1976), pp. 83-106, 128-50. See also José Nun, "The Middle-Class Military Coup," in Claudio Véliz, ed., *The Politics of Conformity in Latin America*, pp. 66-118.

61. Jaime Larraín García-Moreno, *Mejoramiento de la vida campesina* (Santiago, 1936), pp. 18-19.

62. Heise González, *La constitución de 1925*; Donoso Letelier, "Régimen presidencial."

63. See ch. 5, p. 109, and ch. 6, pp. 129.

64. René Montero Moreno, *La verdad sobre Ibáñez* (Buenos Aires, 1953); Luis Correa Prieto, *El Presidente Ibáñez* (Santiago, 1962); Echaíz, *Evolución histórica*, pp. 159-63.

65. On the depression, see P. T. Ellsworth, *Chile: An Economy in Transition* (New York, 1945). On the Socialist Republic, see: Jack Ray Thomas, "Marmaduke Grove: A Political Biography" (unpublished dissertation in history, Ohio State University, 1962); Thomas, "The Socialist Republic of Chile," *Journal of Inter-American Studies*, 6 (1964), 203-20; and Drake, *Socialism and Populism*, pp. 71-83, 99-108. The naval revolt is discussed in Nunn, *The Military in Chilean History*, pp. 199-202; and Patricio Manns, *Revolución de la escuadra* (Valparaíso, 1972).

66. Drake, *Socialism and Populism*, pp. 371-402, has an extensive bibliography

including numerous works on the hegemonic crisis. See also Drake, "Political Responses," and two works by Carlos Keller: *La eterna crisis chilena* (Santiago, 1931), and *Un país al garete* (Santiago, 1932).

67. Rafael Luis Gumucio V., *El deber político* (Santiago, 1933), p. 17, quoted in Drake, *Socialism and Populism*, p. 121.

68. Nunn, *The Military in Chilean History*, pp. 218-33; Terence S. Tarr, "Military Intervention and Civilian Reaction in Chile, 1924-1936" (unpublished dissertation in history, University of Florida, 1960).

69. On the parties during the crisis period, see Echaíz, *Evolución histórica*, pp. 117-27; Stevenson, *Chilean Popular Front*, pp. 49-56; and Claudio Orrego Vicuña, ed., *Horacio Walker y su tiempo* (Santiago, 1976). On contemporary corporatist thought, Paul W. Drake, "Corporatism and Functionalism in Modern Chilean Politics," *Journal of Latin American Studies*, 10 (1978), esp. 90-101.

70. Pike, *Chile and the United States*, p. 245.

71. Alessandri, *Recuerdos de gobierno*, vol. 3; Stevenson, *Chilean Popular Front*, pp. 57-72; Echaíz, *Evolución histórica*, pp. 135-36.

72. See *Acción Social*, published monthly after about 1933; also Eduardo Cruz-Coke Lassabe, *Pensamiento de Cruz-Coke* (Santiago, 1974).

73. On the Popular Front, see Stevenson, *Chilean Popular Front*; Alberto Cabero, *Recuerdos de don Pedro Aguirre Cerda*, 2nd ed. (Santiago, 1948); and Richard R. Super, "The Chilean Popular Front Presidency of Pedro Aguirre, 1938-1941" (unpublished dissertation in history, Arizona State University, 1975).

74. Ministerio de Salud Pública y Bienestar Social, *Acción Social*, año VII, no. 68 (Apr. 1938), unpaginated.

75. For a summary of the SNA's continuing developmental activities, see Correa Vergara, *Agricultura chilena*, 1, 169-226; and *El C*, 70 (1938), edición extraordinaria.

76. *El Siglo*, Nov. 12, 1940, p. 5.

3

Forging an Agrarian Gremio

When the era of mass politics dawned in Chile and landowners' prerogatives began to be challenged, the SNA was still essentially the same voluntary association it had been for fifty years: a small elite dedicated primarily to the technological progress of Chilean agriculture. Its purview had broadened by the turn of the century to include political defense of landed interests, but during the Parliamentary Period its defense role required little more than the Society's articulation of the "agricultural" interest. The political system, characterized by limited participation and rural predominance in Congress, could be relied upon to screen out any real threat to the landowner. The SNA's main sources of power were the quality of its members—their aggregate social, economic, and political power—and the reputation of the institution itself. With the advent of reform, when landowners turned to their voluntary association for defense against serious threats, the institution as then constituted was ill prepared for effective action in the new political context.

The SNA's greatest political liability was landowners' extremely negative image, which tended to prejudice their case with the urban population. This situation preoccupied the Society's directors throughout the period of reform and proved very difficult to combat. Beyond that, the SNA's small size was a handicap in mass politics: it could not demonstrate strength of numbers, which counted for much more after 1919, and thus was vulnerable to the charge of representing only a tiny fraction, a special interest within the rural population. Moisés Poblete Troncoso's analysis, written in 1919, reflected the common perception of the SNA: "The Sociedad Nacional de Agricultura . . . is composed almost exclusively of the large agriculturists of the center of the country, of the large landowners, whose economic interests are opposed to those of the small and medium landowners."[1] The SNA was quite aware that its size and lack of true representativeness reduced the "*fuerza moral*" (moral suasion) that it might exercise.[2]

On the other hand, the SNA had both actual and potential strengths for competing in the evolving political system. The elite nature of its membership—particularly of its board of directors—was still a distinct advantage after 1919. Because ownership of rural land was so common among the upper classes, the SNA was able to recruit as members and directors men of political influence—deputies, senators, ministers, or officers in the Conservative, Liberal, or Radical parties. The aggregate wealth of the membership gave the SNA a source of strength that was translatable into political power in various ways. Not the least of its advantages in a deferential society such as Chile's was the social status and prestige of a large part of its membership and most of its directors. The notoriously *siútico* (social climbing) middle-class politician or official was not immune to co-optation through selective conferral of upper-class status symbols such as membership in clubs or invitations to social affairs, or simply through social or business intercourse with an Echenique or a Larraín.[3]

Despite its small membership (787 members in 1918) the SNA had a potential strength in numbers to complement its qualitative advantage. There was considerable room for expanding membership among large landowners throughout the country, the great majority of whom had traditionally ignored the SNA's mission and its implicit offer of membership. Beyond that, the potential for building a mass base was virtually unlimited so long as the hierarchical fabric of rural society held together. Landowners had direct control over an agricultural labor force of some 400,000 workers throughout the country and normally exercised important influence over some 150,000 smallholders who looked to them for credit and seasonal employment.[4] As long as labor unions and left-wing parties could be kept out of the countryside, the SNA had the potential to harness the rural masses to its political machine.

First Steps

Landowners and the SNA were caught unawares by the postwar political crisis, and their initial response was confused and inconsistent. On the one hand, a series of issues which had heretofore been academic suddenly became political; for example, the need to improve inquilino housing had been an occasional topic of discussion and debate for several years, but in 1919 a bill was introduced in Congress to compel landowners to action.[5] To a group accustomed to complete freedom of action, the threat of compulsion was shocking and dismaying, particularly so in that it came in response to demands by the lower orders. Even more shocking was the eruption of strikes in the countryside and the threat of "bolshevism." In the heat of the postwar crisis and the first sign of threat to the established order, the SNA's public pronouncements on issues were equivocal and often contradictory.

Another factor which contributed to the SNA's uncertain response was the question of the role of the Society itself. For ideological, public relations, and juridical reasons, the SNA had always maintained its "above politics" facade, based on a distinction between party and interest group activities. The difficulty in 1919 was that calls for land reform, social improvements in the countryside, price controls, and other matters of direct concern emanated from factions and parties that formed the core of the political establishment.[6] If the SNA became involved in defending landowners' interests, its actions would inevitably be construed as "political." The question then was whether to respond through the SNA, to establish a separate "political" organization of landowners, or, as many hoped could be done, simply to wait for the storm to blow over.

The SNA's initial decision was to remain aloof from political matters in a direct sense, while indirectly marshaling opposition to the legislative threats of 1919. The device chosen was an "assembly of agriculturists," a purportedly national and independent congress of agriculturists based on representation from all the country's agricultural departments. Of the 650 delegates, some 500 were SNA members; and although Society directors occupied the most prominent positions in the assembly, they did so as representatives of a particular geographic area, not as SNA directors. The assembly's express purpose was to examine the rash of threatening legislative proposals and to forward its recommendations to Congress. The assembly also debated general strategy for confronting the emerging urban reformist alliance, a question which turned on whether to reform the SNA to make it an effective pressure group. Although a minority of the delegates favored that approach, the majority preferred to keep the Society out of "politics" by forming a separate Agrarian Union as the landowners' political arm.[7]

The Agrarian Union was based on the precedent of the short-lived Agrarian League, which the SNA had established in 1905 to coordinate the battle over the cattle tax.[8] The purpose of the Agrarian Union was expressly political—to unify agriculturists, articulate their interests, and lobby for the policies they desired. The strategy was to create an electoral bloc for the 1921 congressional elections, and the method was to urge landowners' support, within their own parties, of candidates pledged to the union's legislative program. No means of pressure beyond conferring or withholding votes was contemplated and none could have been applied, given the multiple party affiliations of the rural elites. In endorsing the concept of an agrarian electoral bloc, the SNA argued for voting the economic interest:

> It is frequently said that agriculturists make up 70 percent of Congress; however, it is fitting to observe that fundo owner does not mean the same as agriculturist, and that even supposing such a proportion among the legislators,

> there has not been until now a program to which they could apply their parliamentary initiative. Given the popular prejudice against agricultural producers, the legislative bills which emanate from those [socialist] currents of thought are not favorable to producers and, moreover, threaten them with formidable burdens. Agriculturists must not . . . abandon the nomination [of candidates] to city politicians.[9]

Although ostensibly independent, the Agrarian Union was in fact closely tied to the SNA. It received office space in the SNA building, the use of Society personnel and facilities, and a subsidy; it was privately considered "a branch of the Society."[10]

Formed to serve lobbying and electoral purposes, the Agrarian Union soon assumed the function of uniting landowners at the local level to meet the threat of social unrest in the countryside. The early 1920s witnessed the beginnings of rural labor organization and strikes in the central provinces, while in the south unresolved tenure questions resulting from the haphazard occupation of Araucanian lands after 1850 gave rise to sporadic violence. Expressing an exaggerated but genuine fear of "bolshevism in the fields," landowners began to organize chapters of the Agrarian Union at the *comuna* (local government) and department levels in 1921.[11] By 1923 local chapters had appeared throughout the central agricultural heartland and by 1925 had spread throughout the south. Because these grass roots organizations maintained only nominal affiliation with the central office in Santiago, the number of local units and their total membership are impossible to ascertain; but in many parts of rural Chile the Agrarian Union provided landowners their first organizational experience and made them receptive to the SNA's subsequent overtures.[12]

Although reasonably effective at the local level, the Agrarian Union was too amorphous to strengthen the landowner interest in national politics. Its efforts had no discernible impact on the 1921 election, which actually increased the reformist forces in Congress. Moreover, by 1921 it had become apparent to most observers that irreversible change had occurred in politics and that the threat of adverse policy would not simply evaporate. Newly elected SNA director Arturo Alemparte used the public forum of *El Mercurio* in July 1921 to make precisely that point and to urge the Society itself to assume the political role assigned to the Agrarian Union, with two constraints: it should not form a separate agrarian party nor "become involved in labor or social problems of an urban character."[13] In response to this and to common accusations of "little effective action," the SNA in 1922 reversed itself and called for strengthening the landowner political voice under its own auspices: "The obstinate struggle of vested interests requires us to live closely united. It is obvious that if the agriculturist continues as he has until now, isolated, indifferent, supporting with resignation the effects of poorly studied laws as he does the inclemencies of the weather, he will fall defeated in the struggle where rival interests are disturbingly active."[14]

The SNA thus set out to give concrete expression to the notion of the *gremio*—the functional grouping of all men who worked the soil. In competition with the Marxist idea of class struggle, the gremio concept emphasized class harmony and community of interest within the fraternity of agriculturists. In a typical call for unity, the *Boletín* explained that "AGRICULTOR is not only the great hacendado, owner of thousands of hectares; he is also the owner of the smallest parcel of cultivated land in any point of the republic; he is the renter of any producing plot; and he is any individual who derives his living from cultivating the soil. [Therefore] the smallholder, the modest sharecropper, and the most humble inquilino should join the great hacendado, since all are interested in defending our agriculture."[15] This unity and strength of the gremio were necessary for agriculturists to "defend their position against the city."[16] The common enemy came in many guises—from "urban political elements, foreign and sometimes hostile to agriculture," to "subversive elements" who came from the city to preach "class hatred" in the countryside and who, incidentally, undermined the desired image of class harmony within rural society.[17] To organize, strengthen, and control this ethereal but potentially powerful agrarian gremio, the SNA launched a three-part program of recruiting new members, incorporating the middle and lower rural strata in nonmember status, and bringing the independent agricultural societies into the SNA.

The Growth of Membership

The SNA began the first membership drive in its history in 1922, with the goal of reaching 2,000 members. This ambitious endeavor was an attempt to overcome what the Society had periodically lamented as the "absence of the spirit of association" among Chilean agriculturists.[18] By this time, however, developments in national politics, the eruption of rural unrest, and the experience of association through the Agrarian Union had greatly reduced landowners' resistance to organization, facilitating the Society's efforts.

Beyond appealing to landowners' sense of self-preservation, the SNA also enhanced the practical benefits of membership to attract recruits. The most visible change was the growth of commercial operations. The SNA had imported a relatively small volume of machinery, seeds, and other articles for sale to its members since the 1870s. In the twenties and thirties the commercial department expanded the range of its offerings and, by selling to members at a discount, multiplied the volume of its business severalfold. In addition, the Society established its own fundo and experimental stations to produce improved seeds, serums, and other products for sale to members at reduced prices. It also instituted various new services including legal aid, tax preparation, an enlarged library, technical consultation, and a bureau which specialized in cutting through the growing volume of red tape concomitant to expanded government regulation. To accommodate its commercial operations, enlarged staff, and new services, in 1924 the Society constructed a four-story building on Tenderini Street in downtown Santiago. More than just another office building, the imposing SNA edifice was seen by some contemporaries as symbolizing a new political force on the national scene.[19]

Another means of attracting and retaining members was to represent more effectively the needs of specialized producers. As early as 1903, when it absorbed the National Society of Viticulture, the SNA had established a "section" open to members with particular interest in viticulture. Provision was also made for other commodity sections, but only two or three were set up before the 1920s and they functioned intermittently.[20] By the twenties Chilean agricultural production had diversified considerably, and as government controls over the agricultural economy were instituted in the 1930s the need for political representation of special commodity producers increased accordingly. The complexity of price, marketing, and taxation policy for individual commodities was so overwhelming that in 1931 the Society's directors appealed for the formation of more sections: the council "cannot neglect its primary role and occupy itself with details which it could not materially cover."[21]

The challenge was to represent special interests effectively enough to preclude the fragmentation of landowners and producers into numerous competing and disunited associations. To improve the situation of the commodity sections the revised statutes of 1929 granted a seat on the board of directors to the president of each section. By 1940 the Society had at least five sections with fairly stable existence, representing producers of wine, cattle, dairy products, fruits, and poultry. And underscoring the SNA's continuing aristocratic character was a section with no political purpose whatsoever—the section of riding horses.[22]

The membership campaign, the expansion of services, and, not least, the threats to landowners generated considerable interest in joining the Society. After an intensive recruitment drive throughout the southern agricultural region, the SNA reached its 2,000 member goal in 1926. Membership declined during the depression, as a matter of economics and of dissatisfaction with SNA positions.[23] Then, with economic recovery, the introduction of new political challenges, and a renewed recruitment drive, membership more than doubled during the second Alessandri and Popular Front governments. By 1940 the SNA had reached the size it maintained, with some fluctuation, through the 1970s (see Table 5).

Table 5
Total SNA Membership, 1901-78

Year	Total Members[a]	Number Change	Percent Change	Year	Total Members	Number Change	Percent Change
1901	380	—	—	1940	3721	75	2.1
1902	429	49	12.9	1941	3835	114	3.1
1903	465	36	8.4	1942	4079	244	6.4
1904	605	140	30.1	1943	4123	44	1.1
1905	651	46	7.6	1944	4248	125	3.0
1906	563	−88	−13.5	1945	4241	−7	−0.2
1907	573	10	1.8	1946	4183	−58	−1.4
1908	702	129	22.5	1947	4024	−159	−3.8
1909	704	2	0.3	1948	3741	−283	−7.0
1910	775	71	10.1	1949	3538	−203	−5.4
1911	757	−18	−2.3	1950	3246	−292	−8.3
1912	800	43	5.7	1951	2987	−259	−8.0
1913	778	−22	−2.8	1952	2996	9	0.3
1914	729	−49	−6.3	1953	3259	263	8.8
1915	767	38	5.2	1954	3311	52	1.6
1916	766	−1	−0.1	1955	3393	82	2.5
1917	772	6	0.8	1956	3462	69	2.0
1918	787	15	1.9	1957	3545	83	2.4
1919	851	64	8.1	1958	3594	49	1.4
1920	834	−17	−2.0	1959	3938	344	9.6
1921	743	−91	−10.9	1960	4019	81	2.1
1922	716	−27	−3.6	1961	4078	59	1.5
1923	919	203	28.4	1962	3921	−157	−3.8
1924	1119	200	21.8	1963	3938	17	0.4
1925	1931	812	72.6	1964	3947	9	0.2
1926	2076	145	7.5	1965	4478	531	13.5
1927	2095	19	0.9	1966	4886	408	9.1
1928	1974	−121	−5.8	1967	4970	84	1.7
1929	1920	−54	−2.7	1968	4688	−282	−5.7
1930	2043	123	6.4	1969	4217	−471	−10.0
1931	1891	−152	−7.4	1970	3767	−450	−10.7
1932	1638	−253	−13.4	1971	3329	−438	−11.6
1933	1608	−30	−1.8	1972	3404	75	2.3
1934	1838	230	14.3	1973	3662	258	7.6
1935	2072	234	12.7	1974	3931	269	7.3
1936	2507	435	21.0	1975	4379	448	11.4

Table 5
Total SNA Membership, 1901–78

Year	Total Members[a]	Number Change	Percent Change	Year	Total Members	Number Change	Percent Change
1937	3012	505	20.1	1976	4333	−46	−1.1
1938	3387	375	12.5	1977	4088	−245	−5.7
1939	3646	259	7.6	1978	3658	−430	−10.5

[a]These figures are for direct memberships, including business firms as well as individuals. They do not include indirect members who belonged to the SNA through membership in an affiliated organization (such as the Sociedad Agrícola del Sur, after 1929, or the Confederación de Pequeños Agricultores de Chile, after 1970). Cf. figures in Appendix 1, which include only individual members (no corporate members).

SOURCE: SNA, "Nómina de Socios," Membership Section Archive.

Developing a Territorial Organization

From the adoption of its growth policy in 1922, the SNA did not rely on the simple expansion of its regular membership. Even had it recruited all the landowners of sufficient means to pay the incorporation fee and annual dues, the numerical strength of the Society would have been unimpressive in comparison with that of competing interests such as labor, foodstuff processors and merchants, and consumers. In order to develop a mass base, the SNA had to look to the middle and lower strata of rural society. In addition to augmenting its numbers, by incorporating smallholders and other segments of the rural population the SNA could hope to substantiate its claim of representing a gremio united across class and geographic boundaries. At the same time, the Society observed the implicit constraints imposed by the structure of rural society and by its own historical experience as an organization of the larger landowners and producers. Thus it did not reduce dues and hedged but did not drop the traditional requirement of sponsorship for new members.[24] Instead, the SNA's solution to the challenge of appending a mass base to an elite organization was to establish degrees of association through a hierarchical, territorially-based structure which encompassed smallholders and even some landless sharecroppers and workers in nonmember status while preserving the dominance of the large landowners.

The basic unit of the Society's territorial organization was a department-level committee of all members who resided or owned property in that department. The explicit functions of the "departmental committees" were to communicate local conditions and needs to national headquarters, recruit members, carry out SNA policy, and represent the Society in all matters at the department level. Departmental units were formed of existing

Society members wherever possible; in departments where few or no members owned land, prominent local agriculturists were invited to join the Society and constitute its departmental committee. The latter approach was particularly useful as an instrument for expansion into the south, where there were few SNA members before the 1920s. During 1923 and 1924, forty-two departmental committees were established in the sixty-eight agricultural departments between Freirina in the Norte Chico and Llanquihue in the south.[25]

Departmental committees were restricted to full-fledged Society members. In order to harness some of the thousands of small farmers to its political machine without jeopardizing control by the upper strata, the SNA set up complementary department- and comuna-level "agrarian assemblies" wherever conditions were propitious. Though controlled by Society members or the large operators of each locality, these assemblies incorporated the smaller farmers who were too poor to pay regular Society dues or too plebeian to participate on an equal footing with the local gentry. The agrarian assemblies were formed from local chapters of the Agrarian Union, where they existed, or were instituted by Society members. Their functions were similar to those of the departmental committees.[26]

Organization of the assemblies varied in detail, but two examples will illustrate the general tendencies. In the comuna of San José de la Mariquina (department and province of Valdivia), membership was by invitation. Dues were proportionate to the assessed value of the member's property, although landownership was not a condition for membership; small owners or renters paid as little as twelve pesos per year, in contrast to Society dues of eighty pesos. Control of the assembly was assured by the provision that a majority of its directors be Society members.[27] The local assembly in the comuna of Talagante (department and province of Santiago) was organized along similar lines, but its board of directors was structured differently. Of the ten directors, two were to be sharecroppers or laborers, two owners or tenants of plots under 100 hectares, and six owners or renters of properties exceeding that size. Thus in Talagante efforts were made to reach into the lower rural strata to fortify the SNA's structure.[28]

To complete the Society's territorial structure the departmental committees were encouraged to elect eight-man provincial councils, which would coordinate activities and speak for the organized agriculturists of their provinces. After 1929 each functioning provincial council in provinces that did not have independent agricultural associations was granted a seat on the Society's council.[29] The complete territorial organization of the Society after 1925 thus paralleled the state's administrative structure.

One of the most important functions of the comuna- to province-level associations was to organize resistance to labor union and left-wing political recruitment within their jurisdictions; in that role they replaced the local units of the Agrarian Union. A second major aspect of their activity was to work with SNA headquarters in pursuit of national and local objectives. From Santiago the Society could mobilize its chain of command for petition campaigns via telegram and produce hundreds of communications from all parts of Chile. In several instances, the SNA attempted to turn out the rural vote through the medium of its national structure. There were also practical benefits for provincial agriculturists in the area of problem resolution. Due to the extreme centralization of Chilean public administration, decisions from the capital were normally required for resolution of local complaints about railroad service, road maintenance, or the actions of public officials, and for local improvements. With its vertical organization, the SNA established a system of local-center linkages that paralleled those provided by the political parties and became an alternate kind of political broker between the capital and outlying districts. By enlisting the aid of SNA headquarters, landowners in remote areas could frequently expedite the redress of local grievances.[30]

The degree of activism, even the lifespan, of the local, departmental, and provincial organizations was primarily a function of conditions in the countryside. The initial organizational flurry in the early twenties coincided with the first union activities and strikes in rural areas. Calm was restored to the countryside after 1925, and many of the grass roots organizations seem to have become inactive or lapsed altogether. A new factor encouraging landowner organization was the Ibáñez government's corporatist policy of refusing to entertain petitions from individual or unorganized groups of landowners; this may have kept some of the SNA's local units at least nominally alive.[31] Several of them were reported to be reforming in 1931 as a means of exerting greater pressure for relief from the effects of the depression.[32]

The revival and intensification of leftist activity in the countryside under the Popular Front stimulated another wave of landowner organizing throughout the country, particularly in the central zone. Provincial councils established in Colchagua, O'Higgins, Curicó, Ñuble, Linares, Aconcagua, and Valparaíso during those two years claimed their seats on the SNA board of directors, while dozens of local and departmental committees and assemblies were formed or resuscitated throughout the country. In response to the high degree of organizational activity, the SNA in 1939 established a special coordinating committee of gremio action to set guidelines for and maintain contact with the mushrooming agrarian groups.[33]

The absence of documentation makes it impossible to know with certainty which and how many of the SNA's subsidiary units were active at any given time. Figure 1 depicts the post-1929 SNA organizational struc-

Figure 1
SNA Organizational Structure, Bío-Bío Province, after 1929

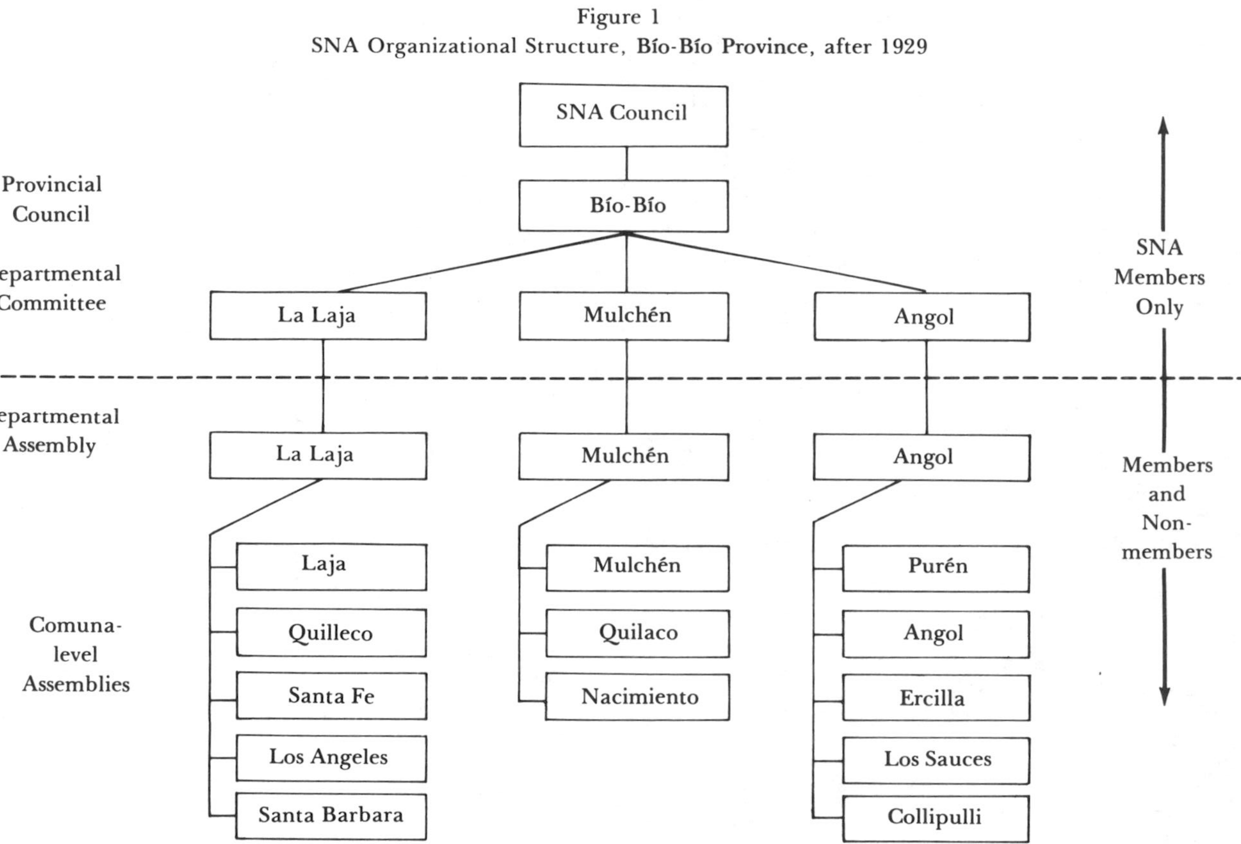

ture as it would have functioned in a province that was completely organized according to prescribed norms.

Unification of the Agricultural Societies

To round out the formation of a national agrarian bloc, the SNA in the twenties began to foster close cooperation with the four independent regional agricultural societies. Relations had traditionally been good but not close between the SNA and the Sociedad Agrícola del Sur, founded in 1887 at Concepción; the two societies periodically exchanged visits and occasionally pronounced or petitioned together on matters of common interest.[34] Three other societies formed after the turn of the century also retained their regional autonomy: the Sociedad Agrícola del Norte, founded in 1907 at La Serena; the Sociedad Agrícola y Ganadera de Osorno, established in 1917; and the Sociedad Cooperativa y de Fomento Agrícola de Temuco, founded in 1918. The challenges to landowners that arose after 1919 heightened the importance of nationally coordinated action; and although some members of the regional societies had also joined the SNA, all the associations sought a means of institutionalized cooperation.

In 1925 a southern regional agrarian congress took the first steps toward unified action by drawing up a twelve-point national agrarian program which all the societies were asked to endorse.[35] In 1929 agreement was reached on formalizing a merger, when the SNA revised its statutes to provide a seat on its board of directors for the president or a delegate of every legally constituted agricultural society in the country. It was also agreed to hold periodic consultations on political matters and to coordinate lobbying efforts on matters of common concern. The accord implicitly recognized the primacy of the SNA while preserving the regional societies' identities and individual spheres of action.[36]

A Profile of the New SNA

Reflecting on the growth of agrarian organization and the SNA's role in that process, *El Campesino* editorialized in 1938: "Some years ago it would have been improper to speak of the gremio of agriculturists. . . . The impetus for change . . . came from the SNA, which, by virtue of its location, the tradition it has maintained, and its natural influence, was called to serve as the nucleus of the gremio movement."[37] Thus by the thirties, when faced with increasingly difficult challenges to their prerogatives, landowners were much better prepared for defense than they had been in 1919. The organized national agrarian bloc formed under the SNA's tutelage provided an alternate source of power for the rural elites who had become vulnerable as the oligarchy of the Parliamentary Period lost its political hegemony.

Irregular record keeping, subsequent losses of data, and overlaps and fluctuations in membership among the multiple agrarian associations preclude establishing with any precision the membership characteristics of the organized gremio.[38] The numbers, names, social and economic status, and political experience and preferences of the thousands who joined the agrarian groups in some capacity other than as regular SNA members are largely unknown. To understand the nature of the agrarian bloc, then, we must rely on examining the changes in the SNA's membership as the Society responded institutionally to the advent of reform politics.

The most fundamental question to ask about the SNA is whether it remained a large landowners' association after its expansion. On the one hand, the indirect evidence suggests that despite the SNA's recent interest in the whole of rural society, regular membership was still designed for the large landowner or producer.[39] The annual livestock shows, for example, continued to be important social events where the visitor would observe in the flesh what George McBride called the "master-man relationship." While their *mozos* paraded pedigreed specimens before the judges, well-manicured, impeccably tailored landowners observed at a safe distance to avoid dirtying the hands or offending the nostrils.[40] One advertised benefit of joining the SNA was the discount which the telephone company offered to members who maintained phones in both city and country residences, and in 1938 the SNA's membership application forms asked for both city and rural addresses.[41] The Society's journal often contained articles on landscape gardening for the parks which graced all respectable fundos and on the care and grooming of thoroughbred dogs; and when a women's section was added to broaden the journal's appeal, it instructed members' wives on beauty secrets and amusements rather than on baking or canning.[42] Overall, the tone and style of the SNA strongly suggested a continuing identification with the values of the elite.

The direct evidence about SNA members as landowners is limited to a single sample, based on the only reasonably complete set of land tax records for this period, that of 1928. One therefore cannot authoritatively describe the SNA of 1940 in relation to land tenure, but it is possible to make certain projections. Another limitation in identifying SNA members within the ranks of landowners is that the tax records were not subdivided into useful analytical categories. In order to provide better perspective on the distribution of landed property by value, the findings of the 1935–36 agricultural census are provided in lieu of the 1928 tax records in Table 6.[43]

The tax rolls bear out the suspicion that the SNA was still essentially a large landowners' association in 1928. Rural property of $200,000 mini-

Table 6
Chilean Rural Landholdings in 1935-36

Category by Value (pesos)	Number of Holdings	Percent of Total Holdings	Thousands of Hectares	Percent of Total Surface	Value in Millions	Percent of Total Value
0-4,999	113,673	58.90	778	2.93	221	3.53
5-19,999	49,352	25.58	1,580	5.97	460	7.34
20-49,999	14,045	7.28	1,689	6.38	427	6.81
50-99,999	6,375	3.30	2,113	7.98	441	7.03
100-199,999	4,058	2.10	2,604	9.84	562	8.96
200-499,999	3,114	1.61	3,905	14.75	961	15.33
500-999,999	1,388	0.72	3,575	13.50	952	15.18
1m-1,999,999	651	0.34	4,429	16.73	891	14.21
2m-4,999,999	262	0.14	2,851	10.77	734	11.71
5m & over	51	0.03	2,951	11.15	621	9.90
	192,969	100.00	26,475	100.00	6,270	100.00

SOURCE: Adapted from Dirección General de Estadística, *Agricultura, 1935-36: censo*, p. 6.

mum assessed value was checked against the SNA membership list. The $200,000 figure was used to obtain a value, adjusted for inflation, roughly equivalent to the values selected to define large holdings in 1874 and 1908.[44] Table 7 reveals the findings on SNA members as large landowners in 1928 and includes data from earlier years for comparison.

Large properties—those of $200,000 assessed value and over—com-

Table 7
SNA Members as Large Landowners, 1874, 1908, and 1928

	1874	*1908*	*1928*
Total SNA membership[a]	231	698	1,777
SNA large landowners:			
number	134	321	927
percent of total membership	58.0	46.0	52.2
Total large properties	2,197	4,060	5,466[b]
SNA-owned large properties:			
number	245	510	1,376
percent of total large properties	11.2	12.6	25.2

[a]Individual members only (see n. 44).
[b]1935-36 total.
SOURCE: Table 2; *MSNA* (1928), pp. 57-93; Dirección General de Impuestos Internos, *Rol de avalúos . . . 1928*.

prised only 2.8 percent of all landholdings in Chile in 1935-36. For a more detailed perspective on patterns of land tenure among SNA members, the tax records of the same seven geographically representative departments scrutinized for 1908 were examined for 1928. The SNA membership list was checked against all properties valued between $50,000 and $200,000 to determine the incidence of Society membership among owners of smaller but still substantial holdings. Together with the properties of $200,000 and over, these represent the most valuable 9.2 percent of all agricultural properties in the sample departments.

Confirming the earlier pattern, the results indicate that in the sample departments the incidence of SNA ownership increased in direct proportion to assessed value; that is, SNA members were found more frequently as owners of large than of more modest properties. While Society members held some 30 percent of the large properties in the seven departments, they owned only 11 percent of the smaller properties assessed between $50,000 and $200,000. Moreover, of the 98 members found to own these more modest fundos, 67, or two-thirds of them, also owned one or more large properties in the same department or elsewhere. There were 206 individual SNA-affiliated large landowners, who collectively controlled 255 large holdings, and only 31 SNA members who owned substantial but not large properties. Eighty-five percent of the Society members owning property in the sample departments, then, held large estates (see Table 8).

One of the SNA's primary goals after 1919 was to organize all of the country's large landowners. Table 9 illustrates the degree of progress achieved in the seven sample departments by 1928, using the figures for 1908 as a base. There are several factors to consider, however, that bear upon the figures for 1928. First, 302 of the 843 (40.6 percent) of the large holdings in the sample departments belonged to women, companies, estates, religious corporations, the Sociedad de Beneficencia, or government entities. Collectively, these groups were underrepresented in the SNA in proportion to their importance as landowners. For example, while only nine (0.5 percent) of the SNA's 1,777 individually identified members in 1928 were women, females owned 182 (21.6 percent) of the large holdings in the seven departments.[46] Eliminating the corporately and female-owned estates, the figures indicate that SNA members owned 47.1 percent of all large properties held privately by males in the seven departments. Considering that the Society's membership doubled between 1928 and 1940, the SNA's representation among large holders must have increased substantially. Members of regional societies who did not hold regular SNA membership must also have owned some of the large holdings in the departments where those societies operated. Based on this combination of hard and soft evidence, it would seem that by 1940 the organized agrarian

Table 8
SNA Members as Owners of Properties Assessed at $50,000 and over in Seven Sample Departments, 1928[45]

Department and Province	Total Properties $50,000–99,999	Number SNA-Owned	Percent SNA-Owned	Total Properties $100–199,999	Number SNA-Owned	Percent SNA-Owned	Total Properties $200,000 and over	Number SNA-Owned	Percent SNA-Owned	Total Properties $50,000 and over	Number SNA-Owned	Percent SNA-Owned
La Serena (Coquimbo)	38	3	7.9	44	5	11.4	60	14	23.3	142	22	15.5
San Felipe (Aconcagua)	39	2	5.1	34	4	11.8	81	23	28.4	154	29	18.8
Melipilla (Santiago)	26	4	15.4	25	2	8.0	121	55	45.4	172	61	35.5
San Fernando (Colchagua)	33	1	3.0	33	13	39.4	119	39	32.8	185	53	28.7
Talca (Talca)	87	6	6.9	99	8	8.1	207	45	21.7	393	59	15.0
Angol (Malleco)	129	6	4.7	100	15	15.0	148	27	18.2	377	48	12.7
La Unión (Valdivia)	132	13	9.8	103	16	15.5	107	52	48.6	342	81	23.7
Totals	484	35	7.2	438	63	14.4	843	255	30.2	1,765	353	20.0

SOURCE: *MSNA* (1928), pp. 57–93; *Rol de avalúos . . . 1928*; Dirección General de Estadística, *Agricultura, 1929*, pp. 44–57.

Table 9
SNA Members as Large Landowners in
Seven Sample Departments, 1908 and 1928

	Total Large Properties			Number SNA-Owned Large Properties			Percent SNA-Owned Large Properties	
Department	1908	1928	Percent Change	1908	1928	Percent Change	1908	1928
La Serena	36	60	66.7	2	14	600.0	5.6	23.3
San Felipe	66	81	22.7	1	23	2200.0	1.5	28.4
Melipilla	168	121	−28.0	32	55	71.9	19.0	45.4
San Fernando	159	119	−25.2	52	39	−25.0	32.7	32.8
Talca	228	207	−9.2	23	45	95.7	10.1	21.7
Angol	41	148	261.0	9	27	200.0	22.0	18.2
La Unión	39	107	174.4	0	52	—	0.0	48.6
Total	737	843	14.4	119	255	114.3	16.2	30.2

SOURCE: *MSNA* (1909); *Indice de propietarios rurales . . .* (1908); *MSNA* (1928), pp. 57–93; *Rol de avalúos . . . 1928*; Dirección General de Estadística; *Agricultura, 1929*, pp. 44–57.

gremio had succeeded in enlisting the majority of the country's male large landowners.

The SNA, then, was as much a large landowners' association after 1919 as it had been up to that time. An important change had occurred, however, in the geographic distribution of its members' holdings. By 1928 the SNA could legitimately claim the national scope implied in its name. While membership showed some growth in the core area stretching from Aconcagua through Curicó between 1908 and 1928, it expanded more rapidly in the north and most impressively in the southern frontier and lake areas where there had been few members previously. The success of

Table 10
Geographic Distribution of SNA-Owned Large Properties, 1874, 1908, 1928

	Core (Aconcagua-Curicó)			South		
Year	Number of SNA Holdings	Percent of Total SNA Holdings	Percent Change	Number of SNA Holdings	Percent of Total SNA Holdings	Percent Change
1874	197	80.4		35	14.3	
1908	396	77.6	101	106	20.8	203
1928	629	45.7	59	707	51.4	567

SOURCE: *MSNA* (1873, 1909, 1928); *Impuesto agrícola* (1874); *Indice de propietarios rurales* (1908); *Rol de avalúos . . . 1928*.

the SNA's expansion drive is reflected in the fact that in 1928 over half of the large properties owned by members were located south of the core and fully a third south of the Bío Bío River. There is no hard evidence about geographic trends over the next decade, but the indications are that membership in the south held steady or increased while more of the large landowners of the central area joined the Society in the middle and late thirties.[47] Table 10 indicates the geographic evolution of the SNA's landed base.

As was true prior to its expansion, the SNA in 1928 had many members who were not identifiable as large landowners. There is some evidence that owners of smaller but still substantial fundos were joining the SNA in greater numbers by this time. In the seven sample departments, 31 of 237 (15 percent) of the SNA landowners held property assessed between $50,000 and $200,000 without simultaneously owning an estate classified as large.[48] In the south, where most membership growth occurred and where mean agricultural property values were lower than in the center and north, the SNA had absorbed considerable but indeterminate numbers of these less-than-large proprietors.[49] The number of more modest SNA-affiliated fundo owners may have increased also in the zone around the capital, where land continued to divide and change hands readily, where landowners enjoyed easy access to the Society's expanded services, and where the incidence of labor agitation was greatest in the 1920s.[50] Overall, it would be reasonable to estimate that at least 10 percent of the SNA's members in 1928 were landowners not in the "large" category.[51]

Of those remaining members who owned neither large nor more modest but substantial rural property, a majority were probably associated through kinship, service, or business ties with the owners of these estates. Some certainly were relatives of the 927 SNA members who collectively owned 1,213 large estates and uncounted smaller ones: 43 percent of the

North			Total SNA Holdings	
Number of SNA Holdings	Percent of Total SNA Holdings	Percent Change	Number	Percent Change
13	5.3		245	
8	1.6	– 39	510	108
40	2.9	400	1376	170

SNA members who did not own large property in 1928 shared paternal surnames with members who did.[52] Given the large landowners' penchant for living in the capital, their estates usually required the services of administrators or were rented out; both renters and administrators, whether relatives of the landowner or not, may have joined the Society for its practical benefits and to defend the interests of agricultural proprietors and producers. By the Popular Front period, significant numbers of nonlandowners may have joined the SNA as a symbolic political act.[53]

Although still composed primarily of the rural elites, as it grew numerically and expanded geographically the SNA inevitably attracted more members from beyond the traditional national oligarchy. Whereas nearly a fourth of the membership between 1898 and 1918 had held congressional seats or ministerial appointments during their lifetimes, the proportion in the next two decades fell to just under 10 percent. And compared to the 55 percent of SNA members who belonged to the Club de la Unión in 1918, only a fourth belonged in the sample year of 1933.[54] In the course of its expansion, then, the Society had recruited among the landowning elites throughout the country, in the process reaching beyond the traditional SNA member—the central zone landowner who formed part of the national economic, social, and political establishment.

Leadership of the New SNA

While the character of the SNA's membership showed a pronounced change as the result of growth, the collective biography of its board of directors adhered more closely to the historic pattern. Even after the 1929 structural changes in the board of directors (see Figure 2), the Society's leadership was almost as thoroughly representative of the old national oligarchy in the thirties as it had been before 1919. For example, thirty-two of the thirty-seven (86.5 percent) directors in the sample year of 1933 belonged to the Club de la Unión. The incidence of political participation remained at the same high level as during the SNA's first fifty years: 57.7 percent of directors in sample years between 1919 and 1940 held national office at some time during their lives. Several directors, including Héctor Rodríguez de la Sotta, Arturo Lyon Peña, Carlos Briones Luco, and Francisco Garcés Gana, served as president or vice-president of major political parties. Twenty-two of the thirty directors in 1928 owned large estates, most of them in the central heartland. As indicated in Appendix 5, most directors with ten or more years' service had extensive economic interests outside of agriculture and many had professions unrelated to agriculture; some are described in biographical dictionaries without any mention of a connection with agriculture or land.[55]

Figure 2
SNA Council, ca. 1938

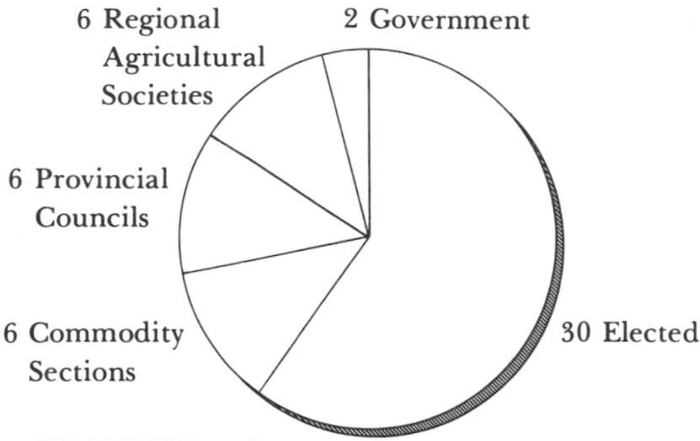

SOURCE: Based on *MSNA* (1938), p. 1.

Of the various factors which contributed to the continuing predominance of the traditional type of Society member in the board of directors, perhaps the most basic was geographic. Half of the thirty elected positions were filled in annual elections in which members had to vote in person at the SNA building; this effectively disenfranchised the provincial member who did not live in or frequently travel to Santiago.[56] A council member had to be able to attend weekly or biweekly meetings in Santiago. Since attendance was expected and perennial absentees were replaced, this requirement clearly favored the member who resided in or very near the capital. As the Society's business became more political, selection of members who held public office or other positions of influence became increasingly important, and this pointed to the traditional type of SNA member. The inclusion of regional society and provincial council representatives in 1929 did little to alter the character of the board; in order to be effective representatives, these men had to live in or travel regularly to the capital, making it quite probable that they had business, professional, or political interests in Santiago.

In contrast to the earlier years, following 1919 the Society's presidency increased vastly in importance. As the organization grew and its work assumed greater significance to landowners, the need for constant, day-to-day authority and direction likewise increased. These needs were partially filled by a full-time secretary general and a host of other salaried officials;[57] but the president now had to be in constant touch with Society business and generally had to spend several hours daily at his job. The obituary of Luis Larraín Prieto, president in the twenties, reveals something of the burdens of office which could not have been written about an SNA president before 1919: "He came to the Society's offices in the mornings and spent almost the whole day there. This interest and activity were a stimulus and an example for everyone."[58] As the job entailed neither salary nor appreciable perquisites, the president had to be a man of independent means. Moreover, with the SNA frequently involved in the public limelight, the president had to present the most politically advantageous image that the Society could offer.

During the twenties, the SNA had only one long-term president, Luis Larraín Prieto, who simultaneously served as minister of agriculture for nearly a year in the government of Emiliano Figueroa Larraín. After two brief presidencies, the SNA in 1932 elected Jaime Larraín García-Moreno to its highest office. In the following eight years, Jaime Larraín demonstrated to the fullest the potential and the responsibilities that the Society's presidency carried in the era of mass politics.[59]

Jaime Larraín met the SNA's traditional criteria for the presidency in every way except age; whereas the job usually went to senior members, Larraín was elected at age thirty-seven. Being SNA president was something of a family tradition among Jaime's branch of the Larraín clan. Rafael Larraín Moxó, his grandfather, had held the office in the 1880s, and Luís Larraín Prieto of the twenties was his uncle. In addition to the family tree, Jaime Larraín had the other standard credentials of the national elite establishment—membership in the Club de la Unión, a law degree, a varied personal investment portfolio. He also had the political vocation of the traditional upper classes: prior to his election as SNA president he had served three years as a deputy; after his retirement from the Society's top position, he went on to found and lead the Partido Agrario Laborista, to be a precandidate for president of the republic in 1946, and to serve twelve years in the Senate. At the same time, Larraín was the embodiment of the serious and progressive landowner. He was an agronomist who regularly visited and personally directed his fundo, La Esmeralda in O'Higgins. It boasted silos, sophisticated machinery, dairy installations, and imported breeds of cattle. The inquilinos' houses were modern, roomy, constructed of cement with zinc roofs; there was a workers' cooperative, clubhouse and theatre, and a school. Overall, the fundo was a model for the technologically and socially progressive landowner.

In other ways, Larraín's election was hardly consistent with SNA tradition. Above all, his politics were controversial within the conservative establishment. As a student he came into contact with the Christian social philosophy of Jacques Maritain and became a leader of the progressive Catholic youth of the 1910s. He showed an activist bent while still a student, setting up workers' schools in Santiago and founding the first taxi drivers' union in Chile. He was elected deputy for the Conservative party in 1921 on a platform whose advanced positions, in the words of a contemporary magazine, "raised fears and protests." In Congress, the article continues, "embracing by conviction the advanced ideas of Christian Democracy, he has dedicated himself to fighting for them."[60] Although he was associated with Eduardo Frei, Bernardo Leighton, and other future prominent Christian Democrats in the twenties, Larraín chose to remain in the Conservative party rather than joining them in forming the Falange Nacional in 1937; this choice may have reflected the partial generational gap which separated them, as well as the responsibilities of the SNA presidency.

Jaime Larraín, then, combined impeccable credentials as a member of the aristocracy with a well-deserved reputation as a progressive agriculturist and politician. Although he remained in the mainstream of the political establishment until after his SNA presidency, he emphatically did not give up the Christian social precepts which marked his early career. Larraín's election to the SNA presidency was a clear indication of the Society's need to innovate in meeting the threat of reform. Some of his stances were controversial and his program for "improvement of peasant life" even threatened to destroy the unity of the agrarian bloc because it was too advanced for many landowners.[61] Yet when he resigned in 1940 he was widely acclaimed for his success in guiding the institution through the period of greatest political challenge that Chilean landowners had faced. It turned out to be the most difficult period for landowners before the 1960s.

Notes

1. Moisés Poblete Troncoso, *El problema de la producción agrícola y la política agraria nacional* (Santiago, 1919), p. 165.
2. *BSNA*, 55 (1924), 308.
3. Drake, *Socialism and Populism*, pp. 118-20, cites expansion of the Club de la Unión to incorporate middle-class elements of the Radical party and the armed forces as evidence of co-optation. See also Guillermo Viviani Contreras, *Sociología chilena* (Santiago, 1926), pp. 58-60. Appendixes 1, 3, and 6 shed further light on SNA members and directors as politicians; note esp. in Appendix 6 the growth of SNA members in a single Congress, the 37th.
4. See Tables 6 and 7.
5. See ch. 7, under "Opening Round."
6. Throughout the twenties and thirties, the Society continued to deny involvement in "politics." In 1925, the SNA and other societies declared themselves united for "economic purposes, without engaging . . . in politics, a realm of activity left to the parties." *MSNA* (1925), p. 23. In 1939 the SNA president drew a distinction between actions proper to an "institution of development" and those that could be construed as "political." Minutes, Mar. 14, 1939, in *El C*, 71 (1939), 385.
7. MSNA (1919), pp. 6-20; *El Agricultor*, 50 (1919), 198-99.
8. Thomas C. Wright, "Origins of the Politics of Inflation in Chile, 1888-1918," *Hispanic American Historical Review*, 53 (1973), 250-52.

9. *El Agricultor*, 51 (1920), 235.

10. Minutes, July 14, 1924, in *BSNA*, 55 (1924), 521; *MSNA* (1924), p. 33.

11. McBride, *Land and Society*, pp. 285-313, discusses the southern property question; see ch. 7, under "Opening Round."

12. Minutes, Aug. 29, 1921, in *BSNA*, 53 (1922), 46; *ibid.*, 54 (1923), 285; *ibid.*, 56 (1925), 329-30.

13. *El Mercurio*, July 3, 1921, p. 5.

14. *BSNA*, 53 (1922), 626-27, 628-44.

15. *Ibid.*, 56 (1925), 302, 304-5.

16. *Ibid.*, 62 (1930), 700.

17. *El Agricultor*, 51 (1920), 235.

18. Ch. 1, p. 7; *BSNA*, 53 (1922), 643-44.

19. McBride, *Land and Society*, pp. 228-29, pointedly wrote that the SNA's building was part of the "little Chile" of the politically powerful. The purpose of the SNA's expansion of services was frankly political, as revealed in Minutes, Dec. 18 and 26, 1922, in *BSNA*, 54 (1923), 221-29. Growth of the SNA's services and commercial section is described in *El C*, 70 (1938), edición extraordinaria, 3-12; *ibid.*, 72 (1940), 742-47.

20. *MSNA* (1902-3), pp. 10-11; Minutes, Nov. 21, 1921, in *BSNA*, 53 (1922), 157; Minutes, Aug. 27, 1928, in *ibid.*, 60 (1928), 684; *ibid.*, 59 (1927), 791-93.

21. *BSNA*, 63 (1931), 457.

22. *MSNA* (1938), p. 1.

23. See ch. 4 under "Strategy for Defense" for analysis of the SNA's problems during the depression.

24. *BSNA*, 62 (1930), 699-700; *El C*, 70 (1938), unpaginated.

25. SNA, *La SNA en las provincias: labor de la delegación de la SNA en su jira por el sur del país* (Santiago, 1924); SNA, *Congreso Regional Agrario*, p. 21; *MSNA* (1923), p. 5; *BSNA*, 55 (1924), 307-8.

26. Minutes, Apr. 20, 1925, in *BSNA*, 56 (1925), 311; *ibid.*, 329-30.

27. *Asamblea de Agricultores de la Comuna de San José* (Valdivia, 1925).

28. *MSNA* (1925), pp. 20-23; *BSNA*, 56 (1925), 559; Minutes, Sept. 28, 1925, in *ibid.*, 819.

29. SNA, *Estatutos de la SNA*, (Santiago, 1930).

30. The directors requested in 1930 that all petitions from local and departmental organizations be routed through the SNA central office for its action. Minutes, Aug. 18, 1930, in *BSNA*, 62 (1930), 612. Valenzuela, *Political Brokers*, pp. 193-210, describes the parties' role during this period as brokers between central and local levels.

31. See ch. 4, pp. 90-91, 99*n*.

32. *MSNA* (1931), pp. 5-7; Minutes, July 6, 1931, in *BSNA*, 63 (1931), 444; Minutes, Aug. 24, 1931, in *ibid.*, 497.

33. Minutes, Dec. 11, 1939, in *El C*, 72 (1940), 55; *El Mercurio* often reported news of these developments, e.g., Apr. 1, 1939, p. 19; July 31, 1939, p. 26; Nov. 30, 1939, p. 18; Apr. 21, 1940, p. 35; Dec. 15, 1940, p. 55.

34. One of many examples was reported in *BSNA*, 30 (1901), 479-82.

35. SNA, *Congreso Regional Agrario*, esp. pp. 22-23, 33-72.

36. SNA, *Estatutos*.

37. *El C*, 70 (1938), edición extraordinaria, 277-78.

38. To illustrate the problem of numbers, the Sociedad Agrícola y Ganadera de Osorno reported but did not identify 1,068 members in 1939, leaving no evidence as

to overlap with SNA membership. *Agricultura Austral*, año VI, no. 78 (July 1939), unpaginated. Moreover, some of the regional societies had their own local affiliates, but it is not clear whether these consisted only of regular members or included smallholders or workers in nonmember status.

39. One of the Society's publications, *SNA en provincias*, p. 48, announced the hope of recruiting all the country's agriculturists "de importancia."

40. McBride, *Land and Society*, pp. 3-14. The best evidence about the livestock shows is pictorial: see the November edition annually in *BSNA* and *El C*.

41. *El C*, 70 (1938), unpaginated.

42. E.g., *El C*, 72 (1940), 136-39, 192-93, 307-8; see esp. the section "Ella y su hogar."

43. The total estimated value of rural property in the country rose from $6,069,251,362 in 1928 to $6,270,000,000 in 1935-36, or only about 3 percent. Therefore the use of 1935-36 figures reflects the situation of 1928 quite accurately. Moreover the 1935-36 census figures should be more reliable than the tax rolls in identifying agricultural property, since the former are based on rural property with primary or secondary agricultural exploitation. This should have eliminated numerous suburban and small town plots, as well as mines, that the tax rolls would have classified as rural but which had no relation to agriculture.

44. The figure of $200,000 as the definition of large property was obtained by adjusting the figure used in 1908 by the approximate increase in the total value of taxed rural property between 1909 and 1928. From a total of $1,208,312,591 in 1908, rural property had risen to $6,069,251,362 in 1928, an increase of 500 percent. Although this would suggest a minimum figure of $250,000 for defining large property, I rounded it downward in order possibly to locate more SNA landowners on the tax rolls. Corporate and company members (69) were not checked or counted in Table 7, since they would reveal little or nothing about the SNA's members as landowners unless all partners and associates in corporate and company holdings could be identified—an impossible task. There is a discrepancy of 128 members between the list published in *MSNA* and the total reported membership (Table 5). Those whose dues were in arrears, or who had joined quite recently, may have been omitted from the published list but still reported as members.

45. The total number of holdings of $50,000 and over reported in *Agricultura, 1929*, is approximately 5 percent larger than the number located by hand counting from the tax rolls. The hand-counted figure is used here.

46. *MSNA* (1928); Dirección General de Impuestos Internos, *Rol de avalúos: tasación general practicada el año 1928* (Valparaíso, 1929), 63 vols.

47. The growth of local, departmental, and provincial organizations in the core area indicates that enough landowners were now joining in that area to sustain those associations. Note that most of the large sheep-ranching operations in Magallanes were organized as companies or corporations. While some of these joined the SNA, they do not show up as landowning members since only individual members were checked against the tax rolls.

48. See above, pp. 66-67.

49. The tax rolls for Valdivia through Chiloé were examined for properties assessed as low as $100,000 and yielded forty-one SNA members who did not own "large" estates. This unsystematic check suggests that closer scrutiny of the tax rolls throughout the south might turn up considerably more members.

50. See ch. 6, under "Intellectual and Political Background," on subdivision of property; ch. 7, under "Opening Round" and "Rural Labor," on labor distur-

bances. The area immediately surrounding Santiago could not be analyzed with any accuracy for 1928, given the increased urban sprawl and resultant difficulty of distinguishing between urban and agricultural land use.

51. This very rough estimate is based on the risky premise that the ratio of smaller but substantial SNA landowners ($50,000-200,000) to large SNA landowners ($200,000 and over) in the seven sample departments (31 exclusively smaller, 206 large) can be projected throughout the country. If this is done, it gives a figure of 140 smaller landowners nationally (8.3 percent of the SNA membership). Taking into account the higher incidence of less-than-large SNA landowners in the south, and the probability of a higher incidence around Santiago, the projected figure might be raised to 10 percent of the total membership (178 members). This estimate seems more likely to be low than high.

52. *MSNA* (1928), pp. 57-93.

53. *El Mercurio*, May 4, 1940, p. 9, mentions by name two of the hundreds of individuals who joined the SNA during the Popular Front government: the Radical minister of defense, Alfredo Duhalde Vásquez, and the former president of the Radical party, Florencio Durán Bernales. They may or may not have been landowners, but they joined at the time when the Radical party was divided between siding with its Marxist allies or with the SNA in a showdown discussed in ch. 7, under "Landowners, Communists, and National Politics." Florencio Durán Bernales, *El Partido Radical* (Santiago, 1958), pp. 98-100, confirms the political motive of numerous Radicals for joining the SNA during the same period. See also the cartoon in *El Siglo*, Oct. 22, 1940, p. 5.

54. Appendixes 1 and 2.

55. Appendixes 3, 4, and 5. *MSNA* (1928); *Rol de avalúos . . . 1928.*

56. SNA, *Estatutos*. A revision in 1939 altered the details but not the basic method of voting. *El C*, 71 (1939), 22.

57. The administrative structure is outlined in *El C*, 72 (1940), 743.

58. *El C*, 70 (1938), 181.

59. The ensuing sketch of Jaime Larraín is based on the following sources: interview, Jaime Larraín García-Moreno, Santiago, Dec. 6, 1968; interview, Gerardo Larraín Valdés (son), Santiago, Aug. 3, 1976; photos of fundo La Esmeralda from the 1930s; Pedro Pablo Figueroa, *Diccionario biográfico de Chile*, 4th ed. (Santiago, 1897-1901), 3, 643-44; Cortés and Fuentes, *Diccionario político*, p. 266; A. Sotomayor, "La vida que pasa," *Sucesos: Semanario de Actualidades*, año XX, no. 1023 (May 4, 1922), unpaginated; and several articles in *El C*.

60. Sotomayor, "La vida que pasa," unpaginated.

61. See ch. 4, pp. 80ff.

4

The SNA and the Politics of Reform

Expansion of the SNA and creation of an agrarian bloc provided landowners a vital tool for the defense of their interests. Beyond that, the SNA was obliged to develop an overall strategy and methods of action appropriate to the changing political context after 1919. The fundamental strategic question was whether to try to defend the status quo in its entirety or to offer concessions in an attempt to preserve the essentials among landowners' rights and privileges. Within the latter option were several variants: (1) make minimal concessions under immediate pressure to forestall mass movements, revolutions, or coups d'état; (2) remedy or eliminate the most glaring situations or institutions that the left could successfully exploit to its advantage; or (3) offer substantive but moderate reforms in the hope of creating a more stable society and political system, thereby making landowners' essential prerogatives more secure. In developing methods of political action the SNA had to take into account the liabilities of the landowner image and the substantial changes in the decision-making process that resulted from the democratization of politics and the expansion of state activity in the social and economic realms.

A Strategy for Defense

In 1919 and the decade of the twenties, the SNA adopted no consistent attitude toward the major problems raised by the advent of mass politics. This inconsistency merely reflected the uncertainty and vacillation characteristic of the upper-class establishment as a whole when confronted with the initial challenge of reform. The Society, like most individuals who participated in the great debate over the "social question" after the turn of the century, had generally staked out progressive public positions and urged the opportune resolution of social and labor problems before they assumed a graver character.[1] However, when suddenly faced with a mobilized working class demanding substantive reform the SNA, along with much of the oligarchy, abruptly reneged on its commitment to reform and dug in its heels against change. Such was the general reaction of landowners as expressed in the conclusions of the 1919 Asamblea de Agricultores: years of SNA editorial support for increased subdivision of large holdings, improvement of inquilino housing, and better conditions for agricultural labor were thrown out the window, and landowners asserted that the rustics' vicious and nomadic ways were simply "the consequence of the mental backwardness produced in Chile, as in all of Spanish America, by the crossing of the conquistador with the aboriginal race."[2]

One senses that the SNA, along with much of the upper class, was in a prolonged state of shock and confusion between 1919 and the early thirties, bewildered by the changes taking place and unable to develop a broad and consistent strategy for reacting to them. Landowners were psychologically unprepared to deal with demands for change backed by threats. Their earlier advocacy of progressive solutions was premised on the understanding that they, the directing classes, would prescribe and administer reforms of their own volition, and that the lower elements would show their gratitude through strengthened bonds of loyalty, greater productivity, and rejection of the blandishments of "agitators" who sowed the seeds of class hatred. The attitudes of the SNA's directors in 1919 were essentially unchanged from the sentiment expressed in a 1906 *Boletín* editorial dealing with pressure from the masses: "The public powers cannot proceed under the pressure of such a threat, nor even take it into account. To give way under such conditions would be to establish the most lamentable of precedents; that would be equivalent to not only confessing weakness and impotence, but also to stimulating disorder, to contributing to sanctioning the success of the social and political agitators who thrive on popular tumults."[3]

In the early twenties, then, the attitude of the SNA leadership, reflecting that of the conservative majority of the political establishment, was to reject most social legislation as illegitimate and unnecessary. Combined with this attitude there seems to have been an unstated hope that the problems raised in 1919 would soon go away. Concurrently, however, the Society continued to advocate voluntary paternalistic improvements in rural life as a moral obligation of the *patrón* and as a matter of prudence.[4]

Along with the rightist majority the SNA began to exhibit more flexibility toward reform after 1924, especially when it could dictate the terms. In 1926, for example, it drafted a moderate bill for the subdivision of large properties, and made an important concession on the unpopular livestock tariff.[5] Although the SNA leadership viewed the Ibáñez reforms with considerable apprehension, it generally chose to cooperate when possible rather than trying to obstruct. Ibáñez's low tolerance for dissent and his heavy emphasis on investment in agricultural development undoubtedly made the choice easier.

After the severe economic and political crisis of 1930-32, a majority within the conservative political establishment adopted, in varying measure, the progressive strategy of flexibility and concession. The SNA leadership generally accepted the same approach, although on specific issues affecting landowners' interests it normally took a tougher line than did, for example, the Alessandri government. However, there were several voices of dissent within the SNA council. Among the most intransigent of those was Héctor Rodríguez de la Sotta, onetime president of the Conservative party, presidential candidate in 1932, and SNA director during most of the thirties, whose attitude toward reform can be inferred from the following pithy statement: "The suffering and the mean circumstances which beset the poor and which sociologists say is wrong, we Christians say is proper. . . . For in our concept as Christians, poverty is the estate most rich in the means through which man realizes his eternal destiny."[6] Rodríguez and a few other directors, including Jorge Silva Somarriva, Nicanor Allende, and Luis Correa Vergara, consistently hewed to the laissez-faire line and opposed most social reform and state intervention.[7]

Jaime Larraín's election to the SNA presidency in 1932 confirmed the ascendancy of the progressive line within the board of directors. Don Jaime offered a competing interpretation of Christian social doctrine: in his view, it was the duty of "the directing class and . . . those who possess means of fortune to resolve in a Christian manner the problem of misery and to apply in the realm of labor the moral norms about the social use of wealth."[8] For the benefit of those less Christian than himself or don Héctor, he hastened to add the practical argument that such action would also "put an end to the injustice which engenders the movement of agitation and the adherence of the masses to revolutionary credos."[9] Larraín's sincere and consistent Christian professions cannot be taken as anything but statements of his personal ideology. Comprised as it was of political leaders and partisans of various persuasions, the SNA would not have formally embraced a particular set of ideological guidelines any more than it would have aligned itself with a single political party. Stripped of ideological overtones, however, Larraín's pronouncements accurately reflected the SNA council's majority view that material improvement and spiritual guidance of the masses would strengthen the bonds of class harmony, preserve the essence of the social order, and defeat the efforts of revolutionaries to win over the populace.

Under Larraín's presidency the SNA followed the principle that landowners' interests could best be defended by a strategy of timely concessions, both substantive and token. The SNA was unwilling to give up as much as some of the right would have it do, but rather than trying to preserve the status quo in its entirety the Society attempted to defend that which was essential and that which was defensible while compromising in peripheral areas. It generally followed the "insider" approach to reform issues: rather than directly opposing prejudicial measures the SNA usually attempted to work within Congress or the administration to produce policy that contained a maximum of good intentions and a minimum of teeth. Larraín recommended the insider approach in the following terms: "It is useless [to try] to detain social evolution. It is necessary to put oneself on the side of it in order to guide it. Let us not be agents provocateurs of demagoguery and disorder."[10]

In the case of legislation, the SNA normally took a low-key approach in order not to reinforce the unpopular image of landowners and further strengthen the left's case against them by appearing reactionary. It generally expressed publicly its agreement with the principle and purpose of reform legislation that it actually opposed, pointed out the bill's defects, and then offered its collaboration and expertise in tailoring the legislation for the peculiar setting of rural life. The desired outcome was either a safely diluted law, which would nonetheless demonstrate landowners' sense of social responsibility and willingness to cooperate in peaceful change, or failure to resolve differences among competing proposals, resulting in no law at all. In the case of legislation already enacted the SNA rarely called directly for its repeal, which in most cases it would not have been able to achieve anyway; rather, it often appealed for temporary suspension of the law's enforcement until, with the SNA's help, the law could be "reformed."[11]

The SNA infrequently took the initiative in proposing reform legislation of its own confection. One such case occurred in the mid-thirties when rural social and working conditions were coming under heated attack from left and right. The SNA leadership decided that since its encouragement of voluntary improvement had failed, it had better turn to internal regulation to prevent the imposition of far harsher terms. The Society thus offered to work with the government in drawing up legislation for minimum wages in agriculture and the improvement of inquilino housing and simultaneously, with great fanfare, launched its campaign for "the improvement of peasant life," also known as the "policy of the good patrón."[12]

The fate of the SNA's attempt at internal regulation showed the limits of its progressive strategy. Although the proposed legislation was practically unenforceable, to many landowners, including some SNA members, it appeared dangerous and severe. At least two SNA directors who served on the bill-drafting committee opposed it, and several public denunciations were forthcoming from dissident landowners. President Larraín had to take to the radio and make a special trip to the south to explain his program and try to preserve harmony within the agrarian bloc. The gremio only narrowly avoided an open rupture in 1936–37, and the experience forced Larraín and the SNA to refrain from supporting subsequent measures of this kind.[13]

Jaime Larraín later identified the opposition to the campaign for "improvement of peasant life" as "those who, wedded to individualist economic doctrines, deny the Church and the State major intervention in private relations."[14] The widespread opposition to the progressive strategy, however, was based on much more than the ideological discrepancies that Larraín cited. Within the agrarian bloc and within the SNA itself there had emerged by the thirties two very different and often incompatible approaches to defining the landowner interest. The real difference between the two views was frequently obscured by the use of stock phrases such as "state intervention" or "social justice," which tended to place the conflict within an ideological framework; but more important than matters of principle were geography, economic interests, and political experience. The divergence of interpretations was primarily a result of the changing composition of the SNA—and in a broader sense, of the agrarian gremio—and of the differences in collective traits between the membership and the board of directors.

As was discussed in chapter 3, the SNA's board of directors after 1919 exhibited many of the same social, economic, and political traits that had characterized the Society's leadership during the SNA's first half-century. The majority of board members were large landowners of the central zone, commonly were active in politics at the national level, practiced a profession, moved in the highest national social circles, had diversified economic interests, and lived most of the year in Santiago. The obituary of long-term director and former president Pedro Ruíz Tagle, published in the SNA journal, is very instructive as to the multiple interests characteristic of the Society's leadership: it emphasized "the utmost affection that he had for agriculture, *which he made his only profession*" (italics added).[15] At the risk of oversimplification, one could affirm that the Society's leaders were men of the national elite by birth, wealth, politics, or commonly all of the above, and that as a result they had a national upper-class view of the world. Guillermo Barros Jara, Máximo Valdés Fontecilla, or Alberto Correa Valenzuela quite naturally saw the political priorities and interests of landowners within the context of, and as one variable in, the broader upper-class interest. In the case of conflict between the immediate economic interest of landowners and the long-range welfare of the upper social strata, the latter was likely to take precedence.

By 1930 the preceding statement would not have applied to a majority of SNA members. As a result of the Society's numerical growth and geographic expansion, the central area landowner who was simultaneously a member of the national upper class had gone from majority to minority status within the association and to a fraction of the total within the entire agrarian bloc. The new majority of Society members were landowners or producers in the frontier and lake regions of the south, and the independent affiliated societies were strongest and most numerous in the same area. Hard data on regional societies' membership are lacking, and the vast majority of the SNA's southern members do not grace the pages of the biographical dictionaries; nonetheless it is possible to draw some generalizations from known cases.

A few SNA members whose landed base was in the south had been integrated at least marginally into the national upper class through business or politics. Julio Buschmann, one of the largest landowners in the south, was a dentist in Osorno and a founder and president of the Sociedad Agrícola y Ganadera de Osorno. For several years he represented that institution in the SNA board of directors and exercised political power on the national level as senator from Llanquihue.[16] The four Möller Bordeu brothers from Concepción became large landowners throughout the lake and frontier regions, ran various businesses, and brother Víctor was an SNA director in the thirties. All the brothers were powerful in the Radical party: two of them served in various ministries from the thirties into the fifties and another was a deputy for several years.[17] The economic and political biography of Cristóbal Sáenz, a Radical leader and SNA member, reads very much the same way.[18]

The Möller Bordeus, Julio Buschmann, and a handful of other SNA members bridged the gap between the provincial and the national realms of activity. The Schillings of Osorno and the Schleyers of Chillán provide the far more typical examples of SNA members among the landowning elite whose frame of reference was provincial or regional. The four Schilling brothers each owned large rural properties and ran mills, warehouses, and other businesses throughout the lake district. Brother Hugo was president of the largest bank in the south, the Banco de Osorno y La Unión, and Enrique was a *regidor* (councilman) in the municipality of Osorno for several years.[19] The three Schleyer brothers operated several fundos around Chillán with their father, owned a distillery, and were involved in municipal government.[20] These men exemplified the local or regional elites: like the traditional Society member they owned businesses, practiced professions, lived in town, and belonged to the prestigious clubs, but rather than in Santiago they operated in Temuco, Puerto Montt, or Los Angeles.

There were two important factors that tended to give the southern landowner a different view of the landowner interest than that generally adopted by the SNA board of directors. First, the entire economy of the frontier and lake regions, excluding the industrial enclaves of Concepción and Valdivia and the coal-mining area of Lota and Coronel, was geared to agriculture—primarily to wheat and secondarily to cattle raising and dairy farming.[21] Thus even the landowner who also owned retail stores and practiced law was ultimately dependent on the price of wheat, the tariff on livestock, the cost of labor, and railroad rates. Second, the southern landowner generally had little direct political experience, either as an observer of mass politics or as a public or party official beyond the local level. The majority, living in or near small, quiescent provincial towns, had not experienced at first hand the postwar mobilization, seen proletarian mobs, heard radical speeches, or witnessed the legions of unemployed during the depression; nor had they learned, from experience in Congress or in the executive committee of the Liberal party, the tactic of the timely concession or the art of gently castrating a reform bill.

The tendency of the southern landowner, then, was to interpret the landowner interest in black or white terms, while the more sophisticated Society directors viewed it within the context of the broader class interest. A majority in the council recognized that a rise in the price of wheat entailed a rise in the price of bread, and possibly a rise in urban social tensions; to the southerner, dependent on the price of his wheat, the price of bread was irrelevant. To the politically experienced SNA board member, a concession to the left, such as funding the Ministry of Labor, might be an investment in the next congressional election and in the long-term class interest; to the provincial southern member, it meant the bother of keeping written contracts and fending off meddlesome labor inspectors. To the board in the mid-thirties, taking the initiative in rural social legislation was an attempt to preempt the forces of revolution; to the southern landowner it was unwarranted intrusion into his private matters and a threat to his profits.

An exchange between SNA directors in two council meetings in 1932 aptly illustrates the divergent approaches to policy formulation—the broad class interest versus the immediate economic welfare of producers. The essence of the conflict is best understood if the reader makes a slight editorial change, substituting "upper-class" for "general" interests. Although a dissenter on issues of reform and state intervention, Jorge Silva Somarriva nonetheless stated the common view within the board that

> the opinions of this institution should not favor exclusively the interests of the gremio, but on the contrary consider, above all, the general interests of the collectivity. . . . [The policy in question] would have brought within a short time the brusque reaction that it was logical to expect from the preponderance of the interests of some to the detriment of those of the rest, since it was based on the sacrifice of interests also worthy of being considered and respected.

In the following meeting director Kenneth Page reacted: "The opinions of the SNA should consider exclusively the interests of the industry which it represents, without allowing considerations of a general nature to interfere with the expression of purely agrarian needs." Silva Somarriva in turn responded by restating his position con brío: "Whenever the Society defends exclusively gremio interests which perturb the higher interests of my country, I shall forget that I am an agriculturist and remember only that I am Chilean."[22]

Discrepancies over defining and defending the landowner interest were endemic, but the Great Depression and the accompanying social and political crisis brought the conflict into high relief. After the fall of the Ibáñez government in July 1931, the political system was in chaos, the economy in shambles, and unemployment high and still mounting. The main concern of the conservative political establishment was to patch together a government that could at least preserve the institutional structure from revolution or military coup, and in the interest of unity the right and center parties coalesced behind Radical acting president Juan Esteban Montero as their candidate for the October election.[23] In the frontier and southern areas, meanwhile, landowners were mobilizing to demand additional price supports, suspension of mortgage payments, emergency credit, and other measures to ease the impact of the continuing decline in agricultural prices. The agrarian association of San Carlos called for a new national organization "to defend the common interests of landowners," and several militant new local and regional agricultural associations sprang up.[24] Dissatisfied with the attitudes of the major parties and the acting Montero government, a sizeable group, primarily of disaffected Radicals, formed the Agrarian party in August 1931 and began seeking a presidential candidate.[25] The southern agricultural societies immediately announced their support of the new party and asked for the SNA's endorsement.

This placed the SNA squarely in a dilemma: its response would either jeopardize the fragile electoral coalition of right and center and thus invite political disaster, or endanger the unity of the newly formed agrarian bloc. The Society's prestige in the south was already tenuous. As a director reported upon returning from the south, "agriculturists do not adhere to the Society because they believe it does not defend their interests."[26] On the other hand, the upper-class priority clearly was to elect and support a "national" government that would be capable of surviving the nadir of the depression and forestalling revolution. The SNA's response was an unconvincing compromise: it expressed "satisfaction" at the founding of the Agrarian party and concurrently took the unprecedented step of formally endorsing Montero in exchange for the inclusion of a mild agrarian program in his campaign platform.[27]

After his election, Montero proved quite ineffectual in coping with the crisis, and his inaction further alienated southern landowners from the government and from the SNA, which continued to support the regime.[28]

Finally, in an effort to explain its position to landowners, the Society published a manifesto on December 27, 1931, which pithily stated its dilemma and its criteria: "A dual responsibility exists for this venerable corporation: that of safeguarding the interests of agriculture . . . and that of maintaining the support which elements of order and enterprise must lend the government and its decisions."[29] Although the SNA's efforts were insufficient to sustain the weak regime in power, the first minister of agriculture in Alessandri's second government later commended the SNA for "having viewed at every moment, and above all gremio interests, the permanent interests of the country."[30]

The restoration of constitutional government under Alessandri and the gradual economic recovery allowed the agrarian bloc to survive the depression relatively intact. The Agrarian party remained active and consistently drew well in the frontier area, but most of the agricultural associations formed in protest against the SNA's attitude either died or merged with other societies during the thirties. However, as the reaction to Jaime Larraín's progressive policies demonstrated, the basic divergence of criteria was not susceptible to permanent solution, and it cropped up periodically. The same conflict underlay the formal split between the SNA and the southern wing in 1961 over the agrarian reform issue.[31]

The SNA in the Political Process

In contrast to the relatively modest political role it had played prior to 1919, after that time the SNA was constantly involved in the political process. When not actively lobbying on particular pieces of legislation or administrative rulings, the SNA's leaders and professional staff were continuously alert to the rise of threats or of opportunities to further landowners' political objectives. In addition to the pressures for reform from both left-center and right, the SNA had another problem which was new to the twenties. Whereas governments previously had routinely consulted the Society on all matters affecting agriculture prior to taking action, after Alessandri's election the Society no longer enjoyed the same automatic access to the inner councils of government and to the decision-making process.[32] Its occasional and partial exclusion from policy planning was in part the result of periodic government hostility, but more important, it was a byproduct of the developmentalist state, which had its own dynamic for generating policy affecting agriculture.

As indicated earlier, the SNA's primary form of political action prior to mass politics had been the articulation of the agricultural interest. With the exception of a few issues of unusual importance, the Society had stated its position on pertinent matters and relied on its institutional prestige and the favorable disposition of the authorities to achieve its purpose. In the majority of issues over which the SNA was concerned, the stakes were so low that the outcome did not really matter much. In the context of mass politics, however, various means of generating and applying pressure had to be used: rewards for supporting SNA positions and sanctions against opposing them had to be applied or suggested. The pressure tactics that the SNA used were quite standard for business interest groups anywhere but tailored to the Chilean situation and to the Society's overall defense strategy.

Articulation and dissemination of landowner views and stands on particular issues were of course still essential to effective lobbying. The SNA's journal, articles volunteered for the daily press, and direct correspondence with the appropriate political pressure points were constant and standard activities of the president, directors, and staff. The Society had a special budget for paid advertising, circulars, pamphlets, and the like. As the political system evolved and matters affecting landowners became key national issues, the SNA viewpoint became newsworthy and received extensive free coverage. Written communication was supplemented by personal contacts when possible. The president or delegations of directors continually solicited and usually obtained personal interviews with congressional committees, the president, ministers, and bureau chiefs, and this form of lobbying was considered very important.[33]

Beyond expressing its position on particular issues, the SNA after 1919 attempted in various ways to combat the liability of the negative landowner image. On the one hand it tried to project an alternate image by featuring in its journal articles about modern fundos and their progressive owners and by exploiting anything that cast landowners in a positive light. It simultaneously attempted to disassociate itself from the negative stereotype by depicting the Society as representative of all segments of the agricultural population.[34] One rather transparent effort to shed the large landowner identification was the adoption in 1933 of a new name, *El Campesino*, for the monthly journal. The most innovative step in the campaign to influence public opinion was the acquisition in 1936 of a commercial radio station, followed immediately by the establishment of a national network of cooperating stations over which the SNA broadcast its message throughout most of the country. The radio station generated revenue for the Society through the sale of advertising, and it permitted more effective communication of agricultural news such as technical improvements, current prices, and new laws and regulations. Most important politically, however, competitive popular programming gave the SNA access to mass audiences and thus provided a tool for communicating the Society's views on the issues and for subtly attacking the villain landowner image.[35]

Because of its preference for the insider approach, the SNA seldom resorted to full mobilization of the power resources represented by the agrarian bloc—and this may be one reason why historians have tended to ignore the seriousness of the challenge to landowners before the sixties. By the thirties, the tough language, the telegram blitzes, the implacable opposition to a bill or an administrative order were used very selectively; these were saved for the critical issues rather than squandered on minor points or on matters that could be safely compromised or rendered ineffectual at some further point in the decisional process. The SNA neither employed nor seriously considered some forms of economic pressure used by agrarian interest groups, such as the withholding of produce from market and destruction of crops or animals. Moderation in the use of pressure tactics made the occasional strong stand newsworthy and effective.

On matters that were especially threatening and at times of particular stress to the landowner position, the SNA utilized certain established methods of generating pressure by demonstrating the numerical strength and the unity of the organized rural sector. Telegram blitzes by all societies and the SNA's provincial, departmental, and local units were occasionally used to impress the authorities. On weighty matters a public letter, memorandum, or report might be sent to Congress or the president in the names of all the agricultural societies and over the signatures of their presidents. In cases of serious threat, emergency meetings of all society and provincial assembly presidents were held to consider the issue at hand and to articulate the "national" agrarian position with the appropriate publicity.[36]

Beyond responding to specific threats, the societies also tried to keep their strength and views in the public eye by holding periodic national conventions of all the societies and affiliates. These meetings normally addressed landowners' current policy objectives and drew up an "agrarian program" for the molding of public opinion and the enlightenment of the politicians. The first such conclave was held in 1925, and by the late thirties they had become annual events.[37]

In 1919 and again in 1939 the SNA sponsored congresses or assemblies of another type, which were designed to be even more authoritative than the intersocietal meetings. Both of these occurred in times of crisis—the first during the postwar mobilization, the second early in the Popular Front government. In both instances the intention was to create the impression of complete national rural unity, above and beyond the landowner organizations. There were two main objectives in the 1939 Congreso de Agricultores. The first was to attract prominent Radicals from the party's landowner wing, whose presence at the congress would bring pressure to bear on the Popular Front government for moderation on rural issues. The second was to project an image of complete interclass solidarity within the agrarian gremio by seating delegations allegedly representing smallholders, recipients of government-distributed parcels, and even inquilinos.[38] The latter was a contrivance of the most transparent nature, but the tactic nonetheless elicited the reluctant admiration of the Communist party's agrarian department: "In the recent activities of the National Society of Agriculture we can see a tactic developed which tends to group the middle strata of the peasant population around the latifundista, as the so-called Congress of Agriculturists pretended to do."[39]

The SNA after 1919 participated in electoral politics on an irregular basis and under the constraints imposed by its charter and by landowners' conflicting party preferences. The political loyalties of SNA members were still distributed among several parties—primarily the Liberal, Conservative, and to a lesser extent the Radical, but also among a few smaller parties and factions. While the challenge of reform brought the Liberals and Conservatives closer together after 1924, they still often disagreed on strategy and tactics and thus backed separate congressional and even presidential candidates, as in 1932. Since the Radical party was frequently in opposition to the Liberals and Conservatives, and the Agrarians, Nazis, and other groups took independent stands, endorsement of candidates or other partisan actions would almost inevitably conflict with the party allegiances of some members and associates of the SNA. Moreover, among the Society's directors at any given time one would find men high in the councils of the Conservative, Liberal, or Radical parties, for whom party loyalty might take precedence over SNA business. Thus the Society generally avoided all actions that might be construed as partisan and consistently discouraged suggestions that it form or support an independent agrarian party.[40]

When it came to electoral involvement, then, the SNA normally limited itself to exhorting landowners to vote their economic interest above all other considerations and to educating the parties to landowner needs. As Francisco Encina saw it in 1919, even rural congressional districts were generally represented by "lawyers and young intellectuals" unfamiliar with agricultural problems, because "the majority of agriculturists do not exercise the electoral influence that they might. They do not bother to attend [party] assemblies and abandon the designation of candidates to the professional politician (*politiquero*) or the local pharmacist."[41] The SNA *Boletín* repeated Encina's theme in 1922: "Wholly agrarian provinces send to Congress representatives who view everything related to the most permanent and solid of industries . . . with the most sovereign indifference; other provinces, agricultural also, find their representatives among people who, although they own fundos, do not know the necessities of agriculture. The action of this kind of representative is necessarily deficient."[42]

As noted, the Agrarian Union of the early twenties was an attempt to remedy that situation. In 1925 the agricultural societies tried further to raise the political consciousness of landowners by asking them to vote only for candidates pledged to a twelve-point program of agrarian demands. The SNA also encouraged landowners to utilize the full electoral potential of the rural populace: prior to the elections for the 1925 Constituent Assembly, for example, it called on members and other landowners to register themselves and their friends, inquilinos, and neighboring smallholders in order to offset the growth of the city vote. This approach of course rested on the assumption that the landowner could still deliver the votes to his candidate.[43]

The two elections in which the SNA endorsed candidates were exceptional cases, and in both instances its involvement was unsuccessful. Although its candidate won in 1931, Montero survived only six months in office and his ineffectual administration opened the way for the Socialist Republic. In 1938 the capitalist sector was so fearful of a Popular Front victory that it mobilized all its resources behind conservative Gustavo Ross and placed the relatively new and politically untainted Confederación de la Producción y del Comercio in the forefront of the campaign to marshal the country's "productive forces." The SNA was a major component of this confederation, and Jaime Larraín was president of both organizations. His prominence in the campaign and the very visible activity of other SNA directors made the Communist charge that the SNA building was "general headquarters of the Ross campaign" fairly plausible; given the landowner image, moreover, the SNA activity in Ross's behalf may have been counterproductive.[44] In any case it was detrimental to the SNA for the first few months of the Popular Front government in that the normal channels of communication with the administration were shut off until the rancor stirred up by the bitter campaign began to fade.[45]

In contrast to the Parliamentary Period when Congress was the source of most important decisions affecting landowners, after 1925 the SNA's lobbying efforts were directed increasingly toward the executive branch and its burgeoning bureaucracy. Because of the complexity of legislating in matters of social welfare, labor relations, and economic regulation and because of the need for flexibility and adaptability in the administration of that kind of law, Congress normally enacted very general legislation and left to the designated administrative agencies the authority to establish operating regulations and procedures. This created a situation in which many of those agencies exercised de facto legislative power and, moreover, interpreted and enforced their own rules. The abrupt emergence of a well-developed welfare and developmentalist state out of a strongly parliamentary, basically laissez-faire system involved a drastic modification of decisional procedures affecting public policy and shifted the locus of decision-making sharply away from Congress.[46]

The SNA developed various methods for dealing with postlegislative decision-making and the proliferation of administrative agencies. In matters of economic regulation, for example, the Society set up a special section to gather economic data for use in policy formulation. The minister of agriculture in friendly governments was a valuable intermediary between organized landowners and the administrative dependencies of other ministries, particularly those of the Ministries of Labor and Social Welfare, whose routine functions affected landowners in generally negative ways. A receptive minister of agriculture could inject the landowner view into all policy calculations at the highest level and lobby from within. Between creation of the ministry in 1924 and 1940, thirty-three men occupied the position; nine of them were current SNA directors, who collectively occupied the office 35 percent of the time.[47] Overall, the SNA's most effective device for defending landowner interests within the myriad of new and expanded government agencies was corporate representation.

Corporate Representation

The decades of the 1920s and '30s witnessed the growth of corporatist sentiment among segments of the Chilean upper and middle classes. Although corporatist practices in government were not new to that period, as the SNA's history illustrates, the government of Carlos Ibáñez was the first to consciously and systematically develop the rudiments of a corporate state. Taking inspiration from the European fascists, Ibáñez fostered the corporate organization of society and government as a means of offsetting the growing political power of the masses. Ibáñez did not go so far as to restructure the legislative power along functional lines, as Vargas did soon thereafter in Brazil; rather, Ibáñez's approach was to leave the institutions of the liberal democratic state intact while building into them an important element of functional representation.[48]

As a necessary condition for functional representation, the Ibáñez government encouraged the formation of functional organizations among the populace according to economic role. For labor, Ibáñez repressed the leftist-controlled FOCh and replaced it with the government-sponsored and controlled Confederación Republicana de Acción Cívica (CRAC). Industrial and agricultural producers were informed that the government would no longer entertain petitions from individuals. In order to interact with government, they would have to organize or join existing producers' associations and obtain the association's endorsement of their petitions. The government also tried in various ways to exercise control over the functional organizations. In the case of agriculture, Ibáñez attempted unsuccessfully to group all landowners into a single structure by urging the independent societies to disband and merge into the SNA. He also requested and obtained seats on the SNA board of directors for two high bureaucrats, the subsecretaries of agriculture and commerce. Another means of control was the requirement of legal status for all associations and their inscription in a registry as a condition for dealing with the government. The thrust under Ibáñez, then, was to make membership in functional associations compulsory, to centralize them, and to bring them under partial government control.[49]

The integration of functional organizations into government was done primarily at the administrative level. Ibáñez began implementing the labor legislation of 1924, instituted new social programs, and established governmental power to regulate the economy and direct its development. In setting up the state's socioeconomic administrative system, his regime incorporated the affected interest groups directly into the administrative apparatus in the numerous "semiautonomous" agencies and boards established to run specific programs. Under Ibáñez's approach of compulsory and universal membership in corporate associations, entities brought into the administration would in theory have been truly representative of their economic functions. After Ibáñez, the functional system of representation was maintained and expanded, but the attempt to compel membership was abandoned. The result was the anomaly of private voluntary associations, which set their own membership requirements and internal governance and which in reality represented privileged minorities within their own economic sectors, exercising critical decisional powers within the public administration in the name of their entire sectors. This system of privileged corporate representation continued to expand into the 1960s.[50]

As noted earlier, the SNA's reaction to the rise of the welfare and developmentalist state was ambivalent, and even through the thirties there were occasional objections to "state intervention" voiced in meetings of the board of directors. Nevertheless, the realists recognized the new situation as a fait accompli and saw in corporate representation a device which gave landowners important residual power to offset the decline of the right's electoral strength and moral authority. Moreover, corporate representation gave the SNA the flexibility it needed to follow the progressive strategy: it could acquiesce in or support reform legislation with the expectation that such laws could be rendered harmless in the administrative process.

Having created a strong national organization, and being recognized as the representative of the agrarian sector, the SNA stood ready to take advantage of the opportunities provided by Ibáñez's institutional reforms. By the early thirties it publicly embraced corporatism and encouraged the strengthening of functional representation, as Jaime Larraín revealed in a 1934 speech: "We advocate a State in which all national activities are represented and in which each material or spiritual function has its organ and expresses its aspirations. We advocate a State that is above all groups and is capable of developing a grand national policy. We advocate a State which controls, which stimulates, and which promotes the organized activities."[51] And to participate effectively in a corporate system, "we must strengthen our gremio organization. We must carry it to its ultimate consequences. The gremio will be the intermediary between the citizen and the State, the legitimate mouthpiece of the aspirations of labor. From its bosom will come forth genuine representations and not delegations divorced from the mass of citizenry."[52]

Throughout the thirties, the Society consistently pressed for extension of the corporate system and for representation in all relevant agencies. By 1940 the SNA had participated in at least twenty-nine permanent or long-term boards and eighteen ad hoc commissions of regulatory, administrative, or advisory character. Some of these organisms, such as the Superior Council of Equestrian Development or the Supervisory Council of the Army's Factory and Armory, were marginal to landowners' basic interests; others, including the Central Bank, the Exchange Control Commission, and the Chilean Development Corporation (CORFO), were critical to regulating the national economy as a whole; and agencies such as the Agricultural Colonization Board, the Agricultural Export Board, and the Council of the State Railroads were clearly of direct relevance to landowners and agricultural producers. Table 11 lists some of the agencies of a long-term nature in which the SNA had voting representation.

Composition of the boards and agencies varied according to the nature of their responsibilities. In most cases a combination of bureaucrats and presidential appointees assured the government a voting majority, although disagreement among governmental agencies could, and occasionally did, undermine any attempt to impose an official policy. In boards which dealt exclusively with agricultural matters, representatives from some or all of the regional associations were included along with delegates from the SNA and personnel from the agricultural bureaucracy. In agencies with broader purviews—such as the Central Bank, the Labor Council, or CORFO—the national industrial, mining, commercial, and agricultural associations, and occasionally the Chilean Labor Federation, were represented along with bureaucrats and government appointees. In general the system was weighted in favor of business over labor and the government over combinations of private interest.[53]

Corporate representation offered benefits both to government and to participating groups. Both sides of course stood to benefit if cooperation and close consultation yielded better, more workable policies than could otherwise be developed. From the viewpoint of government, hearing and

Table 11
Some Corporate Agencies in Which SNA Obtained Representation, 1925-40[a]

State Railroads Council, 1925
Agricultural Education Council, 1925
Factory and Armory of the Army, 1925
Agricultural Council, 1925
Roads and Communications Council, 1925
Central Bank, 1925
Agricultural Credit Agency, 1926
Epidemics Council (Ministry of Agriculture), 1926
Appeals Tribunal for Land Tax, 1928
Agricultural Colonization Board, 1929
Superior Council of Equestrian Development (Ministry of War), 1929
Exportation Commission, 1929
Agricultural Export Board, 1930
Normalization Commission, 1930
Central Customs Board, 1930
Advisory Committee, Exchange Control Commission, 1931
Staples Commission, Municipality of Santiago, 1931
National Savings Administration, 1933
Council on Nutrition, 1933
Conciliation and Arbitration Board, Province of Santiago, 1933
Superior Labor Council, 1934
National Economic Council, 1934
Administrative Commission for Cold Storage Facilities, 1934
National Housing Authority, 1937
National Council on Nutrition, 1937
Chilean Development Corporation (CORFO), 1939.

[a]Society participation began in the years indicated.
SOURCE: *BSNA*, 55-65 (1924-33); *El C*, 65-72 (1933-40); *MSNA* (1924-40).

assessing the inputs of functional representatives made it possible to perform political cost-benefit analysis of proposed policies and thus to avoid the inadvertent alienation of important interest groups. As a result of participating in the decision-making process, corporate representatives assumed a share of the responsibility for measures adopted; thus when landowners disagreed with some aspect of agricultural credit policy, they might blame their representatives on the Agricultural Credit Board as well as the government.[54] Finally, governments could hope to exercise some suasion over participating associations by the implicit threat of canceling their privileged representation.

For business organizations, the advantages of participation greatly outweighed the liabilities of shared responsibility and potential restrictions on freedom of action. Most fundamental for the SNA, corporate representation guaranteed access to the policy process in areas of vital importance to its constituents. Given the great degree of power exercised by some of the administrative and regulatory agencies, the SNA could sometimes thwart congressional or presidential intent. In the Agricultural Export Board, for example, a unified landowner bloc could determine policy unless unanimity prevailed among government representatives. In other cases the Society could at least muster the votes to mitigate or eliminate particularly undesirable measures. Even when the SNA was unable to affect decisions significantly, its participation in the agencies could yield valuable intelligence that alerted the Society to apply pressure at other points in the political process. Finally, corporate representation provided a valuable tool for dealing with unresponsive but generally friendly governments, such as Montero's. By withdrawing or threatening to withdraw its representatives from particular agencies, as it did on occasion, the SNA was able to condemn specific policies without denying its support to the moderate governments that it felt constrained to uphold.[55]

By 1929 the SNA had developed the previously latent landowner-producer interest into a powerful national bloc, but, to carry corporatism to its logical culmination, it set out under Jaime Larraín's direction to establish an intersectoral peak organization of business associations. Much of the groundwork had been laid by the time concrete steps were taken in the early thirties. The emergence of redistributive issues as the substance of politics after 1919 affected landowners and other entrepreneurs in similar ways and fostered movements to organize for self-defense. The Ibáñez government's corporatist policies also strengthened the trend toward association. The result by the early thirties was the existence of a plethora of business interest groups based on product, general sector, or geography. A 1933 government report named a total of eighty-three legally constituted entrepreneurial groups and admitted its list was incomplete.[56] While most of the organizations were probably affiliated with one of the four main national sectoral associations, there was no single peak entity comparable to the Chilean Confederation of Labor to defend the common interests of the business sector.

Precedents for the institutional unification of economic associations dated from the late nineteenth century. The SNA had often coordinated its lobbying efforts on measures of common interest with the SOFOFA and other groups, and in 1896 a National Chamber of Commerce had been proposed to link the agricultural, industrial, mining, and commercial associations. No such organization prospered, however, until the beginnings of reform jolted the business establishment into action.[57] The postwar economic crisis and radicalization of the labor movement touched off the greatest wave of unionization and strike activity in the Chilean experience, and the Alessandri government's unwillingness to suppress labor with the traditional dispatch created difficult problems for employers in all sectors of the economy. In response to the urgent need for labor peace, the Asociación del Trabajo, or Labor Association, was founded in 1921.

The Labor Association, modeled after an organization recently founded in Argentina, at first served primarily as an employers' union for member firms and was so considered by the government's labor office. It attempted to forestall labor disturbances through a combination of propaganda, paternalism, and blacklisting of suspected or known organizers. By way of propaganda it published a weekly paper, *Horizontes Nuevos*, to "illuminate the worker's mind" and distributed patriotic pamphlets in schools, labor headquarters, and military barracks.[58] In the hope of "creating solid ties of owner-worker harmony," it encouraged voluntary improvements by employers by loaning money for construction of workers' housing and selling group medical and accident insurance. When its efforts failed and member firms were struck, the association backed the employer by mediating or breaking the strike.[59] In effect, the Labor Association filled the void created by the new tolerance for union activity and strikes in the absence of a functioning official system of labor relations. From the beginning, the Labor Association also extended its sphere of action beyond labor relations to speak for the common interests of all Chilean entrepreneurs. It continually called for "reform" of the 1924 social legislation and in 1926 and 1927 sponsored national taxpayers' assemblies to articulate the uniform business opposition to higher taxes.[60] After reaching a maximum membership of 1,650 firms with 160,000 employees in 1926, the Labor Association gradually declined in the ambience of social peace created by the Ibáñez government.[61]

Although Ibáñez effectively suppressed organized labor and the left, his developmental and social policies had serious implications for the capitalist sector, and the chaotic economic and political situation of 1931 and 1932 brought additional threats and complications for business. Reflecting the surge of corporatist sentiment among the upper classes, representatives of the national mining, industrial, commercial, and agricultural associations met at the SNA's invitation in 1933 to coordinate political strategy and lay the groundwork for future institutional relationships. The following year, Jaime Larraín called for a full convention of all the country's entrepreneurial associations:

> The origin of this proposal obeys a natural and instinctive impulse—the defensive attitude one adopts when his life is endangered. Industrial, agricultural, and commercial firms feel their prosperity and even their existence threatened by the exuberant development of social and tax legislation in

> Chile, which does not dissimulate a spirit of open hostility toward capital. The idea of harmony [in social legislation] has given way to truly fanatical persecution of capitalists and employers.[62]

Under the presidency of Jaime Larraín, the convention of June 1934 established the Confederación de la Producción y del Comercio for the stated purpose of "assuring that national legislation proceeds in accordance with the just interests of commerce and production."[63] Unlike the Labor Association, this was a true confederation of national and regional, general and specialized agricultural, industrial, mining, and commercial associations in a national peak organization. The proliferation of voluntary economic associations in the twenties and thirties is illustrated by the number of charter member groups: thirty-five agricultural, sixty-five industrial, eleven mining, and eighty commercial associations signed the confederation's charter, and dozens more joined in subsequent months. The primary concerns of the business sector were reflected in the reports presented in working sessions at the convention: thirty-four on state intervention, twenty-six on taxation, twenty-three on social legislation.[64]

Jaime Larraín was elected president of the confederation and served in that capacity through 1938, simultaneously with his SNA presidency. The confederation generally confined itself to issues that affected most or all of its member organizations, leaving the specialized associations to grapple with sectoral, commodity, or regional issues. One of its early accomplishments and a triumph for the corporatist strategy was convincing Alessandri to establish the Consejo de Economía Nacional (National Economic Council), an advisory board which provided organized business an official and very advantageous mechanism for influencing economic policy and the general governance of the country. Since it had to be consulted on all economic policy, the council partially compensated for the loss of automatic access that the SNA had enjoyed before 1918.[65] The confederation also became very visible in the 1938 presidential campaign: it was to the Ross forces what the labor movement was to the Popular Front effort—an organism above political parties which appealed to all the country's "productive forces." The Confederación de la Producción y del Comercio in general provided Chilean capitalists a valuable tool for strengthening their position in the corporatist order.

When their vital interests were first challenged by the urban working and middle classes, landowners had turned to the SNA as a means of defense. After the Society's growth, the organization of the agrarian gremio, and the adoption of new strategies and tactics for pressure group politics, the SNA had emerged as a powerful tool in the landowners' struggle to preserve their prerogatives. The next three chapters examine the SNA's handling of the most critical issues facing Chilean landowners in the twenties and thirties, the same issues they faced in the sixties and seventies—price controls, agrarian reform, and rural unionization and welfare.

Notes

1. See ch. 6, under "Intellectual and Political Background," and ch. 7, under "Intellectual Background," for the SNA's early positions on subdivision of land and rural social conditions. The *BSNA* published very enlightened editorials on more general social problems, e.g., *BSNA*, 31 (1900), 759-64; *ibid.*, 38 (1907), 349-50; ibid., 39 (1908), 1-8, 67-75.

2. Francisco Encina *et al.*, "La subdivisión de la propiedad rural en Chile en 1919," *Mapocho*, tomo V, vol. 13 (1966), 22. Also in *MSNA* (1919), pp. 6-20.

3. *BSNA*, 37 (1906), 164.

4. *Ibid.*, 55 (1924), 541-43; see also ch. 7, under "Opening Round."

5. *BSNA*, 57 (1926), 573-77; *MSNA* (1926), pp. 3-6.

6. Quoted in Pike, *Chile and the United States*, p. 201.

7. These directors often expressed their positions in the board meetings. For examples, see Minutes, Dec. 26, 1932, in *BSNA*, 65 (1933), 52; Minutes, Dec. 4, 1933, in *El C*, 66 (1934), 210; Minutes, Aug. 5, 1940, in *ibid.*, 72 (1940), 602. Also Rafael Zuaznábar de la Barra, "La Sociedad Nacional de Agricultura" (Memoria de Prueba, Universidad de Chile, 1947), pp. 38-43; and Comisión de Salarios, Acta de la Sesión del 14 de abril de 1936, in *AN*, Min. de Agr., Informes Comisión Salarios, 1936.

8. Jaime Larraín García-Moreno, "Concepto cristiano del problema social agrario," *El C*, 72 (1940), 776.

9. *Ibid.*

10. Larraín, *Mejoramiento de la vida campesina*, pp. 18-19.

11. See chs. 5 and 7 for examples.

12. Larraín, *Mejoramiento de la vida campesina*; also ch. 7, under "The 1930s."

13. *AN*, Min. de Agr., Informes Comisión Salarios, 1936; Zuaznábar de la Barra, "La Sociedad," pp. 38-43; Gonzalo Santa Cruz Errázuriz, "El mejoramiento de los trabajadores agrícolas y la sindicalización campesina" (Memoria de Prueba, Universidad de Chile, 1941), p. 62.

14. *El C*, 72 (1940), 777.

15. *Ibid.*, 66 (1934), 56.

16. *Diccionario biográfico de Chile*, 3rd ed. (Santiago, 1940), p. 166.

17. *Ibid.*, p. 632.

18. *Ibid.*, p. 836.

19. *Ibid.*, pp. 864-65.

20. *Ibid.*, pp. 866-67.

21. McBride, *Land and Society*, pp. 281-348; Corporación de Fomento de la Producción, *Geografía económica de Chile*, texto refundido (Santiago, 1965), pp. 453-548.

22. Minutes, Aug. 16, 1932, in *BSNA*, 34 (1932), 474; Minutes, Aug. 22, 1932, in *ibid.*, 479.

23. Cortés and Fuentes, *Diccionario político*, p. 320; Drake, *Socialism and Populism*, pp. 65-70.

24. Dirección General de Estadística, *Anuario agropecuario 1934-35* (Santiago, 1936), p. 73, gives wholesale prices by index; Minutes, Aug. 31, 1931, in *BSNA*, 63

(1931), 540; Minutes, Aug. 22, 1932, in *ibid.*, 64 (1932), 479.

25. Cortés and Fuentes, *Diccionario político*, pp. 10-11.

26. Minutes, Dec. 19, 1931, in *BSNA*, 64 (1932), 149.

27. *Ibid.*, 63 (1931), 437-38; Minutes, Aug. 31, 1931, in *ibid.*, 540-41.

28. As late as April 1932, the SNA president and delegations from the other major business associations publicly reiterated their full support of the Montero regime "in order to aid, in that fashion, in the maintenance of the present governmental regime." Minutes, Apr. 11, 1932, in *BSNA*, 64 (1932), 234-35. On the Montero government's ineptness, see Drake, *Socialism and Populism*, pp. 69-74.

29. *BSNA*, 63 (1931), 627-29. The 1931 SNA *Memoria* phrased it this way: "The Society has tried to maintain the situation which its antiquity and prestige have given it to the present, echoing the common aspirations of agriculturists and at the same time avoiding creating, with excessive and exclusively gremio petitions, difficult situations for the government, which must make its decisions taking into consideration the general interest." *MSNA* (1931), pp. 6-7.

30. *BSNA*, 64 (1932), 494.

31. See ch. 8, under "Alessandri."

32. As pointed out in chs. 5-7, several major reform bills affecting landowners came to the SNA's attention only after they were drawn up by government officials.

33. See examples of personal contacts in chs. 5-7.

34. E.g., *BSNA*, 56 (1925), 303-5.

35. *El C*, 72 (1940), 750-51; *El Mercurio*, Apr. 22, 1938, p. 21.

36. See chs. 5-7 for examples.

37. SNA, *Congreso Regional Agrario; El C*, 72 (1940), 237, 313-15.

38. On the 1919 Asamblea de Agricultores, see *MSNA* (1919), pp. 6-20; on the 1939 Congreso de Agricultores, see *El C*, 71 (1939), 635, 691-706.

39. Chacón Corona, *El problema agrario*, p. 33.

40. A survey of SNA members of Congress in eight sample years between 1895 and 1936 revealed the following party affiliations (deputies and senators are combined): Conservative, 36.1 percent; Liberal, 34.2 percent; Radical, 11.9 percent. The remainder belonged to the older National and Liberal Democratic parties, which went defunct in the twenties, were independents, or could not be identified by party. Note that the thesis linking landowners to the Conservative party is not borne out in the case of SNA members who were active politicians. This survey is based on Valencia Avaria, *Anales de la República,* 1 and 2, and the Santiago press for Mar. and Apr. 1895, 1901, 1909, 1918, 1924, 1928, 1933, and 1936.

41. Francisco Encina, "Nuestra situación agraria," *Revista Chilena*, año III, tomo IX, no. 27 (Nov. 1919), 212-13.

42. *BSNA*, 53 (1922), 626-27.

43. Minutes, Sept. 21, 1925, in *BSNA*, 56 (1925), 740-41; circular of May 1, 1925, to Chilean agriculturists, in *ibid.*, 303-5. See Heise González, "El caciquismo político" on landowners and the rural vote.

44. *El Mercurio*, July 24, 1938, pp. 37-41; *ibid.*, Oct. 15, 1938, p. 3.

45. Marta Infante Barros, *Testigos del treinta y ocho* (Santiago, 1972), examines the 1938 campaign.

46. Urzúa Valenzuela and García Barzelatto, *Diagnóstico de la burocracia*.

47. Valencia Avaria, *Anales de la República*, 1, 402-44; *MSNA* (1924-40).

48. On corporatism in Chile, see José Luis Cea Egaña, *La representación funcional en la historia constitucional de Chile* (Santiago, 1976), and Drake, "Corporatism and Functionalism." Recent works on corporatism in Latin America in-

clude: Frederick B. Pike and Thomas Stritch, eds., *The New Corporatism: Socio-Political Structures in the Iberian World* (Notre Dame, Ind., 1974); and James M. Malloy, ed., *Authoritarianism and Corporatism in Latin America* (Pittsburgh, 1977).

49. Adolfo Ibáñez B. (Ministro de Fomento), circular no. 1, in *Boletín de la Asociación del Trabajo*, año III, no. 30 (Nov. 25, 1927), 3. Several communiques from the minister of fomento indicate that the policy of rejecting individual petitions was actually enforced, e.g., Oficios, Dec. 6 and 15, 1927, *AN*, Min. de Fomento, Oficios 1927. See also Minutes, Nov. 18 and 25, and Dec. 2 and 16, 1929, in *BSNA*, 62 (1930), 311-17; and *ibid.*, 555-57.

50. Menges, "Public Policy"; Drake, "Corporatism and Functionalism," pp. 101-5.

51. *MSNA* (1934), p. 126.

52. *Ibid.*, p. 127.

53. For example, the SNA shared a representative with the SOFOFA on the governing board of the Central Bank, whereas in the Agricultural Export Board (as originally constituted) there were three representatives of the agricultural societies and four government appointees. *BSNA*, 63 (1931), 9-11. Menges, "Public Policy," outlines the composition of some public agencies in 1967.

54. In 1924 the SNA refused a seat on the Agricultural Council of the Ministry of Agriculture (which it later accepted), claiming that it "would have no function other than sharing responsibilities." *MSNA* (1924), p. 14.

55. Minutes, April 11, 1932, in *BSNA*, 64 (1932), 236; Minutes, Apr. 3, 1933, in *ibid.*, 65 (1933), 290. Note that landowner representation on the Agricultural Export Board was reduced in 1935.

56. Dirección General de Estadística, *Sinópsis geográfico y estadístico de Chile, año 1933* (Santiago, 1934), pp. 108-9.

57. Ministerio de Industria y Obras Públicas, *Memoria . . . año 1896* (Santiago, 1896), pp. 60, 132.

58. *Boletín de la Asociación del Trabajo*, año I, no. 9 (Feb. 28, 1926), 2; *ibid.*, año II, no. 24 (May 20, 1927), 6-7. Poblete Troncoso, *Organización sindical*, pp. 53-54, classifies the Labor Association as a "sindicato patronal."

59. *Boletín de la Asociación del Trabajo*, año I, no. 2 (June 30, 1925), 1. The minutes of the association's governing council often repeat or paraphrase the following cryptic phrase: "Satisfactory intervention of the association in defense of social peace, in diverse conflicts produced in affiliated firms." *Ibid.*, no. 1 (May 30, 1925), 8.

60. *BSNA*, 57 (1926), 784-88; *El Mercurio*, Jan. 6, 1927, pp. 10-11.

61. *Boletín de la Asociación del Trabajo*, año I, no. 10 (Mar. 30, 1926), 2. Although there was no institutional connection between the sectoral economic associations and the Labor Association, there was some overlap in their governing boards: in 1926, for example, two of the ten directors of the Labor Association were current SNA directors.

62. *El C*, 65 (1933), 613-14.

63. Confederación de la Producción y del Comercio, *Estatutos* (Santiago, 1938), p. 14, quoted in Menges, "Public Policy," p. 345.

64. *El Mercurio*, June 10-16, 1934; *MSNA* (1934), pp. 123-40; *El C*, 66 (1934), 318-25; Drake, "Corporatism and Functionalism," p. 102.

65. Oscar Alvarez Andrews, *Historia del desarrollo industrial de Chile* (Santiago, 1936), pp. 351-56.

5

The Struggle over Food Price Inflation

Inflation became a regular feature of Chilean life in the decade after the War of the Pacific. The circumstances of its beginning are complex and varied. Chile adopted unbacked paper money in 1878 as a temporary measure which became, with few interruptions, permanent policy that constantly swelled the money supply. Expansion of money in circulation led to constant devaluation of the Chilean currency, causing the peso cost of all imports to rise and concurrently allowing competing domestic products to find high and inflating price ceilings. In the decades after the war, the captured nitrate fields generated a period of unprecedented national prosperity and a substantial growth of consumer demand, which also contributed to inflation.[1]

In the case of foodstuffs, the rapid increase in urbanization after 1880 combined with large-scale migration to the arid nitrate provinces, which imported all foodstuffs, greatly extended demand. Internal migration roughly doubled the domestic market for commercial agriculture between 1875 and 1895 and again by 1920.[2] Inflation of food prices resulted from the growth of demand and a relative inelasticity of supply. Despite the considerable modernization that occurred, Chile's traditional agrarian structure, characterized by a dichotomy of large inefficient holdings and subsistence minifundia, was unable to respond quickly and freely to market incentives. Moreover, during the period of quickening economic development after 1880, landowners found attractive investment opportunities outside of agriculture while the new wealthy frequently bought rural estates as much for prestige, recreational opportunities, and expected inflation of land values as for the income they produced. Both these factors deterred investment in agriculture and contributed to food price inflation.[3]

The struggle of the urban poor against inflation is as old as inflation itself. From the 1880s organized workers struck for wage increases to compensate for inflation, and the constant fight to keep abreast of rising prices was a major factor in the development of working-class political consciousness, organization, and radicalism.[4] For the unorganized majority of the working and middle classes and for the large *lumpen* elements of the cities, however, the only way to fight the rise of prices was to control inflation itself; and given governmental hostility toward strikes, pursuit of price controls also recommended itself to organized labor. Thus the popular response to inflation had a dual character—pursuit of wage adjustments and of price controls under various guises.

From the onset of inflation, efforts to control prices focused on foodstuffs, because food constituted the major expense of the urban poor. Survey data from the 1910s through the recent past have consistently revealed that over half the average Chilean working-class budget—often much more than half—has been dedicated to feeding the family, and even so without providing adequate nourishment.[5] Landowners and the SNA were directly involved in the conflict because the urban poor identified producers, rather than processors or distributors, as being primarily responsible for rising prices. The struggle was long, sometimes violent, and frequently a threat to social and political stability. When a system of price controls finally was established in the 1930s, its purpose was to prevent revolution and not, as some economists contend, to promote the industrialization of Chile.[6]

The Cattle Tax and Inflation, 1888–1918

The tentative beginnings of organized popular opposition to food price inflation date from the decade after the War of the Pacific. Between 1888 and 1918, the urban poor directed their frustration over rising prices at a customs duty on imported livestock commonly known as the "*impuesto al ganado*" or cattle tax. Although the duty was not an important factor in the overall rise of food prices, the circumstances surrounding its proposal and enactment transformed it into the symbol and, in the popular mind, the primary cause of food price inflation. The struggle to block and later to repeal the cattle tax was the first round of the protracted conflict between landowners and the urban masses. Thirty years of intermittent conflict over the cattle tax hardened popular resistance to inflation and contributed immeasurably to the development of political consciousness among the urban masses. It demonstrated to the upper classes the potential power and radicalism of the urban poor and encouraged the timely adoption of price controls and other preemptive measures.[7]

The SNA's 1888 proposal to establish a tariff on livestock was the first major step toward agricultural protectionism in Chile. Although Chile had been a minor exporter of livestock products prior to 1850, the ensuing wheat boom led to the extension of cultivation at the expense of rangeland; as a result, Chile became a cattle-importing country and by the 1880s consumed an average of 63,000 head of Argentine cattle per year.[8] In 1887 the government awarded a guaranteed contract for completion of the Chilean segment of the transandean railroad. This development threatened to inundate the Chilean market not only with the scrawny *criollo* cattle of the Cuyo region but also with the superior meat cattle of the rapidly modernizing pampas to the east. The SNA took a dim view of the prospect of heightened competition for Chilean cattlemen, in light of the current decline of wheat exports, which had sustained the rural economy in the 1860s and '70s. Thus the SNA sponsored legislation the following year to assess a moderate but protective duty on livestock.[9]

The SNA bill proved highly controversial and unpopular due, in large measure, to its timing. On one hand, food prices had been rising moderately but insistently since the War of the Pacific;[10] on the other, a self-proclaimed "party of the working people" had entered the Chilean political arena in 1887.[11] The SNA bill offered the Democratic party a welcome opportunity for publicity and for reaching the urban poor by exploiting a potentially popular issue. In leading the opposition to the cattle tax, the Democrats showed their perception of the real but still largely inarticulate popular frustration over inflation and of the exploitable image of landowners. In tying the cattle tax to inflation they could court the growing but effectively disenfranchised urban masses, while simultaneously attacking the economic interests of the landowning elite whom they viewed as the core of the oligarchy.

The Democrats contended that the cattle tax would affect even the largely vegetarian urban poor, in that it would lead to the conversion of cropland to pasture or range and thus cause food prices to rise at an accelerated rate. They launched a campaign of pamphleteering, public rallies, and strikes which touched off a lively debate in the press and Congress and which, in the estimation of the leading Santiago daily, made the cattle tax bill "the great issue of the day."[12] Malaquías Concha, founder and mentor of the party, cast the cattle tax proposal in terms of the class struggle and artfully exploited the existing negative image of landowners, claiming the duty would amount to "taking from the poor to give to the rich; oppression does not cease to be such because it is clothed in legal forms, and a people whose ration of meat is subject to taxes is an enslaved people, paying tribute to a handful of proprietors whose domains are burdened with mortgages and whimsical encumbrances."[13] In view of the high level of popular agitation and other problems besetting his government, President Balmaceda persuaded the SNA to withdraw its bill.[14] Thus, quite implausibly, the disenfranchised poor thwarted the SNA's will, and the Democrats had discovered an issue which they would exploit periodically for over thirty years while laying the groundwork for future social and political reform.

Nine years later a similar SNA proposal was enacted as part of a general tariff reform law.[15] Passage of the cattle tax in 1897 raised little opposition and no public outcry, probably because the Democrats supported the industrial protection embodied in the law and because, in the current climate of deteriorating relations with Argentina, a measure directed against Chile's largest transandean import was both popular and patriotic.[16] However, repeal of the cattle tax quickly became a favorite issue of the labor unions—stronger and more militant by the turn of the century—and of the Democratic party, which by then was established throughout the republic and had two deputies in Congress.[17] With a massive issue of paper money in 1905 and the onset of a strong inflationary surge, the cattle tax issue returned to center stage.

The popular response to the 1905 inflation showed clearly the mixture of myth, opportunism, and hatred of landowners on which the cattle tax issue was based. The urban poor were deprived of their small ration of meat that year, not as a result of the minor rise in meat prices but because staples such as beans, potatoes, and bread shot up precipitously.[18] Yet the rallying cry against inflation was "down with the cattle tax," indicating that the duty had become synonymous with food price inflation. Among the urban masses, years of exposure to anti-cattle tax propaganda and the negative landowner image had conditioned them to identify the landowner as the villain and the cattle tax as his instrument for exploiting the consuming poor. For leaders such as Malaquías Concha, who would grasp the actual situation, the cattle tax was a useful if not a valid issue. Yet given the current political realities, effective solutions to inflation, such as price controls or sound monetary policy, were beyond the Democrats' reach. An emotional issue such as the cattle tax at least offered an indirect method of attacking the oligarchy and of building political consciousness among the urban population.

In September 1905, labor organizations and the Democratic party formed a Central Committee to Abolish the Cattle Tax. The SNA, determined to preserve the cornerstone of its agricultural development policy but reluctant to take "political" action, countered by forming the "Agrarian League"—an ostensibly independent and totally ineffectual organization designed to elect a produty Congress in the elections of March 1906.[19] The issue came to a head, however, on October 22, 1905, when anti-cattle tax forces held simultaneous rallies in several cities and towns. In Santiago an orderly protest of between 30,000 and 50,000 participants degenerated into two days of violence in which proletarian mobs roamed the city at will, looting stores and attacking the property and persons of the wealthy. This event, known as the "Red Week," stands out as the bloodiest uprising in the history of Santiago before 1973; over 300 persons were killed and at least 1,000 injured.[20]

More noteworthy than the casualty figures of the Red Week was the manner in which the authorities attempted to contain the mobs. The Santiago army garrison was away on maneuvers, and a disturbance of such unprecedented magnitude easily overwhelmed the municipal police. As the situation deteriorated the volunteer fire department, commanded and largely staffed by the capital's elite, was pressed into service. Subsequently arms were distributed to the Club de la Unión, whose officers mustered the younger members into an impromptu "guard of order" to reinforce the beleaguered police and firemen.[21] The ensuing direct, face-to-face class warfare, without the usual intermediaries, was a unique and haunting experience for both parties. To the elites, facing the proletariat over rifle barrels translated the "social question" from an academic abstraction to sobering reality and undoubtedly impressed on them the explosive potential of unmitigated inflation.[22] On the other hand, the massacre perpetrated by the gilded youth in defense of their fathers' cattle tax could only intensify the sense of alienation and class hatred among the poor, as the following extract from a labor newspaper suggests: "The people were assassinated with great zeal and treachery by the brutal raids of the young bourgeois horde who on that occasion revealed the savage cannibalism which they artfully conceal beneath the veneer of an infamous education without humanitarian sentiments or respect for the lives of others."[23]

In the aftermath of the Red Week, accusations of responsibility flew freely. While the SNA emerged as the main culprit, its defense placed the blame on political agitators:

> The cattle duty is nothing more than a pretext exploited by agitators who pursue purposes far different from reducing meat prices. The truth is that the people did not even realize the existence of the duty until certain agitators exploited it as the synthesis and expression of the class hatred which they themselves are whipping up among the lower classes. They have presented the cattle duty as an abuse perpetrated against the poor man in benefit of the rich.[24]

More detached observers viewed the Red Week as a symptom of "social disequilibrium" and the result of "the miserable condition of the working and middle classes."[25]

Despite the impact of the Red Week, the SNA and its allies successfully blocked congressional action on the cattle tax until the winter of 1907, when another acceleration in the rate of inflation inspired prudent action. Even then Congress only suspended the cattle tax for two years. At the end of that period the government requested another year's suspension, but the SNA sought resumption of the duty as scheduled. In the absence of substantial opposition, the landowner view prevailed and the cattle tax was restored in December 1909. Moderate inflation continued over the next decade but without radical upswings in the rate until the end of 1918; thus opposition to the cattle tax remained largely rhetorical.[26]

Although the SNA remained steadfastly insistent on protection for the cattle industry, which it considered the most lucrative branch of the rural economy, it was clear that after 1905 its leadership was highly sensitive to food price inflation. In order to avoid future outbreaks such as the Red Week, and to preserve the cattle tax, the Society began to advocate a host of indirect measures to combat food price inflation—at no cost to landowners. From 1905 on, particularly at times of accelerating inflation, it urged reduction of railroad rates for livestock and agricultural produce, modernization of the Santiago slaughterhouse, establishment of farmers' markets to eliminate middlemen, and it even endorsed voluntary subdivision of land near cities to promote more efficient production of truck crops.[27] Although prior to 1919 it never advocated outright price controls, its promotion of indirect measures to combat rising food costs indicates the SNA's recognition of the dangers of unmitigated food price inflation. As later events showed, the lesson of the Red Week was not lost on the governing elites either; in contrast to the SNA, however, they generally proved very willing to sacrifice landowners' economic interests in times of stress as a means of preserving social and political stability.

The Postwar Crisis and Its Aftermath

The post-World War I economic crisis in Chile brought the food price issue back to the forefront of public attention. Although rising food prices were but one aspect of the complex economic situation, the popular reaction was directed initially toward securing relief from inflating food costs.[28] This was a logical and sensible focus for a number of reasons. Food was not only the primary lower-class expenditure, but the impact of food price inflation was generalized among the poor, working or not. Moreover, there was no effective way to remedy the crisis of unemployment, which had its origins abroad and which was far too massive to be resolved by a government that lacked both the funds and the machinery to do so. Finally, the focus on food prices reflected the continuing importance of the landowner image and the experience of the anti-cattle tax battle of the turn of the century.

The volatile situation produced by the economic collapse gave rise to the largest and most widespread popular mobilization yet seen in Chile. The labor unions raised the first cry against inflation in the customary Independence Day rallies on September 18, 1918. A month later the FOCh and allied political leaders formed the Asamblea Obrera de Alimentación Nacional (Workers' Assembly of National Nutrition), an umbrella organiza-

Table 12
Food Price and Cost-of-Living Index, 1913–25

Year	Domestic Foods	Imported Foods	General Cost of Living
1913	100	100	100
1914	116	112	108
1915	128	136	120
1916	109	144	117
1917	112	141	118
1918	110	151	121
1919	132	238	143
1920	165	256	168
1921	151	230	169
1922	146	227	173
1923	152	236	176
1924	164	240	186
1925	200	217	202

SOURCE: Dirección General de Estadística, *Sinópsis estadístico, año 1925*, p. 118.

tion patterned after the anti-cattle tax committee of 1905, to coordinate the drive against food price inflation. Besides the national body, local committees were established in larger cities and towns throughout the country. In addition to organized labor and the political left, a variety of middle-class groups, including the Chilean Student Federation, the Federation of the Middle Class, and the National Educational Association, soon joined forces with the Workers' Assembly. In contrast to the 1905 situation, then, the Workers' Assembly represented a broader-based multiclass coalition of mobilized consumers, which gave the movement both more sophistication and wider appeal.[29]

In its first few months of activity, the Workers' Assembly mobilized hundreds of thousands of people throughout the country, issued ultimatums to the authorities, and elicited important concessions from a government unaccustomed to responding to demands by the masses. Simultaneous protest rallies in Santiago and several provincial towns launched the campaign on November 22, 1918.[30] From then through the summer of 1919, the Santiago press provided almost daily coverage of the "*problema de las subsistencias*"—the staples problem—and the activities of the Asamblea Obrera, which met nearly every night.[31] The asamblea threatened but did not carry out a general strike in December and scheduled another round of protests for February 7, 1919. The government responded by prohibiting the demonstrations and assuming emergency powers in January. Citing the imminent threat of revolution, the government concentrated large detachments of *carabineros* in Santiago for the first half of 1919 and also pressured Congress to enact a long-dormant bill to expand the national police.[32] After the state of siege was finally lifted, the Workers' Assembly carried out simultaneous demonstrations in at least twenty-three towns and cities on August 29, 1919. The principal rally in the capital drew a crowd of at least 100,000.[33]

The program of the Workers' Assembly combined the traditional response to inflation with new, more realistic and sophisticated proposals. From the beginning it demanded repeal of the symbolic cause of inflation, the cattle tax, and an embargo on food exports. In view of the menacing demeanor of the popular mobilization, the government immediately asked Congress to suspend the cattle tax "as a condition indispensable to social stability and economic well-being."[34] Despite the SNA's energetic protests, in December 1918 Congress suspended the duty for three years and simultaneously appropriated $2 million for the acquisition and sale of food staples at cost to the public. Meanwhile the authorities of Santiago and other cities attempted to check rising prices by setting up farmers' markets. The Sanfuentes administration also sponsored a bill to restrict food exports, but in the face of stiff opposition from agricultural interests and the economically orthodox, Congress refused to pass it.[35]

In contrast to 1905–7, the mobilized consumers did not accept suspension of the cattle tax as a panacea. The more extreme nature of the economic crisis, the greater sophistication of the movement's leadership, and perhaps the very willingness and haste of the government to sacrifice the hated symbol of inflation combined to raise popular demands beyond the level of palliatives. Thus the government's initial conciliatory measures had no discernible impact on the movement, which simply shifted its focus to another of the Workers' Assembly's demands—creation of a national agency to regulate food prices and supplies. Beyond specific demands, moreover, spokesmen for the Workers' Assembly began to articulate a new philosophy of the relationship between production and consumption of foodstuffs. The veteran Malaquías Concha described his concept of the social responsibility of agricultural producers as follows:

> The products of the soil belong, first and foremost, to the citizens of the country; they are a social resource, produced by capital, land, and labor in concert. Consumers consider it unjust that landowners should unilaterally claim the right to sell their cereals abroad, causing famine among their compatriots. The right of property is limited by the social interest; consequently, the proprietor cannot use his property in a manner contrary to the general good.[36]

The movement's insistence on a price control mechanism forced the first full-dress discussion of price controls in the Chilean experience, and the debate was joined by a wide range of individuals, officials, and interest groups. The SNA initially rejected the notion of direct price controls. In a note to a special committee of the Chamber of Deputies, it recommended some of the standard alternatives: reducing the urban population, setting up consumers' cooperatives, promoting popular savings, reducing freight rates for foodstuffs, and in one of its more troglodytic statements suggested that "the strict enforcement of laws on alcoholic beverages and abolition of gambling would be the most effective measures which could benefit the working class."[37] Organized landowners, however, stood virtually alone within the oligarchy in opposing price controls. The administration, a group of Conservative deputies, the agronomic society, the SOFOFA, and other elements of the political right proposed or endorsed legislation to establish price control agencies of varying types in the interest of restoring social peace.[38]

In view of the overwhelming sentiment for controls, the Society by early 1919 changed its position to that of apparent collaboration with the moderate forces which favored controls at the retail and wholesale levels but rejected fixed prices to the producer. In pursuit of a preemptive but painless solution the SNA council went so far as to invite the leadership of the Workers' Assembly to discuss and draft a joint price control bill capable of passing Congress. The Society's strategy worked at the initial stage but floundered when the governing council of the Workers' Assembly rejected the compromise bill precisely because it exempted producers from controls. Negotiations went no further on this precedent-setting joint venture; its efforts at compromise rebuffed, the SNA board reaffirmed its adamant rejection of prices pegged to production costs, calling such an arrangement "impracticable" and claiming that it would cause "serious disturbances."[39]

Enactment of price control legislation was hampered, then, by the combination of consensus on principle and disagreement on specifics. As the economic crisis deepened in 1919, moreover, pressures for enactment of price control legislation began to be superseded by more transcendent matters. As its component groups became increasingly radical and mobilized, the Workers' Assembly shifted its focus from inflation toward more sweeping demands of the working and middle classes. From the time of its convention in March 1919, the Workers' Assembly began to broaden its scope to include basic social and political reform: the convention adopted a fifty-point program that emphasized housing, wages, working conditions, electoral reform, and even called for a people's militia.[40] As the crucial 1920 election approached, the price control issue was lost in the general ferment of the heated campaign.

Although no direct price control legislation was adopted during the postwar crisis, developments during the following decade indicate that the struggle over food price inflation had nonetheless entered a new and more realistic phase after 1919. Most fundamentally, the cattle tax—symbolic cause of inflation—disappeared as an important and emotional political issue. After obstinately defending the livestock duty for almost thirty years, in 1926 the Society proposed to depoliticize the old cornerstone of its development policy by substituting for ad valorem rates a sliding duty scale pegged to wholesale cattle prices. The measure, enacted in 1927, effectively removed the cattle tax from further public concern.[41]

With the burial of the cattle tax issue, the question of price controls assumed priority. In response to the lessons of 1905 and 1918–19, and to the heightened power of working- and middle-class groups, the governing elites accepted the political necessity of controlling the extremes of food price inflation. Thus when the general tariff level was raised by 50 percent in 1921, food staples were exempted.[42] Anticipating the results of a severe drought in 1924, the municipality of Santiago established an agency to build and supervise new markets and refrigerated storage facilities; and the national government announced plans, which the brevity of the drought rendered unnecessary, for a price control agency with extensive powers.[43] In 1929 the Ibáñez government sponsored a bill whose provisions went well beyond the limits of what the SNA could support. The proposal would authorize the president to set prices at every level, including to the producer, modify duties on foodstuffs by decree, and even dictate the cultivation of certain crops.[44] The depression temporarily solved the problem of inflation, but the very extent of the powers of Ibáñez's bill revealed governmental sensitivity to inflation and readiness to sacrifice landowners' immediate interests for the long-term welfare of the upper classes. When the decade ended, it still remained for the terms of price controls to be worked out and for the cost to landowners to be determined.

Depression, Radicalization, and Enactment of Controls, 1930–32

The core of the Chilean agricultural and food price control system was created in two separate stages during the depression. With the onset of contracting markets and falling prices in 1930, the SNA called for the formation of an agency to coordinate and subsidize the exportation of surplus commodities. It subsequently collaborated with the Ibáñez government in drawing up legislation for the Junta de Exportación Agrícola (Agricultural Export Board), established late in 1930. The Junta was similar to agricultural price support mechanisms established elsewhere during the depression; it was intended to provide domestic price supports by purchasing and exporting surplus agricultural products, and its operation was financed by existing and new taxes on agriculture and food processing. Consistent with its corporatist orientation, the Ibáñez government granted three of the seven seats on the Junta's board of directors to the agricultural societies—the SNA and the regional societies of Concepción and Osorno. In the SNA's appraisal, the Junta and its policies provided salvation for agriculture during the nadir of the depression.[45]

While the Society strongly supported the establishment and actions of the Agricultural Export Board, it found itself in a difficult situation in April 1932, when agricultural prices ceased their downward slide and began an accelerated rise.[46] With unemployment still running high, the Montero government immediately sponsored price control legislation fully as comprehensive as Ibáñez's in an attempt to ward off increased social and political unrest. Committed to supporting the moderate Montero regime as the best hope against anarchy or revolution, the SNA was thus caught in a dilemma: it could neither approve the legislation, which was too radical to be palatable, nor publicly condemn it without weakening the government's support. As a result, it remained studiously silent on the bill, which Congress passed in May 1932.[47] Given the current atmosphere of crisis, it is unlikely that the SNA's opposition would have prevented enactment of the price control bill; however, its failure to oppose the measure indicated that the Society again had chosen the upper-class over the narrow landowner interest.

Before the price control law could be fully implemented, the coup d'état of June 4 ushered in the Socialist Republic. The SNA virtually ceased its overt political activity during the hundred days of the Socialist Republic. It was not consulted on policy formulation, and given the hostility of some governmental elements toward landowners, it chose to refrain from public actions or statements in order to avoid possible retaliation. As a director argued during a board meeting, "at the present moment it is inopportune to expose the Society to dangers as a consequence of the doctrines it supports."[48] Thus in August 1932, when the government created the Comisariato General de Subsistencias y Precios (General Commissariat of Staples and Prices), the SNA remained inactive and silent.

Unlike the Junta de Exportación Agrícola and most other policy boards established during the Ibáñez years, the Comisariato was not administered by functional representation; thus landowners had neither automatic access to nor voting rights in the agency designated to set the prices of their products. Moreover, the powers of the Comisariato were more extensive than anything hitherto seriously contemplated. It was authorized to determine which products were staples and to set maximum prices on them at each stage of exchange. The same decree-law that created the Comisariato declared all land, transportation enterprises, and commercial establishments involved in the production or distribution of staples to be "of public utility" and authorized the president to expropriate any of them upon the recommendation of the commissar general. In the case of land, any property not cultivated or used as pasture, or whose owner failed to produce staples in the quality or quantity and under the conditions that the Comisariato might dictate, was subject to expropriation. These latter features of course were not immediately implemented; in fact, they remained dead and forgotten letters until the government of Dr. Allende resurrected them in its fight to expropriate the private sector. However, the Comisariato did quickly place maximum prices at all levels upon wheat and its derivatives, meat, milk, and other foods, as well as on nonfood essentials.[49]

In name and in its specific provisions, the Comisariato bore the unmistakable stamp of the Socialist Republic. However, although institutionalization of price controls was the work of the left, that was merely a matter of circumstance. As indicated by the legislative proposals of 1919, 1924, and 1929 and the Montero law of 1932, the right was equally interested in controlling food price inflation, for different reasons. Establishment of price controls was the logical outgrowth of increasing working- and middle-class organization and militancy, combined with heightened upper-class awareness of the dangers of uncontrolled inflation. The subsequent history of the price control system reveals that, despite the vehement objections of landowners and other affected capitalists, a majority of the Chilean political establishment accepted the Comisariato and similar mechanisms as necessary instruments of social control.

By 1932, then, Chilean agriculture and Chilean consumers were subject to two agencies, each with extensive powers, working at cross purposes—one to aid the producer with minimum prices, the other to protect the consumer by setting maximum prices. Both were emergency measures, but both remained and evolved into the vast, complex, and controversial system of controls which the military government drastically pruned back after 1973.

The Second Alessandri Administration and Price Controls

With the restoration of constitutional government and relative stability by 1933, the SNA was able to resume its normal patterns of political involvement. One of its most pressing tasks was to define a position vis-à-vis the new control mechanisms. Its general approach was to work for the preservation of those elements which benefitted agricultural producers and the abolition of those that it deemed harmful. Despite the objections of diehard advocates of laissez-faire like Silva Somarriva and Rodríguez de la Sotta, the Society embraced continuation of the price support system provided by the Export Board.[50] On the other hand, it vigorously sought the

Table 13
Cost of Living in Santiago, 1928–40 (March 1928 = 100)

Year	General Index	Food
1928	107.2	115.6
1929	109.1	119.0
1930	107.9	114.6
1931	107.1	103.3
1932	113.9	115.1
1933	141.4	147.4
1934	141.5	148.5
1935	144.4	155.0
1936	156.6	171.1
1937	176.4	204.8
1938	184.1	214.3
1939	186.7	210.4
1940	210.3	244.8

SOURCE: Dirección General de Estadística, *Anuario estadístico, año 1942. Comercio interior y comunicaciones*, p. 46.

suppression of the Comisariato, which it considered a nefarious and dangerous tool for use against landowners.

The SNA's objective was complicated by the continuation or emergence of various pressures for consumer protection. Most basically, inflation continued irregularly through the 1930s, while unemployment remained higher than normal. Real income for labor lagged behind predepression levels until the Popular Front government, and surveys revealed that in some cases urban workers were spending over 80 percent of their salaries feeding their families—and even then, deficiently.[51] The growth of the left, demonstrated by the 1932 elections, gave increased leverage to spokesmen for the urban poor who advocated strengthening rather than suppressing the Comisariato. The greater appeal of the left also indicated to much of the right that, regardless of its alleged deleterious effects on production, an instrument such as the Comisariato was a necessary element of the long-range upper-class strategy. Beyond these considerations, the SNA was faced in the thirties with organized millers, wholesalers, distributors, processors, and retailers, none of whom would sit passively by while landowners sought to eliminate controls on producers with no benefit to the other parties.

An important new factor in the equation was the emergence of an amorphous but very influential lobby which advocated the improvement of nutritional standards for poor Chileans. The rhetoric of the nutrition lobby was heavily couched in positivist phraseology about the Chilean "race": it constantly lamented the "decadence of the race" and called for measures in "defense of the race." But whereas the turn-of-the-century positivists were concerned with the moral, educational, or economic condition of the race, the nutrition lobby worried about its physiological condition. This loosely knit group advocated a host of solutions, including more production, better distribution of purchasing power, and nutritional education. For the short-term improvement of the lower-class diet, however, price controls on basic foodstuffs were deemed essential.[52]

The nutrition lobby developed in the twenties in response to stimuli from within and outside the country. Despite its relative advancement in many areas of development, Chile suffered one of the hemisphere's highest infant mortality rates. This acute situation, discussed since the turn of the century within the context of the broader debate on the "social question," was attributed in large measure to inadequate nutrition. The postwar Workers' Assembly had called attention to the economics of the working-class struggle to feed a family. In the twenties, the League of Nations' Commission on Hygiene studied the nutritional crisis of postwar Europe, in the process generating widespread consciousness of the technical aspects of human nutrition. The first important survey in Chile was carried out in 1927-28. Following the First National Congress on Nutrition in 1931, nutritional studies proliferated, and an official Council on Nutrition was established in 1933.[53]

In 1932 the government requested the League of Nations' assistance in assessing Chile's problem, and two European authorities, Mssrs. Dragoni and Burnet, arrived in Chile in 1935. Their work, executed with the aid of the universities, was the most ambitious and complete to date. They surveyed 591 families from all socioeconomic levels and all parts of the country, and their findings confirmed the growing conviction that Chile had very serious nutritional problems. Dragoni and Burnet concluded that half the surveyed population was malnourished; that 27.3 percent of the total sample suffered serious malnutrition (1,500 to 2,000 calories per day); and that 10.9 percent were gravely undernourished (fewer than 1,500 calories per day). They also found nutrition to be a function of income and blamed deficient production, distribution, and conservation of foodstuffs, inadequate education, and other factors for the condition they described.[54] With their personal prestige and that of the League of Nations behind their report, it was taken as irrefutable proof of the "decadence of the Chilean race."

The heightened awareness of nutritional deficiencies in the thirties was manifested in various ways. A school of nutrition was founded in the University of Chile, and reports on the effects of undernourishment appeared commonly in Chilean medical journals; a new journal, specifically called the *Revista de Medicina y Alimentación*, began publication about 1935.[55] The Ministry of Public Health was in the forefront of nutrition studies and was particularly active under the tutelage of Dr. Eduardo Cruz-Coke, himself an early investigator of nutritional problems. The ministry's monthly publication, *Acción Social*, helped to raise awareness of the situation by exposing and disseminating information on the social consequences of malnutrition. Under Cruz-Coke's influence, the revised National Council on Nutrition was founded in February 1937. It soon unveiled a comprehensive plan to arrest the decline of the race, which called for palliatives such as subsidized restaurants and farmers' markets and more substantive measures including stricter price controls and agrarian reform.[56] The "decadence of the race" quickly passed into the political lexicon and became the subject of frequent editorial comment and congressional debate. One well-publicized confrontation in 1938, for example, pitted opposition Senator Durán against Alessandrist Senator Lira Infante. Although at loggerheads over the government's record in addressing the problem, the senators could readily agree on the gravity of the situation: Durán lamented that "the health and vigor of our race [are] notoriously in decadence," while Lira Infante averred that "the problem of the race [is] the problem par excellence of the nation."[57]

The SNA and other elements of the entrepreneurial sector found their efforts to abolish the Comisariato hampered by the influence of the nutrition lobby and the other factors described above. Their first tactic was to challenge the legal basis of the Comisariato. To this end, they persuaded Alessandri at the outset of his second term to appoint an honorary commission to determine the constitutionality of all decree-laws issued under the Socialist Republic. Predictably, the decree-law which created the Comisariato was found to be in violation of the constitution; however, the SNA was quickly disillusioned by Alessandri's refusal to abolish the price control agency.[58] Alessandri did not publicly articulate his motives for retaining the Comisariato, but this course of action was consistent with his commitment to the upper-class strategy of concession and conciliation. With prices still rising, moreover, he could hardly eliminate controls altogether without endangering the social and political stability that were gradually and tentatively returning to Chile.

The SNA's drive to dismantle the Comisariato intensified when it discovered that the Export Board and the Comisariato were operating in direct opposition in the area of wheat production. In 1933 the Junta and the Ministry of Agriculture launched a "wheat campaign" to stimulate the recovery of wheat production to predepression levels. The program consisted of several facets, such as credit, improved seed, and other technical assistance, but the linchpin was a minimum price guaranteed by the Junta.

Concurrently, pursuant to its mission, the Comisariato was setting maximum prices for bread, flour, and wheat; however, the Comisariato's maximum prices were not consistently as high as the Junta's minimums.[59] The ensuing chaos and administrative embarrassment provided an opening wedge for the SNA's renewed attack. "The measures enthusiastically sponsored by the Ministry of Agriculture to foster cereal production . . . unfortunately are destroyed by other organisms of the State which impede the advance which could be accomplished. . . . The confidence and incentive necessary to producers . . . are annulled by the disruptive action of an agency of the state which fills the role of generating anxiety and discord."[60]

Despite the considerable pressure and publicity generated by the SNA and other agricultural societies, the Alessandri government remained firm about preserving the Comisariato. However, in order to placate the business sector, Alessandri resolved the conflict between governmental agencies in 1933 with a decree assigning to the Junta exclusive jurisdiction over wheat and its derivatives and confirming the authority of the Comisariato over all other foodstuffs designated as staples.[61] During the remainder of Alessandri's administration, the Comisariato gradually extended its jurisdiction by declaring several genres of foodstuffs as staples, but the budgetary and personnel constraints under which it labored rendered its enforcement powers virtually ineffectual. The Comisariato, however, did survive with its legal powers intact, and landowners during the Alessandri regime lost their best opportunity to destroy one of the pillars on which the weighty apparatus of state control ultimately came to rest.

Further government actions quickly dissipated the SNA's satisfaction over curtailment of the Comisariato. The jurisdictional definition had placed the wheat economy under the control of producers and agricultural technicians, who could set only minimum prices. This greatly reduced the government's leverage over the price of bread—the single most important element in the diet of the poor and one subject to rapid inflation. The Alessandri government moved to remedy that oversight by sponsoring successive bills in 1933 and 1934 whose basic thrust was to transform the Junta from an instrument of producers into an agency capable of reconciling the interests of producer, middleman, and consumer. In order to balance its orientation the Junta would be authorized to buy and sell, export and import, and set absolute instead of only minimum prices for wheat and its derivatives—in short, to exercise complete control over that very important branch of Chilean agriculture. Concurrently, its governing board would be expanded by the new bills in order to reduce the power of the agricultural societies: instead of having three of the seven seats on the board as originally structured, producers would have only three of nine.[62]

The SNA, in conjunction with the regional societies, strenuously opposed these measures, differentiating rather unconvincingly between the Junta's original mission of supporting prices in order to stimulate production and the vast new powers which would result in stringent control. It claimed that the bills were based on "the same philosophy which gave birth to the Comisariato, which the Society has combatted from the beginning."[63] The Society offered a counterproposal to reduce, rather than expand, the powers of the Junta by limiting its function strictly to exportation. However the SNA again represented a minority position: passage of both bills indicated that social control took precedence over landowners' interests.

Having failed to prevent the establishment of price controls on agricultural producers, the SNA responded to the new reality by developing the tools with which to derive maximum advantage from the undesirable situation. Both the Comisariato and the reformed Junta were required to establish prices to the producer, by zone, on the basis of production costs plus a legitimate margin of profit varying between 15 and 35 percent. Whenever the Comisariato declared an article to be a staple and thus subject to control, it was required to solicit cost data from producers' organizations. The Junta was also required to determine the quantities of exportable surpluses on the basis of official crop forecasts and "any other information which it may obtain." Thus the ultimate policies of the control agencies were determined by ostensibly technical and objective, but clearly political, information.[64] In view of the acknowledged inadequacy of government agricultural statistics, the position of landowner representatives on the Junta's governing board, and the regulations governing the Comisariato's operation, the data supplied by the SNA and other societies were very influential in the determination of prices. If not accepted prima facie, they at least established a bargaining position for the annual price-setting sessions.

The SNA's political use of production data was not entirely new to the 1930s. The Society had presented its own data to the Kemmerer financial mission in 1925 to influence the recommendations on agricultural taxation and had tried to affect alcohol tax legislation and tariff policy through the use of production cost studies.[65] However, the institutionalization of production cost data as criteria for price policy made the control and use of "independent" studies one of the Society's most important tools for protecting the producer interest. In order to meet the constant need for studies of high quality and the proper slant, the SNA established its own Economic Studies Department in 1934. The department's purpose was explicitly political: "to orient the government . . . by filling a great void that exists due to the lack of correct information on the cost of production of the various agricultural products."[66] The department, staffed with agricultural economists, produced the crop forecast and production cost studies which constituted the SNA's main weapon in the annual battle over commodity prices.

The SNA's experience with the Popular Front demonstrated that production cost studies were only as effective as governments were disposed to accept them. With a hostile majority in Congress, the Aguirre Cerda government could do little to augment or reform the price control system, but it did make vigorous use of the existing machinery. In a bid to firm up its popular support, it actually rolled back the retail price of many staples in 1939 and in the process also froze or rolled back prices to the producer.[67] Landowners were so incensed by the official price for wheat in 1939 that they complained long and bitterly, and some even threatened not to plant.[68] The Comisariato added a lengthy list of new foodstuffs and other consumer items to the category of staples and thus brought them under the umbrella of price controls. It also added personnel to its inspection staff in an effort to make official retail prices stick in the face of considerable merchant opposition.[69] The SNA and the regional societies constantly protested the Popular Front's price policies and were somewhat mollified by a substantial increase in the 1940 official price for wheat.[70] Overall, the Popular Front government was the first to try to implement the social philosophy of the Workers' Assembly: that producers, processors, and distributors were essentially in business to serve the consuming public.

By the mid-thirties, then, landowners had become subject to the mechanisms of a controlled agricultural economy. They had invited and obtained intervention on their behalf in the Junta de Exportación but had fought unsuccessfully against the establishment and continuance of agencies, oriented toward consumer interests, which served as instruments of social control. The long-term cost of government price policy to producers has been extensively and inconclusively debated. Whatever the exact monetary cost, however, giving up their traditional right to free marketing of produce—with absolutely unforeseeable consequences—was an important sacrifice that landowners were forced to make in defense of the national upper-class interest.

Notes

1. Histories and interpretations of Chilean inflation include: Fetter, *Monetary Inflation*; Pinto Santa Cruz, *Chile, un caso*, pp. 122-47; Albert O. Hirschman, *Journeys toward Progress: Studies of Economic Policy-Making in Latin America* (New York, 1963), pp. 160-223; Joseph Grunwald, "The 'Structuralist' School on Price Stability and Development: The Chilean Case," in Albert O. Hirschman, ed., *Latin American Issues: Essays and Comments* (New York, 1961), pp. 95-123; and Tom E. Davis, "Eight Decades of Inflation in Chile, 1879-1959: A Political Interpretation," *Journal of Political Economy*, 71 (1963), 389-97.

2. Wright, "Agriculture and Protectionism," p. 49.

3. See ch. 6, pp. 123-25; also Bauer, *Chilean Rural Society*, pp. 106-11, 174-203.

4. Ramírez Necochea, *Historia del movimiento obrero. Antecedentes*, pp. 282-312.

5. A survey of eighty-one working-class families between 1911 and 1921 revealed that on the average, 60 percent of their total income was spent on food. *Boletín de la Oficina del Trabajo*, año XII, no. 18 (1922), 97. An ILO survey of 454 working-class households in 1956-57 indicated that 55.5 percent of total expenditures went for food. International Labour Office, *Household Income and Expenditure Statistics* (no. 1, 1950-65) (Geneva, 1967), 89. See also Ismael Canessa Ibarra, "Salario y medicina social," *Acción Social*, año XIII, no. 75 (Dec. 1938-Jan. 1939), 14-16; Universidad de Chile, Instituto de Economía, *Family Income and Expenditures in Greater Santiago: Experimental Survey* (Santiago, 1966); and Peter D. Bennett, *Government's Role in Retail Marketing of Food Products in Chile* (Austin, Tex., 1968), pp. 22-25. There are no similar data for the nineteenth century.

6. The clearest statements that agricultural price controls were instituted to promote industry are by Markos Mamalakis. See his "Public Policy and Sectoral Development: A Case Study of Chile," in Mamalakis and Clark W. Reynolds, *Essays on the Chilean Economy* (Homewood, Ill., 1965), pp. 117-48; and *The Growth and Structure of the Chilean Economy: From Independence to Allende* (New Haven, Conn., 1976), pp. 102-7, 120-43.

7. Wright, "Politics of Inflation."

8. Silvia Hernández, "The Andean Passes between Chile and Argentina: A Study in Historical Geography" (unpublished master's thesis in geography, University of California, Berkeley, 1970), p. 49.

9. Cámara de Diputados, *Sesiones ordinarias en 1888*, 1, 12-13; *El Ferrocarril*, July 11, 1888, p. 2.

10. See the price table in Bauer, *Chilean Rural Society*, p. 233; also see Appendix 7.

11. On the Democratic party, see: Ramírez Necochea, *Historia del movimiento obrero. Antecedentes*, pp. 207-16; Malaquías Concha, *El programa de la Democracia*, 2nd ed. (Santiago, 1905), and Cortés and Fuentes, *Diccionario político*, pp. 144-53.

12. *El Ferrocarril*, July 8, 1888, p. 2.

13. *Representación del pueblo de Santiago*, p. 10.

14. *El Ferrocarril*, July 10, 1888, p. 2.

15. *Boletín de las leyes y decretos del gobierno, año 1897* (Santiago, 1897), suplemento, pp. 690-715.

16. Malaquías Concha later attributed passage of the cattle duty to myopic jingoism: "Chilean patriotism overcame the necessities of the stomach." Congreso Nacional, Cámara de Diputados, *Sesiones extraordinarias en 1905/6*, pp. 77-78. Jaime Eyzaguirre, *Chile durante el gobierno de Errázuriz Echaurren, 1896-1901* (Santiago, 1957), pp. 95-122, 197-289, deals with boundary conflicts with Argentina.

17. Cortés and Fuentes, *Diccionario político*, pp. 144-53.

18. There are no reliable retail price or cost-of-living data for the period before 1913. Wright, "Politics of Inflation," p. 249, provides a wholesale price table for the years 1897-1910.

19. *El Chileno*, Sept. 14, 1905, p. 1; *MSNA* (1905), p. 7; *ibid*. (1907-9), pp. 17-22.

20. Wright, "Politics of Inflation"; Gonzalo Izquierdo Fernández, "Octubre de 1905. Un episodio en la historia social chilena," *Historia*, 13 (1976), 55-96.

21. Izquierdo, "Octubre de 1905."

22. E.g., *El Ferrocarril*, Oct. 25, 1905, p. 1, called on the authorities to take whatever measures were necessary to prevent such outbreaks of anti-inflation protest in the future.

23. *El Alba*, año I, no. 2 (Oct. 15-31, 1905), p. 4.

24. *BSNA*, 37 (1906), 162.

25. José Alfonso, in *El Ferrocarril*, Oct. 26, 1905, p. 1; Enrique Zañartu Prieto, in *ibid.*, Oct. 31, 1905, p. 1.

26. For details, including the 1907 and 1909 votes analyzed by party and region, see Wright, "Politics of Inflation," pp. 255-57.

27. *BSNA*, 36-49 (1905-18); ch. 6 deals with the SNA and subdivision of land.

28. *Boletín de la Oficina del Trabajo*, año VIII, no. 11 (1918), 261-311, featured a long article on the cost of living.

29. Jorge Barría Serón, "Los movimientos sociales de Chile desde 1910 hasta 1926" (Memoria de Prueba, Universidad de Chile, 1960), pp. 117-18, 241-43, 248; *El Mercurio*, Mar. 3, 1919, p. 13; *ibid.*, Aug. 28, 1919, p. 19; Cámara de Diputados, *Sesiones ordinarias en 1919*, p. 1027.

30. *El Mercurio*, Nov. 23, 1918, pp. 17-18; *ibid.*, Nov. 25, 1918, pp. 3, 17; *ibid.*, Nov. 27, 1918, p. 3.

31. See *El Mercurio*, Nov. 1918-Mar. 1919, esp. the series by Antonio Orrego Barros called "Los problemas obreros," in *El Mercurio*, Dec. 7-14, 1918.

32. *El Mercurio*, Mar. 11, 1919, p. 13; Congreso Nacional, Cámara de Diputados, *Sesiones extraordinarias en 1918-19*, pp. 2695-711; Cámara de Senadores, *Sesiones extraordinarias en 1919-20*, p. 209; *Diario Oficial*, no. 12,290 (Feb. 6, 1919); *ibid.*, no. 12,574 (Jan. 20, 1920).

33. *El Mercurio*, Aug. 30, 1919, pp. 19-20; *ibid.*, Aug. 31, 1919, p. 25; Cámara de Diputados, *Sesiones extraordinarias en 1919-20*, pp. 61-64.

34. Cámara de Diputados, *Sesiones extraordinarias en 1918-19*, pp. 682-83.

35. Law no. 3447, *Boletín de las leyes y decretos del gobierno*, libro 87 (Dec. 1918), 2, 1563-64; *ibid.*, 1578-80; Cámara de Diputados, *Sesiones extraordinarias en 1918-19*, pp. 682-84, 793-96; *MSNA* (1920), pp. 7-8; *El Mercurio*, Nov. 27, 1918, pp. 3, 18.

36. *El Mercurio*, Apr. 20, 1919, p. 23.

37. *Ibid.*, Dec. 11, 1918, p. 12.

38. Cámara de Diputados, *Sesiones extraordinarias en 1918-19*, pp. 1006, 1478-84, 2897-907; *Boletín de la Sociedad de Fomento Fabril*, 35 (1918), 795-96.

39. *MSNA* (1919), pp. 20-21; Minutes, Aug. 11, 1919, in *El Agricultor*, 50 (1919), 240; *ibid.*, 51 (1920), 21, 43.

40. *El Mercurio*, Mar. 10, 1919, p. 12; *ibid.*, Mar. 11, 1919, p. 13; also the series entitled "La cuestión social en Chile," in *ibid.*, Apr. 20-24, 1919. Historians have paid far too little attention to the role of the anti-inflation movement of 1918-19 in mobilizing the working and middle classes and preparing the way for Alessandri's election in 1920.

41. *MSNA* (1926), pp. 3-6; *BSNA*, 59 (1927), 350-51. While the SNA continued its efforts to protect the cattle industry, by the 1930s the specific matter of tariff policy had been overshadowed by the complex price and import policy questions.

42. *Boletín de las leyes y decretos del gobierno*, libro 90 (Feb. 1921), 165-73.

43. Inés Torres Moncada, "Alimentación de las clases populares" (Memoria de Prueba, Universidad de Chile, 1938), pp. 71-73; *El Mercurio*, Sept. 23, 1925, p.

11. The activities of the municipal agency for 1928 are recorded in Santiago, Dirección General de Subsistencias, *Memoria, año 1928* (Santiago, 1929).

44. Guillermo Torres Orrego, *El Comisariato General de Subsistencias y Precios de la República* (Santiago, 1947), pp. 18-35.

45. Jaime Larraín García-Moreno, *Orientación de nuestra política agraria* (Santiago, 1932), p. 25; *MSNA* (1931), p. 13; Minutes, Sept. 1 and 8, 1930, in *BSNA*, 62 (1930), 688-94. The following theses from the University of Chile's law school examine the technical and legal basis of the Junta: Guillermo Donoso Vergara, "Estudio histórico-económico de la producción y comercio de granos" (1938); Emilio Undurraga Villegas, "De la Junta de Exportación Agrícola" (1940); Jorge Gómez T., "La Junta de Exportación Agrícola" (1944); León Finkelstein Rosolie, "La agricultura y los organismos de fomento" (1945); Adela Manquilef Vargas, "El Ministerio de Agricultura y la política agraria" (1951).

46. Dirección General de Estadística, *Anuario agropecuario 1934-35*, p. 73, has a wholesale price index.

47. Torres Orrego, *El Comisariato*, pp. 18-35; Gregorio Talesnik Rabinovich, "Intervencionismo del estado y control de precios por el mismo: estudio especial del Comisariato General de Subsistencias y Precios" (Memoria de Prueba, Universidad de Chile, 1940), pp. 42-53.

48. Minutes, Aug. 16, 1932, in *BSNA*, 64 (1932), 475. *MSNA* (1932) refers only to a note of protest to the caretaker government of General Blanche, which succeeded the Socialist Republic.

49. Studies of the Comisariato include the above-cited works by Torres Orrego and Talesnik Rabinovich and Constantino Macchiavello Varas, "Contribución al estudio de nuestro problema de la carestía de la vida frente al problema de las subsistencias" (Memoria de Prueba, Universidad de Chile, 1933).

50. E.g., *MSNA* (1931), p. 13; *El C*, 70 (1938), edición extraordinaria, 331-40.

51. Estimates of real income were given in Arturo Natho D. (Comisario General de Subsistencias y Precios) to the minister of agriculture (Jan. 23, 1940), in *AN*, Min. de Agr., Trabajos Recibidos, 1940. Canessa Ibarra, "Salario y medicina social," pp. 14-16, cites surveys indicating high food expenditures.

52. Little or nothing has been written about what I have called the nutrition lobby, despite its considerable influence.

53. Torres Moncada, "Alimentación," pp. 93-106, traces the growth of concern for nutrition in Chile. Her work lists numerous studies done in the twenties and thirties, as do Jorge Mardones Restat and Ricardo Cox, *La alimentación en Chile. Estudios del Consejo Nacional de la Alimentación* (Santiago, 1942); and Pike, *Chile and the United States*, pp. 435-37. Peter Hakim and Giorgio Solimano, *Development, Reform, and Malnutrition in Chile* (Cambridge, Mass., 1978), cite nutrition studies done between 1930 and 1970. Proceedings of the 1931 nutritional congress appeared as: *Primer Congreso Nacional de Alimentación Popular. Antecedentes y trabajos* (Valparaíso, 1932). See also Salvador Allende, *Realidad médico-social chilena* (Santiago, 1939). Allende was the Popular Front's minister of health in 1939 and 1940.

54. Carlo Dragoni and Etienne Burnet, "L'alimentation populaire au Chile; première enquête générale de 1935," in *Revista Chilena de Higiene y Medicina Preventiva*, 1, nos. 10-12 (Oct.-Dec. 1938), 407-611. Their study was published earlier by the League of Nations.

55. E.g., Jorge Mardones Restat, "El problema de la alimentación en Chile," *Revista de Medicina y Alimentación*, 1 (1935), 367-78.

56. "Plan Integral de Alimentación," *Acción Social*, año V, no. 57 (Feb.-Mar. 1937), 76-80.

57. Durán's speech is in Congreso Nacional, Cámara de Senadores, *Sesiones ordinarias en 1938*, p. 1200; Lira Infante's is in *ibid.*, p. 1289.

58. *El Mercurio*, June 2, 1933, p. 14; *ibid.*, June 6, 1933, p. 3; Cámara de Diputados, *Sesiones extraordinarias en 1932-33*, 1, 972-76; *MSNA* (1932), p. 10.

59. Cámara de Senadores, *Sesiones extraordinarias en 1933-34*, 1, 589-91.

60. *BSNA*, 65 (1933), 161-62; also *ibid.*, 289.

61. *El Mercurio*, May 21, 1933, p. 5.

62. Donoso Vergara, "Comercio de granos," pp. 230-41.

63. Minutes, Aug. 21, 1933, in *El C*, 65 (1933), 496; Minutes, Sept. 3, 1934, in *ibid.*, 66 (1934), 642; Minutes, Nov. 12, 1934, in *ibid.*, 67 (1935), 47-48; Minutes, Nov. 19, 1934, in *ibid.*, 49; Cámara de Diputados, *Sesiones extraordinarias en 1933-34*, 2, 1588-607; Cámara de Senadores, *Sesiones extraordinarias en 1933-34*, 1, 589-91.

64. Talesnik Rabinovich, "Intervencionismo," pp. 66-68; Macchiavello Varas, "Contribución," pp. 65-66; Undurraga Villegas, "Junta de Exportación," pp. 37-41.

65. *BSNA*, 57 (1926), 413-20; Minutes, July 7, 1930, in *ibid.*, 62 (1930), 530-34.

66. *MSNA* (1934), pp. 84-86. Menges, "Public Policy," cites the founding of the SNA's Instituto de Estudios Agrarios (INTAGRO) in 1960 as an important innovation; in reality, it was simply a reorganization of the department founded in 1934.

67. *El Mercurio* had extensive coverage of the price rollback in the first few months of the Popular Front government: E.g., *El Mercurio*, Dec. 28, 1938, p. 21; *ibid.*, Jan. 6, 1939, pp. 3, 18; *ibid.*, Jan. 10, 1939, p. 18; *ibid.*, Jan. 13, 1939, p. 13; *ibid.*, Mar. 1, 1939, p. 3; *ibid.*, Apr. 5, 1939, p. 22.

68. *Ibid.*, Jan. 5, 1939, p. 20; *ibid.*, Jan. 7, 1939, p. 3; *ibid.*, Jan. 11, 1939, p. 17; *ibid.*, Apr. 3, 1939, p. 3; *El C*, 72 (1940), 1; Arturo Olavarría Bravo, *Chile entre dos Alessandri; memorias políticas* (Santiago, 1962), 1, 370-73.

69. *El Mercurio*, Dec. 28, 1938, p. 21; *ibid.*, Jan. 3, 1939, p. 18; *ibid.*, Jan. 7, 1939, p. 23; *ibid.*, Dec. 6, 1939, p. 3. Numerous protests are registered in *AN*, Min. de Agr., Trabajos Recibidos, 1940.

70. *El Mercurio*, May 13, 1940, p. 16; *ibid.*, July 8, 1940, p. 24; *ibid.*, July 11, 1940, p. 16.

6

Landowners and Agrarian Reform

The dramatic change in rural land tenure brought about by the Christian Democratic and Unidad Popular governments between 1964 and 1973 has generated a vast literature on agrarian reform in Chile. These studies have focused on the political, economic, social, and agronomic aspects of the agrarian reform process, while little has appeared thus far on the historical antecedents of the recent phenomenon.[1] Perhaps that gap in the literature explains the common tendency to treat the agrarian reform issue as if it had first appeared on the scene in the 1950s or '60s. Thus Jacques Chonchol, one of the most authoritative writers on agrarian problems, devoted an article to explaining why no "serious discussion" of agrarian reform took place in Chile before the 1960s.[2] In a similar vein, Federico Gil wrote that as late as the 1950s the large estate had remained "unchallenged."[3] And Robert Kaufman's study of Chilean agrarian reform states unequivocally: "It was during Jorge Alessandri's presidency (1958-1964) that land reform first moved from the level of abstract theoretical debate to the more immediate arena of congressional action and legislative decision."[4]

It does not require much probing into Chilean history between the world wars to discover that the land tenure structure came under serious scrutiny during that period. The number of articles and books published on the land tenure question indicates at the least a lively intellectual interest. Campaign promises and party platforms calling for subdivision of the land reveal that agrarian reform had become something more than an academic question. The formation or growth of pressure groups to promote or oppose agrarian reform and related issues suggests that some elements of Chilean society took it seriously as an issue. Finally, the passage in 1928 and 1935 of Latin America's most advanced agrarian reform laws outside of Mexico indicates that the issue was sufficiently pressing to have elicited response from the country's directing groups. The argument that those laws were passed to preempt demand for revolutionary land reform only confirms the existence of a substantial amount of pressure to be undercut.[5]

Those authors who explicitly or implicitly deny the importance of agrarian reform as a political issue prior to the 1950s or '60s may have been unduly influenced by two factors. First, it is as easy as it is erroneous to conclude from the results of the early laws—only 3,253 families settled in thirty years—that there had been little or no demand for agrarian reform.[6] Second, both the agrarian reform issue and the programs enacted in the twenties and thirties were almost invariably described by the term "colonization" even though their primary thrust was the subdivision of existing agricultural properties rather than settlement of unused land. The semantic change to "agrarian reform" by the 1950s suggests a difference in purpose and approach which existed only in degree. This may have led some authors to draw an artificial distinction between the periods or even to misinterpret the nature of the "colonization" phase.

Intellectual and Political Background of Agrarian Reform

The emergence of agrarian reform as an issue in national politics must be examined against the backdrop of Chile's pattern of rural land tenure. Although most criticism of the latifundio suggested a static situation, numerous studies of Chilean land tenure have demonstrated that the pattern of ownership was in reality quite fluid even in the late nineteenth century and more so in the twentieth. In contrast to some parts of America, in Chile large properties changed hands readily and often; and as a result of the abolition of legal impediments to subdivision and growing economic pressures to divide haciendas, the number of large individual landholdings increased substantially in the century after independence from Spain and particularly after 1880.[7]

Most of the subdivision operative through the 1910s seems to have been concentrated in the two extremes of size and value. On the one hand, colonial entails such as La Compañía in Rancagua or haciendas of late colonial vintage such as El Huique in Colchagua underwent division over time into various fundos of high evaluation and large size in their own right.[8] Many original haciendas by the 1910s had been further fragmented into *hijuelas* of still substantial size and value, while former large estates near the cities were subject to even more subdivision. By this process the number of estates with high assessed value, worked by inquilino and seasonal labor, and capable of conferring prestige and substantial income on their owners had increased markedly over the years. At the other extreme, a far greater increase in the number of landholders was found among the owners of small plots of less than five hectares. These minifundia commonly were fragmented well beyond the point of being able to sustain a family even in poverty. In several departments of central Chile in the 1920s, the average size of these smallholdings was well under one hectare.[9]

Up to the time that agrarian reform became a political issue, the process of subdivision had failed to produce a large stratum of medium-sized farms (five to fifty hectares) operated primarily with family labor and capable of producing consistently for the market. Figures for subdivision in the nineteenth century are scarce, but Bauer's data for two departments where land ownership was on the increase between 1854 and 1917 indicate that the number of family-sized farms remained nearly static during that period (see Table 14). However, it is impossible to gauge whether the pattern in San Felipe and Caupolicán was typical throughout central Chile. In the frontier area and south of the Bío-Bío, the small farm was more common, but there also larger estates dominated the better lands.[10]

Table 14
Land Distribution in San Felipe and Caupolicán (Combined), 1854 and 1917

Category in Hectares	0-5	5-50	51 & Over	Totals
1854				
No. of owners	711	778	181	1,670
Percentage of total owners	42.6	46.6	10.8	100.0
Total hectares	1,806	12,890	173,269	187,965
Percentage of total surface	1.0	6.8	92.2	100.0
1917				
No. of owners	4,019	886	322	5,227
Percentage of total owners	76.9	16.9	6.2	100.0
Total hectares	5,235	12,443	246,750	264,428
Percentage of total surface	2.0	4.7	93.3	100.0

SOURCE: Bauer, *Chilean Rural Society*, pp. 126, 128.

Substantial growth occurred in the number of family-sized farms in central Chile between 1917 and the agricultural census of 1935-36.[11] Beyond the statistical data, the Santiago newspapers provide ample evidence of the process in numerous real estate advertisements featuring *hijuelas, quintas,* and *parcelas* of five to thirty hectares and beyond. Yet McBride, writing in the early thirties, still lamented the lack of a substantial rural middle class of the yeoman type.[12] He observed that some of the medium-sized holdings were in areas too remote or on soils too poor to produce much for the market. Moreover, many if not most of the modest-sized holdings carved out of larger estates on good soils near the cities were used primarily as "*quintas de recreo*" by urban middle- and upper-class elements who did not possess proper fundos. In these cases agricultural land was sacrificed to lawns, ornamental gardens, and often to elaborate houses, while the remaining cultivated land was sharecropped or worked by inquilino labor.[13]

Thus after a long trend toward reduction in the size of agrarian holdings and increase in the number of proprietors, the Chilean land tenure structure was still characterized by a dichotomy of large estates and subsistence or sub-subsistence minifundia. A Chilean economist made the claim in 1919 that "in Chile there exists a greater monopolization of agricultural land than in any other country of the world."[14] After four more decades of accelerating subdivision, a North American agricultural economist reiterated the statement, with only a slight caveat: "The concentration of land ownership in Chile today is among the highest in the world."[15] Table 15 provides a summary of the land tenure pattern as it existed in 1935-36.

Table 15
Rural Land Distribution by Size, 1935-36[a]

Surface (hectares)	Number of Holdings	Percent of Total Holdings	Thousands of Hectares	Percent of Total Surface	Value in Millions (pesos)	Percent of Total Value
0-4.9	87,790	49.08	139	0.55	365	5.87
5-19.9	41,437	23.16	469	1.87	435	7.00
20-49.9	21,341	11.93	692	2.76	413	6.64
50-99.9	11,007	6.15	772	3.08	439	7.06
100-199.9	6,958	3.89	965	3.85	573	9.22
200-499.9	5,323	2.98	1,678	6.69	1,005	16.16
500-999.9	2,220	1.24	1,525	6.08	663	10.66
1,000-1,999.9	1,342	0.75	1,823	7.26	632	10.16
2,000-4,999.9	838	0.47	2,542	10.13	573	9.22
5,000 & over	626	0.35	14,486	57.73	1,120	18.01
	178,882	100.00	25,091	100.00	6,218	100.00

[a]Totals differ from those in Table 6 because fewer proprietors reported the extension of their holdings than reported assessed value.

SOURCE: Adapted from Dirección General de Estadística, *Agricultura, 1935-36: censo*, p. 6.

The rural property structure had been subjected to criticism from time to time during the nineteenth century, as for example during the protracted debates of the 1850s over the abolition of entails. The rise of a large floating population in the countryside also led to occasional conjecture about the possible connection between rootlessness and limited access to landed property.[16] Debate over the autonomous comuna law of 1891 raised the question of the relationship between rural property and political democracy.[17] However, the land question received more sustained attention after the turn of the century, when Chile entered a period of national introspection and self-criticism in response to the economic stagnation, political frustration, and social unrest which characterized the Parliamentary Period.

Two phenomena in particular directed scrutiny toward the rural property structure. One factor was a new concern with agricultural productivity. While food price inflation was commonly attributed to paper money or the cattle tax, various signs pointed also to the suspected low productivity of Chilean agriculture, and the new agricultural statistical service, founded in 1909, quickly demonstrated that yields of basic crops were actually declining.[18] This evidence led to some inquiry into the possible relationship between agricultural productivity and the structure of landed property. The second factor was the general concern with the "social question" which derived from the emergence of a combative mining and urban proletariat in the first years of the twentieth century. Although there were as yet no visible signs of unrest among the rural population, there was some worry that the rustics might be contaminated by the example of militant nitrate and urban workers. The notion of wider dissemination of property as an antidote to revolution became commonplace in the early 1900s, leading to legislation on worker housing in 1906 and spawning considerable discussion of the potential benefits of more widespread ownership of agricultural land.

The SNA through its *Boletín* was a participant in the early discussion of land tenure and generally favored the creation of smaller holdings for both economic and social reasons. A lengthy editorial in 1904 stated the potential social and political problem:

> It is a fact that the "agrarian problem" exists latent in Chile, although it is not visible to everyone: in a country of eight hundred thousand square kilometers there are only a few landowners and an innumerable quantity of proletarians. Many prudent spirits affirm the necessity of openly stating the problem and beginning immediately to work toward the tranquil and beneficial solution, which is nothing other than distributing the land better, creating small property, making farmers. The farmer everywhere is the most solid basis of social tranquility, order, and national prosperity.[19]

A decade later the *Boletín* explicitly tied production to property:

> Our agricultural production is so limited that often it is insufficient for our own consumption. The explanation for this phenomenon is found in two facts: on the one hand, rural property is too extensive to be efficiently cultivated; and on the other, only 10 percent of those who work in agriculture are landowners; the vast majority is composed of the renter, the inquilino, the peón, the vagabond, who cannot be directly interested in the improvement of alien property.[20]

At the same time the Society strongly endorsed a congressional bill to authorize the country's main mortgage bank, the Caja de Crédito Hipotecario, to buy, divide, and resell land within ten kilometers of railroad stations. It also recommended that future road and railroad construction be accompanied by expropriation of large holdings along the rights-of-way.[21] Thus the SNA and segments of the Chilean public elites, influenced by European and North American practices and ideologies, had embraced a concept completely alien to the Chilean experience and value system: the notion of the productive, social, and civic superiority of the family farm.

In common with several elements of the general "social question," the land tenure matter suddenly moved from the academic to the political sphere as a result of the postwar popular mobilization. While the most immediate goal of the Workers' Assembly was price controls, it also demanded land distribution for two purposes: in the long run, to improve agricultural productivity, thereby in its view attacking the root cause of food price inflation; and in the short run, to provide means of subsistence for some of the thousands of currently unemployed workers. Along with a program to subdivide large estates, the Workers' Assembly also called for a progressive land tax to encourage voluntary subdivision.[22]

Spurred by the demands of the Workers' Assembly and the sense of urgency they evoked, a wide spectrum of the articulate public endorsed land reform. Some called for such measures simply to appease the mobilized masses, some to buy time, but others in the genuine belief that better distribution of agricultural property would contribute to solving some urgent national problems. The Society of Agronomists, for example, stated in a note to Congress that "enormous extensions of land in the hands of a single owner, true agrarian fiefs, have been an obstacle to the progress of our agriculture and the cause of inflation" and called for an immediate "agrarian reform."[23] *El Mercurio*, reflecting generally conservative views, editorialized that "our vast system of agricultural production . . . sadly is distinguished by the scarcity of its fruits, its high costs, and the backwardness of its methods." It recommended rapid division of the land to improve productivity and as a preventive social measure, since "where everyone is a proprietor, there is no anarchism or revolutionary socialism."[24]

Moisés Poblete Troncoso of the University of Chile made the most influential statement on rural property in a book, published in 1919, which argued the following thesis: "The rise of the prices of staples is, above all, a problem of production, which is deficient . . . due principally to the poor division of agricultural property. A greater division of agricultural property will intensify production and well-being and realize a democratic ideal in dividing the wealth."[25] Poblete Troncoso also expected other benefits to flow from agrarian reform: greater public-spiritedness and patriotism inherent in smallholders, stemming of rural-to-urban migration, reduction of delinquency, and an end to subversion.[26] Thus by the time of the post-war crisis, a broad segment of Chileans had adopted the alien ideal of the family farm and offered it as a panacea for the country's ills at the moment of the greatest economic and social crisis that Chile had experienced.

Action on the land issue followed quickly in the crisis atmosphere. First a group of Conservative party deputies offered a bill in early 1919 to authorize the Caja de Crédito Hipotecario to purchase, divide, and resell land near major cities—expropriation was not to be permitted.[27] On June 30, 1919, President Sanfuentes introduced a similar bill, whose lengthy preamble constituted a thorough condemnation of the large estate by a man who was himself a substantial landowner:

> The main, if not the only, cause of deficient production should be sought . . . in the circumstance that rural property is concentrated in such a small number of proprietors. . . . In this is the origin, beyond doubt, of the high prices at which agriculturists can sell their products. [The concentration of property] has created in the country a relative prosperity for a small part of the population and few elements of well-being for the great mass of the inhabitants, who live outside the normal conditions which social progress requires.

Inquilinos in particular, the president claimed, "remain removed from many of the benefits of civilization." Citing the "unanimity" of public opinion, Sanfuentes called for "the immediate subdivision of agricultural property, in order to reduce production and retail costs as well as to foment on a vast scale property ownership itself."[28]

While the pressure for agrarian reform came from the mobilized urban poor, the initial attempts to legislate it—in very mild form—came from elements of the oligarchy. The willingness to temporize or perform corrective surgery on the body hegemonic, however, was not universally shared. Although neither bill currently under consideration in Congress differed appreciably from that which the SNA had endorsed in 1914, the Society now demurred at the concept of "forced" subdivision. The Asamblea de Agricultores, convened in 1919 to marshal opposition to the various emerging threats to landowner interests, dealt with the land tenure issue and forwarded its conclusions to Congress. The report affirmed the desirability of family property in agriculture but identified the problem as a matter of ability rather than opportunity: "In Chile everyone is a proprietor who desires to be and is capable of being one; and if only one out of every forty-one inhabitants owns property, it is simply because of every forty-one inhabitants only one has the desire and the capability to be a proprietor."[29] Demonstrating a profound insensitivity to the current problem of unemployment, the Asamblea further called for immigration of skilled agricultural workers. Thus faced with the prospect of legislative mandate, the SNA executed the first of its strategic retreats from the progressive and enlightened posture it had adopted on land tenure. Its view prevailed for the moment, as the agrarian reform question was soon eclipsed by the heated 1920 presidential campaign.

The Legislation of Agrarian Reform: 1928 and 1935

Although the urgency of the land issue waned after 1919, discussion of the question continued in the universities, in the press, and in pamphlets and books. As the decade wore on the ideal of the family farm as a boon to production, an antidote to inflation, and a bastion against subversion and revolution came to be more widely held in academic, professional, and political circles.[30] Illustrative of the ascendance of that view was the provision in the 1925 constitution that "the State will foster the convenient division of property and the constitution of family property."[31] The land issue was also kept alive by new legislative proposals in 1922 and 1926, neither of which was enacted. The stillborn bill of 1926 nonetheless was something of a turning point in the history of land legislation in that it was drawn up without express popular pressure by the conservative government of Emiliano Figueroa Larraín, with the active collaboration of the SNA. It thus marked the conversion of the SNA and of part of the conservative establishment to the tactic of moderate, government-sponsored division of land, without expropriation, as a measure of preemptive reform.[32]

Having the SNA's blessing, the Figueroa bill would possibly have become law had not Colonel Ibáñez assumed power before the legislative process was concluded. Under Ibáñez both economic development and social legislation were high priorities, and as the land question involved both concerns, it became the subject of a new and considerably stronger bill drafted in 1928 without the SNA's approval or even its knowledge. In contrast to the SNA-endorsed proposal, Ibáñez's bill envisioned division of large holdings throughout rural Chile, rather than only near cities and transportation lines, and permitted acquisition of property by expropriation when sufficient land was not freely offered for sale. The proposal cited both the economic and social advantages to be derived from dividing the large holdings.[33]

Although opposed to these and other features of the Ibáñez bill, the SNA was not at full liberty to articulate its position under the prevailing political conditions. Its public response, then, was very limited: Director Francisco Encina published an article in *La Nación* supporting the concept of land division in general but warning of the dangers inherent in expropriation. The Society's *Boletín* reprinted the Encina article and made some innocuous comments of its own.[34] These mild public gestures combined with an unknown quantity of private lobbying were sufficient, however, to persuade Congress to water down the provisions regarding expropriation while otherwise passing the bill intact.

Law 4496 of December 10, 1928, created Chile's first instrument for state intervention in the subdivision of agricultural property. The designation of the agency as the Caja de Colonización Agrícola obscured the real purpose of the law. The concept of "colonizing"—settling vacant lands and bringing them into production—had little meaning in that unclaimed land suitable for cultivation without irrigation had virtually disappeared from Chile by the 1920s.[35] The bill explicitly stated that its primary intent was "to subdivide property, intensify and organize production, [and] promote the constitution of family property." Moreover the statement that "thousands" of small owners were to be seated on "our best soils" could not have been an allusion to pioneer colonists clearing the forests of Aysén or conquering the desert in Antofagasta.[36] Law 4496, rather, was contemplated as the cutting edge of a program of agrarian reform for Chile, to be complemented by other rural development measures of the Ibáñez government, including road construction and improvement, extension of credit, fostering of cooperatives, irrigation projects, and other steps designed to modernize the rural sector. Despite the terminology, the Caja de Colonización was designed to carry out a moderate program for gradually replacing haciendas with family farms.

The Caja was established in 1929 as a semiautonomous agency to administer a working capital of $100 million, which it was to receive in four annual installments. Property was to be acquired by purchase whenever possible at no more than 25 percent above assessed value. Expropriation was permitted if sufficient land was not offered for sale, but it could be used only to acquire the following categories of lands: those within 15 kilometers of railroad stations or ports and 5 kilometers of main roads or navigable rivers, those over 300 hectares north of the Maule River or 500 south of it, and those deemed not intensively cultivated. Recipients of parcels were to be experienced agriculturists and preferably landless. Parcels were to be a maximum of twenty hectares. The Caja's governing board consisted of two representatives of settled colonists, two of the agricultural societies, and seven bureaucrats and presidential appointees.[37]

Did law 4496 create an instrument capable of generating sufficient subdivision to have an impact on production and on the overall pattern of the land tenure? McBride was very optimistic about the possibilities of creating family farms through the direct action of the Caja and the stimulus to voluntary subdivision provided by the possibility of expropriation: "It would seem that the end of the excessively large property has arrived or at least that, even if some of these great estates continue to exist, beside them will be created a multitude of small farms which will carry on a great part of the agriculture of the country."[38] But Adolfo Matthei, an agronomist and proponent of agrarian reform, wrote more guardedly of the law: "Although it merits several objections, it would have been able to effect a substantial alteration in the country's agrarian structure, as long as its application were carried out with the right criteria and with sufficient energy to subdivide the large haciendas."[39]

Overall, a less sanguine assessment was probably warranted. The restrictions on expropriation combined with the authorized level of financing would have prevented even the most vigorous administration from making a frontal attack on the hacienda system.[40] On the other hand, and discounting inflation, the Caja de Colonización as originally constituted could have generated by its direct action several hundred family-sized holdings per year and encouraged private division of lands, and within thirty years it might have made significant progress toward its goal of creating a productive rural middle class. The efficacy of law 4496, however, was never put to the test. Due to the onset of the depression the Caja received only a fraction of the promised capital, and unsettled political conditions after 1930 further affected its functioning. By 1935 only some 600 colonist families had been settled.[41]

A new drive for agrarian reform began in 1933 when President Alessandri introduced legislation to revitalize and extend the flagging program. Several factors explain the second attempt to institutionalize a moderate, ongoing agrarian reform. Perhaps most important was the growth of political forces of the left and center to whom agrarian reform had become an article of faith. The Marxist parties and the Chilean Confederation of Labor by now embraced division of large holdings as an end in itself and as a strategy for attacking the oligarchy, while a variety of moderate reformist groups including the Radicals, Democrats, and various Catholic factions viewed it as a means of enacting their democratic social and political ideals.[42] The Democrats, a very moderate party by the thirties, had insisted on Alessandri's endorsement of land division as a condition of their electoral support in 1932.[43] Beyond that, the harrowing experience of the depression and the Socialist Republic had apparently heightened the appeal to conservatives of moderate land distribution as an antidote to the growth of political radicalism. Carlos Keller reflected this view when he wrote in 1932: "Chilean landowners have the alternatives of turning over voluntarily and without compensation a part of their lands, or losing them completely."[44] Within the SNA's board of directors, there was general agreement that wider distribution of agricultural property would serve as a bulwark against revolution.[45]

Alessandri's promotion of agrarian reform was also consistent with his general approach of preventive reform to shore up the social and political system. Moreover, during his early years in office Alessandri attempted to achieve a broad base of support—what he called a "national government"—by carefully balancing his programs, and agrarian reform may be seen in that context. Under extreme pressure from the landowner associations, his government had suspended the right of unionization for agricultural workers in early 1933, without a convincing legal basis for the action. The introduction of his agrarian reform bill shortly thereafter was probably not a fortuitous occurrence but a calculated gesture of conciliation to the center and left.[46]

Yet another factor underlying Alessandri's action, and one cited in the preamble to his bill, was the growth of rural aspirations for land.[47] In the early thirties, there was still little evidence of peasant mobilization for land but there had been indications of interest. During the twenties, for example, there were numerous reports which linked the success of union organizers to their promises to divide the land.[48] More substantive evidence is provided by the unexpectedly large demand for parcels offered by the Caja de Colonización: by 1935 the Caja had enrolled over 4,000 "aspirantes a colonos" (applicants for land) and rejected over 8,000 unsolicited applications for lack of proper documentation. A large proportion of the successful applicants were city dwellers with political connections rather than the intended recipients, but one would suspect that among the applicants rejected for failure to provide the necessary certificates of birth and good character were rural workers ignorant of the requirement or unable to obtain the documents.[49] Some sources reported that it was common for workers to manifest their desire for parcels informally and outside the prescribed channels, particularly when they saw others receiving land. Finally, the well-known incident at Ránquil, in which carabineros killed several campesinos occupying land they claimed was theirs, occurred in 1934 while Alessandri's bill was stalled in Congress. This demonstration of the volatility of the land question may have softened the resistance to the bill's enactment.[50]

Despite having won an important round on unionization, the SNA and other societies showed no tendency toward conciliation on the Alessandri bill. From the landowner viewpoint, the objectionable changes envisioned in the bill included the collectivization of some colonies and a large increase in the Caja's capital endowment. The most crucial and dangerous aspects of the bill, however, were the elimination of most restrictions on expropriation contained in law 4496 and the removal of agricultural society representatives from the Caja's governing council.[51]

Although the SNA had raised few objections to the functioning of the

Caja de Colonización since its inception, it and the other agricultural societies now marshaled their resources to fight the Alessandri bill, which they claimed would involve "the unconditional surrender of the right [of property] to the whims of government."[52] The societies' public actions included petitions to the president and Congress, extensive use of the press, and extraordinary summit meetings of the presidents of all societies to stake out a "national" agrarian position vis-à-vis the bill. McBride reported rumors that at least some landowners advocated using the Milicia Republicana as a last resort to prevent the bill's enactment.[53] The societies' representatives were so concerned about the bill's passage that they publicly proposed as an alternative a progressive land tax to stimulate voluntary subdivision.[54]

An exchange of public letters between the societies' presidents and Alessandri revealed an interesting shift in landowners' views about agrarian reform. Now, under the threat of a law that could be used against them, they implicitly abandoned the ideal of the family farm if it were to be legislated into existence. Their main defense was that passage of the Alessandri law would produce fears and insecurity among landowners, adversely affecting production and clearly jeopardizing the national interest. They affirmed their support of colonization in the strict sense but opposed the pending legislation precisely because its purpose was something else: "We judge that the bill is mistakenly labeled a colonization bill because the majority of its provisions are directed more toward subdividing cultivated property than toward settling new lands for production."[55] Alessandri answered the societies' objections with rhetoric that might have been borrowed from an old SNA editorial, stating that his bill's purpose was "to subdivide property in order to increase agricultural exploitation and production and to tie to the soil the greatest possible number of the inhabitants of the Republic, which will signify greater security and stability of the socioeconomic order."[56]

The new agrarian reform statute, law 5604, substantially altered existing property rights by strengthening governmental authority over agricultural land. The law continued the clear emphasis on subdivision over colonization, removed previous geographic and size restrictions on expropriation, and granted the Caja $100 million and authorized it to borrow $300 million more, thus potentially quadrupling its capital endowment. Congress did amend Alessandri's bill to restore landowner representation in the Caja's governing council; in fact, the agricultural societies' seats were expanded from two to five. However, the council also contained the minister of lands and colonization and his deputy; the president, director, and subdirector of the Caja; and an "independent" agronomist and three colonist representatives, all appointed by the government. Since all business, including the decision to expropriate, required a simple majority vote, government control over nine of fourteen council members assured that the Caja's policies would reflect the disposition of each administration toward agrarian reform.[57]

Despite the enhancement of its authority after 1935, the reformed Caja still operated under two important restraints, irrespective of the regime in power. First, since ample land was always available for purchase, the law precluded use of the Caja's powers of expropriation. Thus the Caja could not force the subdivision of large estates.[58] Second, the Caja was required to pay in cash the full value of all land it acquired. With this limitation, and calculating the total cost of settling a colonist family at $30,000, Matthei estimated that the Caja could install some 10,000 colonists on its initial capital investment. However, the subsequent pace of agrarian reform would be hampered by the lengthy period (forty-two years) over which recipients amortized their debts to the Caja. Without additional funding, or without cutting back on the social overhead investments that constituted a large share of the cost per parcel, the Caja would be restricted to creating additional family farms at a very modest pace.[59]

In its remaining years, the Alessandri government used the new law to revive Caja activity moderately. By this time the problem of inflation—which ultimately proved fatal—had begun to affect the Caja's prospects for future operation. The 4 percent interest that colonists paid on their mortgages was too little to reconstitute the Caja's working capital, and rising credit costs began to limit its ability to borrow at authorized interest rates, hampering the accumulation of investment capital.[60] Thus, when it came to power in December 1938, the Popular Front government assumed control of an instrument with substantial legal powers for creating family farms but also with financial constraints that threatened to jeopardize its mission over the long run.[61]

Agrarian Reform under the Popular Front

Agrarian reform was a more prominent issue in the 1938 presidential campaign than it had ever been before. Juan Chacón Corona, national agrarian chairman of the Communist party, reported that the land question had been central to the Communists' first serious campaign in rural areas: "We carried out a very extensive effort, linking the electoral question with the fight against the latifundio. We gave birth to the agrarian reform issue in Chile."[62] The Popular Front's program also stressed acceleration of land division and formally distinguished between "colonization" and "agrarian reform," emphasizing the latter.[63] And following the election, the Popular Front's new director of the Caja de Colonización asserted in an interview that he considered the agency not simply a colonization service but "a true institute of agrarian reform."[64]

Although consensus existed within the Popular Front coalition on the importance of agrarian reform, there were two basic and ultimately incompatible ideas of what agrarian reform should be. The Marxist groups stood for expropriation of all large private holdings; they not only believed in socialization of property in principle but also considered agrarian reform a strategy for attacking the oligarchy at its most vulnerable and critical spot. The Communist party's secretary general, Carlos Contreras Labarca, called agrarian reform "the central problem of Chile" and the latifundio "the material base of the Chilean counterrevolution."[65] The Socialist party's Central Committee endorsed the thesis that "breaking the latifundio is taking away from the oligarchy its power of preeminence as a class."[66]

The Radicals held a less doctrinaire and uniform vision of agrarian reform. Reflecting the views of its socially diverse component groups, the Radical party advocated the creation of family farms but not necessarily the elimination of large agricultural units. As president of the republic, Pedro Aguirre Cerda was the most prominent Radical spokesman and moreover was the party's leading authority on agrarian problems and a large landowner himself. Aguirre Cerda had long been a proponent of agrarian reform; he had sponsored a land reform bill in 1922 which went beyond the other pre-Ibáñez proposals in its scope. In his book *El problema agrario*, published in 1929, Aguirre Cerda had expressed the view that while the family farm was the ideal agrarian unit, efficient and productive large holdings whose workers were paid and treated fairly were not antisocial and need not be broken up.[67] The president-elect summarized his approach in a postelection interview: "We do not intend to 'Mexicanize' Chile. We can profit from Mexico's advances, but also from her mistakes. . . . If large properties show themselves economically inefficient, their lands will be divided . . . and given to those who want plots and are capable of working them. We desire to increase the number of small farmers and thus provide a social basis for political democracy."[68]

The differing objectives of Radicals and Marxists led to divergent approaches to the common goal of accelerating agrarian reform. Considering existing law inadequate for eradicating the large estate, the left advocated new, stronger agrarian reform legislation. The Radicals, satisfied to create family farms side by side with existing large holdings, sought primarily to remedy the financial constraints that had begun to affect the Caja's operations and to promote subdivision of large property by indirect means. The left's hopes for new legislation were short-lived; the Socialists, acting on their own, sponsored a bill in 1939 to vastly increase Caja powers by authorizing payment for inefficiently exploited land in long-term, low-yield bonds. Lacking Radical support, this bill quickly died in committee without reaching the floor of Congress.[69]

Despite the significant differences between Marxists and Radicals, both elements supported or at least condoned four approaches to intensifying the agrarian reform process, two of which involved legislation. Following the earthquake that devastated the Chillán area in February 1939, the government requested a special appropriation of $180 million for the Caja to establish model colonies in that zone as part of the reconstruction effort. The amount requested would have expanded the authorized capital endowment of the Caja by nearly 50 percent and more than doubled the capital currently available.[70] A second Popular Front initiative was a bill to tax uncultivated lands as a stimulus to voluntary subdivision, such as the SNA had proposed in 1934 as an alternative to Alessandri's agrarian reform bill. The defeat of these two legislative proposals revealed that the rightist majority in the Senate was clearly indisposed to grant the Popular Front any additional leverage over rural property and forced the government to operate within the existing legal and financial constraints.[71]

Therefore, as a third strategy, the Popular Front turned to increasing the tempo and scope of the Caja's activities. In the division of cabinet posts among the coalition parties (the Communists accepted none), the Socialists received the Ministry of Lands and Colonization. The two Socialists who occupied the post, Carlos Alberto Martínez and Rolando Merino Reyes, were much more active and visible than any of their predecessors. The director of the Caja de Colonización, Leoncio Chaporro, was a Socialist agronomist and author of tracts condemning the large estate.[72] Though committed to a more sweeping agrarian reform than existing conditions permitted, these officials proved very adept at the art of the possible.

Under Chaporro, the Caja accelerated the creation of new parcels and increased social overhead investment in its colonies. In its first ten years, the Caja had seated 1,083 families, an average of 108 per year. In 1939 and 1940, the Caja seated 240 and 310 families respectively—an average of 275 annually. A total of 1,083 parcels was granted in 1939 and 1940, compared with 1,325 for the previous ten years. Since large families received extra parcels or portions of parcels, these figures indicate that the number of people receiving land under the Popular Front almost equaled the record of the previous ten years. Concurrently the Caja vastly increased improvement loans to colonists, granting over $14 million in comparison with $9 million between 1929 and 1938. It also established schools and various social and technical services and began installing cooperatives—required by law but heretofore not implemented. Meanwhile it continued acquiring land for future use. Overall, these concrete results of Caja activity indicate something of the potential for agrarian reform within the framework of law 5604.[73]

The final strategy for promoting agrarian reform was less direct and immediate but potentially much more effective in the long run than the Popular Front's other actions. This approach was to generate demand for agrarian reform in order to break down congressional resistance to new legislation or at least to popularize the land issue in the hope of electing a more sympathetic Congress in 1941 and thereafter. This involved a dual strategy of publicizing in the urban context the desirability of agrarian reform and simultaneously promoting the articulation of demands for land among the rural masses. These activities, carried out primarily within the Ministry of Lands and Colonization and the Caja itself, while undoubtedly annoying to the more conservative faction of the Radicals, were tolerated throughout most of the Aguirre Cerda government as a necessary concession to Popular Front unity.

The Caja de Colonización began publishing its own monthly magazine, *Tierra Chilena*, disseminating information on its activities and in general educating the literate urban public to the campesino's situation and desires. It also took out advertisements in various press organs to promote the benefits of agrarian reform for the country as a whole.[74] On the rural front, the Caja launched a campaign to enroll "aspirantes a colonos" through heavy advertising as well as decentralizing and simplifying enrollment procedures. The minister of lands and colonization used the radio frequently to reach rural audiences; and, foreshadowing the activism of agrarian reform officials in the 1960s and '70s, ministry and Caja personnel traveled extensively, meeting with groups of potential land recipients and encouraging them to organize and articulate their desire for land. The government and individual parties of the coalition supported and subsidized several ostensibly national congresses of rural groups which advocated agrarian reform as well as rural unions and other reforms—a Convención de la Tierra in December 1938, and the following year the Congreso de Colonos, the Primer Congreso Nacional del Campesinado Chileno, and others. Meanwhile, enjoying a new relative freedom of access to rural society, the Marxist parties were actively educating the rural masses to organize and demand land.[75]

The result of these activities was, for the first time in Chile, a ground swell of demand for land among the rural populace. News of conventions, demonstrations, and petitions for land suddenly became prominent in 1939, not only in the sympathetic organs but also in the opposition press. Enrollment in the Caja's official waiting list doubled in 1939 and 1940 from approximately 6,000 to 12,000, and Caja officials assured the public that the unqualified urban applicants with political connections had been purged from the registry. Meanwhile thousands more initiated the procedures for enrolling, many of these in collective petitions which were not accepted.[76]

More important and better publicized was the grass roots movement which sprang up throughout rural Chile, presaging the peasant mobilization for land in the 1960s and early '70s. Associations of "aspirantes a colonos" were formed in many localities, held meetings or regional congresses, and petitioned the government for land. Unorganized workers on individual fundos commonly petitioned for division of the land they worked. "Marchas de la tierra" took place in various areas, including a march of over 5,000 persons in Temuco in August 1939.[77] An observer of rural Chile in 1939 or 1940 might well have given credence to the warning expressed in the preamble of the Socialists' stillborn agrarian reform bill: "If this law is not passed, if we do not make agrarian reform a reality, tomorrow the people may try to impose it in their own fashion and by force, because the people are now fully and consciously aware that it is in the land that they will find the well-being which has been denied them until now."[78]

Faced with these Popular Front attempts to accelerate agrarian reform, the SNA adopted a position calculated to contain the process within the existing legal and financial framework. Thus it offered no major objection to the Caja's increased pace of subdivision and investment; indeed, the Caja's lavish expenditures, in the context of inflation, would hasten the collapse of its solvency and, without additional financing, of agrarian reform itself. Secure in the knowledge that the rightist-controlled Senate would tolerate no additional weakening of property rights while the Popular Front was in power, the SNA took no active public role in the defeat of the Socialist agrarian reform bill or the government's bill to tax uncultivated land—both of which it opposed.[79] However, the SNA reacted vigorously to the Marxist-fostered rise of demands for land, which it perceived as the most dangerous of the Popular Front's initiatives to promote agrarian reform, and frequently denounced "actions against property rights on the part of extremist elements who openly preach the complete socialization of the land."[80]

The SNA's strategy for combatting the growth of demands for agrarian reform was inextricably connected with its broader opposition to leftist penetration of the countryside under the Popular Front. Both landowners and the Marxist parties recognized that organization of the rural masses was the key to fully developing the burgeoning demand for agrarian reform and channeling it effectively into the political system. During 1939 and 1940, the Communists and Socialists launched major rural campaigns of proselytization, in which they relied on union and party organization to institutionalize the demand for land and to wrest the rural vote from landowner control. The SNA, then, with the close support of the conservative parties, concentrated on the fight against unionization and free political recruitment as its primary strategy to undercut the incipient campesino mobilization for land. Its success in thwarting leftist penetration of the countryside, discussed in chapter 7, confined agrarian reform within the provisions of law 5604 and, as had been foreseen, soon spelled the end of Chile's first cycle of agrarian reform.

After the collapse of the Popular Front, no government made serious efforts to promote agrarian reform until the 1960s. However, the frustrated agrarian reform of the twenties and thirties is more than a historical curiosity. The outcome of this first cycle of agrarian reform undoubtedly influenced the nature of agrarian reform in the sixties and seventies. The proponents of preemptive, evolutionary agrarian reform such as was embodied in the 1928 and 1935 laws had definite social and political, as well as economic, purposes in mind. They frankly stated their hope of stabilizing the social structure, their intention of distributing property as an antidote to revolution. If their assumptions were correct, and if they had succeeded in creating 20,000 or 30,000 productive, middle-class family farmers by 1960, the more radical Frei and Allende agrarian reforms might not have occurred. As it was, however, when the right and the SNA finally agreed to a second program of moderate agrarian reform in 1962, their efforts were too little and too late to preempt the serious reformers.

Notes

1. University of Wisconsin, Land Tenure Center, *Agrarian Reform in Latin America: An Annotated Bibliography* (Madison, Wis., 1974), 246-303. See the *Handbook of Latin American Studies* for recent items. A preliminary version of this chapter was read at the annual meeting of the Pacific Coast Council on Latin American Studies in October 1976, and published in the council's *Proceedings*, 6 (1977-79), 59-71.

2. Chonchol, "Poder y reforma agraria," pp. 50-87.

3. Gil, *Political System*, p. 78.

4. Kaufman, *Politics of Land Reform*, p. 45.

5. E.g., Loveman, *Struggle in the Countryside*, p. 223.

6. Marvin J. Sternberg, "Chilean Land Tenure and Land Reform" (unpublished dissertation in economics, University of California, Berkeley, 1962), p. 129.

7. Land tenure studies include: Comité Interamericano de Desarrollo Agrícola (CIDA), *Chile: Tenencia de la tierra y desarrollo socio-económico del sector agrícola* (Santiago, 1966); Gene Ellis Martin, *La división de la tierra en Chile central* (Santiago, 1960); Jean Borde and Mario Góngora, *Evolución de la propiedad rural en el Valle del Puangue*, 2 vols. (Santiago, 1956); Rafael Baraona, Ximena Aranda, and Roberto Santana, *Valle de Putaendo: estudio de estructura agraria*

(Santiago, 1960); and Universidad de Chile, Instituto de Economía, *Subdivisión de la propiedad agrícola en una región de la zona central de Chile* (Santiago, 1960). Bauer's *Chilean Rural Society* deals with the historical evolution of landed property in the whole of central Chile.

8. A fine case study of subdivision in the nineteenth century is Arnold J. Bauer, "The Hacienda el Huique in the Agrarian Structure of Nineteenth Century Chile," *Agricultural History*, 28 (1972), 455-70.

9. Bauer, *Chilean Rural Society*, pp. 123-32; McBride, *Land and Society*, pp. 232-42.

10. McBride, *Land and Society*, pp. 240-41.

11. Bauer, *Chilean Rural Society*, p. 129 (Table 26).

12. McBride, *Land and Society*, pp. 253-55.

13. *Ibid.*, p. 243; Borde and Góngora, *Evolución de la propiedad*, 1, 170-75, discuss this phenomenon in a zone relatively near Santiago.

14. Poblete Troncoso, *Problema de la producción*, p. 31.

15. Sternberg, "Chilean Land Tenure," p. 34.

16. Bauer, "Chilean Rural Labor"; *BSNA*, 2 (1870-71), 343-47, 376-78, 386-92.

17. Guillermo Gibbs, *La tierra y el inquilinaje* (Santiago, 1890).

18. Figures (annual) on the declining yields of major grain crops between 1909-10 and 1932-33 may be found in *Sinópsis geográfico y estadístico, año 1933*, pp. 144-45.

19. *BSNA*, 35 (1904), 569.

20. *Ibid.*, 45 (1914), 649.

21. *Ibid.*, 590-91, 719-21.

22. *El Mercurio*, Aug. 28, 1919, p. 19.

23. *Ibid.*, Nov. 4, 1918, p. 15.

24. *Ibid.*, Dec. 7, 1918, p. 3; *ibid.*, Dec. 8, 1918, p. 3.

25. Poblete Troncoso, *Problema de la producción*, inside cover and pp. 69-70.

26. *Ibid.*, pp. viii, ix.

27. I have not been able to locate this bill in the *Sesiones* but it is referred to in various sources, e.g., *El Mercurio*, Dec. 8, 1918, p. 3, and Encina *et al.*, "Subdivisión de la propiedad."

28. Cámara de Diputados, *Sesiones ordinarias en 1919*, pp. 705-11.

29. Encina *et al.*, "Subdivisión de la propiedad," p. 25; also in *MSNA* (1919), pp. 6-20.

30. McBride, *Land and Society*, pp. 168-70.

31. Pan American Union, *Constitution of the Republic of Chile, 1925* (Washington, D.C., 1957), p. 4 (ch. 3, art. 10, no. 10).

32. *BSNA*, 57 (1926), 573-77.

33. Cámara de Diputados, *Sesiones ordinarias en 1938*, 1, 726-30. The SNA council expressed its dismay at discovering the bill had been drawn up in Minutes, May 28, 1938, in *BSNA*, 60 (1928), 407-8.

34. *BSNA*, 60 (1928), 417-20, 547.

35. McBride, *Land and Society*, p. 256.

36. Cámara de Diputados, *Sesiones ordinarias en 1938*, 1, 726-30.

37. *Boletín de las leyes y decretos del gobierno*, libro 97 (1928), 3221-42.

38. McBride, *Land and Society*, p. 275.

39. Adolfo Matthei, *La agricultura en Chile y la política agraria chilena* (Santiago, 1939), p. 155.

40. I believe that McBride misinterpreted the law on this point. He claimed that it was seen by landowners as a serious threat to the social order and considered it an important cause of Ibáñez's fall from office two and a half years later. He failed to sense the willingness of at least some vested interests to tolerate moderate reform. McBride, *Land and Society*, p. 271.

41. Leoncio Chaporro, *Anotaciones críticas sobre el cultivo de la tierra en Chile* (Santiago, 1939), pp. 61-62; Caja de Colonización Agrícola, *Hacia una nueva vida por la colonización* (Santiago, 1941), p. 13.

42. A number of Catholic groups which favored land reform are cited in George Grayson, "The Chilean Christian Democratic Party: Genesis and Development" (unpublished dissertation in political science, Johns Hopkins University, 1967), pp. 75ff. The university theses of two future prominent Christian Democrats, Eduardo Frei and Bernardo Leighton, called for agrarian reform; both were done in 1933. Grayson, pp. 113-16.

43. Echaíz, *Evolución histórica*, p. 121.

44. Keller, *País al garete*, p. 124.

45. Minutes, Apr. 11, 1932, in *BSNA*, 64 (1932), 235-37.

46. See ch. 7, pp. 154-55.

47. Cámara de Diputados, *Sesiones extraordinarias en 1932-33*, pp. 2785-90.

48. E.g., a report in *Revista Comercial*, año XXV, no. 1228 (Sept. 10, 1921), 48,907.

49. Germán Espinoza Ferrari, "Realizaciones económicas y sociales de la ley no. 5604 sobre colonización agrícola nacional" (Memoria de Prueba, Universidad de Chile, 1940), pp. 38-40. Chaporro, *Anotaciones críticas*, pp. 9, 61, mentions a figure of 16,000 "aspirantes a colonos" for some unspecified time in the thirties—apparently referring to the period prior to passage of the Alessandri law.

50. Carlos Keller, *La eterna crisis chilena*, p. 271; *País al garete*, pp. 123-25; Affonso *et al.*, *Movimiento campesino*, pp. 26-30.

51. Cámara de Diputados, *Sesiones extraordinarias en 1932-33*, pp. 2785-90.

52. Letter from Jaime Larraín and seven other presidents or delegates of agricultural organizations to Arturo Alessandri, Sept. 10, 1934, reproduced in *MSNA* (1934), pp. 115-20 (quotation, p. 117).

53. McBride, *Land and Society*, pp. 381-82.

54. Larraín *et al.* to Alessandri, Sept. 10, 1934, in *MSNA* (1934), p. 116.

55. *Ibid.*

56. Arturo Alessandri to Jaime Larraín *et al.*, no date, reproduced in *MSNA* (1934), pp. 121-22 (quotation, p. 121).

57. *Boletín de las leyes y decretos del gobierno*, libro 104 (1935), 395-439; Caja de Colonización Agrícola, *Hacia una nueva vida*, pp. 43-45.

58. McBride, *Land and Society*, pp. 256-77, cites ample land for sale. Adolfo Matthei, *Política agraria chilena*, p. 52, denounces prices paid for land by the Caja in its early years as "truly scandalous." This is confirmed for the later years in Finkelstein Rosolie, "La agricultura y los organismos de fomento," pp. 123-24.

59. Matthei, *Agricultura en Chile*, p. 159; also Fernando Edwards Hurtado, "Estudios sobre política de colonización interior" (Memoria de Prueba, Universidad de Chile, 1939), pp. 52-53.

60. Sternberg, "Chilean Land Tenure," p. 129.

61. The number of university theses written on agrarian reform after 1935 reflected a growth of interest in the question. In addition to the already cited theses of Edwards Hurtado and Espinoza Ferrari, the following theses were done on agrarian

reform (all are from the Facultad de Ciencias Jurídicas y Sociales, Universidad de Chile): Víctor García, "El problema de la colonización" (1936); Eduardo Long, "La propiedad en la ley sobre colonización agrícola" (1937); Rodolfo Fuenzalida Ríos, "El latifundio y el problema de la división de la tierra" (1939); Jorge Marshall Silva, "La lucha por la reforma agraria" (1941); Hugo Trivelli F., "Expansión y estructura agrarias en Chile" (1941); and René Labarca Letelier, "Subproducción agrícola y sistema de propiedad ante la estadística chilena" (1943).

62. José Miguel Varas, *Chacón* (Santiago, 1968), p. 108.

63. The Popular Front program appeared in *El Mercurio*, Apr. 15, 1938, p. 21; see also Stevenson, *Chilean Popular Front*, pp. 82-85.

64. *El Mercurio*, June 25, 1939, p. 38.

65. *El Siglo*, Oct. 7, 1940, p. 4.

66. Partido Socialista de Chile, Comité Central Ejecutivo, *Tesis sindical presentada al V Congreso del Partido celebrado en Santiago en diciembre de 1938* (Santiago, 1939), unpaginated.

67. Aguirre Cerda, *El problema agrario*.

68. C. H. Haring, "Chile Moves Left," *Foreign Affairs*, 17 (1938-39), 622.

69. Cámara de Senadores, *Sesiones ordinarias en 1939*, pp. 1715-31.

70. *El Mercurio*, June 6, 1940, p. 17; *ibid.*, June 7, 1940, p. 13.

71. Cámara de Diputados, *Sesiones ordinarias en 1940*, pp. 3845-53, contains some of the debate on this bill.

72. In addition to his previously cited *Anotaciones críticas*, Chaporro had earlier written *Colonización y reforma agraria: hacia una distribución mas justa de la tierra en Chile* (Santiago, 1932).

73. Caja de Colonización Agrícola, *Hacia una nueva vida*, esp. pp. 9, 13-15.

74. E.g., a full-page ad in *Acción Social*, año XI, no. 91 (Aug. 1940), unpaginated.

75. The best sources for these activities are the daily press and the Caja's *Tierra Chilena*; I have found no reference to the ministers' and the Caja's roles under the Popular Front in the secondary literature.

76. Caja de Colonización Agrícola, *Memoria, años 1939-40* (Santiago, 1942), p. 73. Espinoza Ferrari, "Realizaciones económicas," pp. 38-40, estimated that at least 30,000 individuals had made some "gestiones" to enroll between 1929 and 1940.

77. Reference to these developments in the countryside is found almost daily during much of 1939 and 1940 in *El Mercurio* and the rest of the Santiago daily press. *Tierra Chilena* also reported on the rise of rural demand for land. After its founding in August 1940, *El Siglo* had a daily page dedicated to rural struggles. See also Minutes, Oct. 30, 1939, in *El C*, 71 (1939), 819-20.

78. Cámara de Senadores, *Sesiones ordinarias en 1939*, p. 1724.

79. *El C*, 73 (1941), 435.

80. *El Mercurio*, May 22, 1939, p. 15.

7

Landowners and Rural Labor

The recent revolutionary transformation of the Chilean countryside stimulated considerable historical research into the antecedents of the campesino mass movement. These investigations have uncovered the beginnings of social unrest and political activity in the countryside as far back as 1919 and in the process have convincingly shattered the myth of a passive and completely marginal peasantry prior to the 1960s.[1] Even though the early movements for unionization, the petitions, and the strikes were usually inspired and directed by urban labor cadres, the Chilean agricultural worker proved a willing follower and demonstrated the potential for autonomous collective action. Analysis from the landowner's viewpoint confirms that although relatively little was achieved before the sixties, the issues of unionization and the condition of rural labor were important ones in national politics and major preoccupations of the SNA.

The question of whether agricultural workers were to enjoy the legal right to unionize on the same basis as industrial labor was the greatest direct concern of both landowners and spokesmen for rural workers. As suggested earlier, the formation of unions implied much more than the creation of instruments for regulating labor relations; it would also provide the necessary means of organizing a rural political force independent of landowner control and consequently could jeopardize the conservative advantage in national politics as well as raise the prospect of effective agrarian reform. Unionization was not, however, the only issue involving relations between landowners and their labor force. Minimum wage laws, housing and nutritional standards, and the application of social security legislation were recurring themes between 1919 and 1940. In a general sense the basic issue was whether, and to what degree, the rural working class would attain the benefits of the labor and social welfare legislation of the twenties and thirties, which in general drew no distinction between urban and rural occupations.

Although the prospect of unionization was the paramount concern of landowners, all intrusions of the state into the landowner's traditional autonomy in labor relations and welfare were viewed as challenges to proprietary authority. While the questions of unionization and welfare (wages, housing, social security benefits, etc.) can be and have been treated separately, from the perspective of the political process they form a single complex, multifaceted issue. In fighting the threat of unionization, and against the backdrop of their eroding political power, landowners had to offer increasingly important concessions, both token and substantive, in the areas of housing, wages, and other benefits. In view of their very close interrelationship in the dynamic of politics, then, unionization and welfare will be examined as aspects of a single issue.

The Intellectual Background

About a century elapsed between the visits of the two foreigners who left classic accounts of rural life in Chile. Claudio Gay, the French natural historian, spent several years in Chile in the 1830s, and George McBride, the geographer from UCLA, made his observations in the 1920s and early '30s.[2] There are two things significant for our present concern about their comments on rural labor. First, McBride thought that the labor system he witnessed had not changed appreciably since the visit of Gay, or even earlier, and his belief was apparently widely shared by his Chilean contemporaries.[3] Second, despite his very critical remarks, Gay found the Chilean system of resident or inquilino labor quite acceptable, even desirable, by the European standards of his day, while McBride was deeply offended by the continuation of the "master-man" relationship into the twentieth century.[4] Although his warnings about the awakening consciousness of the peasantry were exaggerated, McBride's concerns were the subject of heated controversy after 1919.

All observers of the rural scene distinguished between the two main classes of agricultural worker—the inquilino, or resident worker attached voluntarily to the fundo, and the *afuerino* or peón, the seasonal worker with no ties to a particular fundo. In exchange for his labor and that of his family and sometimes others, the inquilino normally received a small cash wage, a dwelling of sorts, a ration of food, a small garden plot, and often the right to graze a few animals. Although lacking in prospects of upward mobility, the inquilino did enjoy relative security of tenure and a certain minimum level of subsistence. The peón, drawn from the smallholders and floating population of the Central Valley and the coastal range, worked for a daily wage and ration of food during harvest and other periods of peak labor demand. The peón lacked security altogether, earned barely subsistence wages while he worked, and, as the rural population increased, found it increasingly difficult to eke out a living. The peón, then, was the

Table 16
Composition of the Chilean Rural Labor Force, 1935-36[6]

Categories	Inquilinos (heads of households)	Peones or Gañanes (workers who are members of inquilino or empleado households)	Afuerinos (workers who are not members of inquilino or empleado households)	Empleados (blacksmiths, bookkeepers, warehouse keepers, etc.)	Total Workers
No. of workers	107,906	106,371	94,797	30,598	339,672
Percentage of total	31.8	31.3	27.9	9.0	100.0

SOURCE: Dirección General de Estadística, *Agricultura, 1935-36: censo*, p. 34.

typical migrant to the city, the nitrate and copper mines, and abroad.[5] The 1935-36 agricultural census provided an analysis of rural labor by type (see Table 16).

Contrary to McBride's perception, the labor system had undergone substantial change since colonial times. Rather than being replaced by a more modern system, however, inquilinaje had been tightened up and reinforced in response to Chile's imperfect incorporation into the Atlantic economy, so that the inquilino of 1910 or 1930 worked more for less real wages than his ancestors had. A few critics of the rural labor system, such as Tancredo Pinochet LeBrun, sensed the real deterioration in the inquilino's situation; but once the institution came under fire in the twentieth century, it was damning enough to know that the contemporary labor system was generically the same as colonial inquilinaje.[7]

The institution of inquilinaje was discussed intermittently and generally critically during the nineteenth century.[8] The emigration of thousands of Chileans to Peru in the late 1860s in search of construction jobs on Henry Meiggs's railroads set off a prolonged inquiry into the underlying causes of the exodus. Although the unattached peón undoubtedly emigrated in far greater numbers than the resident worker, the debate—carried out largely in the pages of the SNA's *Boletín*—focused on the nature of inquilinaje and its possible deficiencies.[9] British consul Horace Rumbold wrote in 1876 that "it has become the fashion in this country to attribute most of the evils complained of to the system known as 'inquilinaje.'"[10]

The emergence of an organized and radical proletariat in the cities and the nitrate mines, the spread of strikes, and the bloody repressions following the turn of the century brought the "social question" to the fore in Chile. It became practically de rigeur for a successful or aspiring public figure to enunciate his particular wisdom about the lower orders, so that after 1900 Chile was inundated with books, pamphlets, lectures, university theses, social novels, and newspaper articles analyzing the "social question" and offering prescriptions for its solution.[11] The working classes of the cities and the nitrate zone received the bulk of the attention, since they were the active problem, but the fear that class conflict might spread to the country motivated several inquiries into the condition of agricultural labor.

The most influential social novel of the period, Augusto Orrego Luco's *Casa Grande*, took the upper classes to task for virtually everything, including their use of rural labor. On the protagonist's family estate "the inquilino was considered as the serf of the Middle Ages, and the *patrón* gave orders with sovereign and unappealable authority, despotically." As a result, Orrego Luco affirmed, "the art of exploiting one's neighbor was a highly developed skill" among landowners in general.[12] In the same year, 1908, the SNA published a three-part editorial on the "social question" which dealt primarily with the urban working class, but it also warned that the condition of rural labor required remedial action:

> Although our distinguished habitual readers may feel offended, they will permit us to affirm that most hacendados have done little, very little, to improve the condition of their workers. With rare exceptions, the existence of the inquilinos is as miserable and forsaken today as it was in the most remote times. Dwellings—if certain hovels (*ranchos*) deserve that name—food, moral treatment, everything is so rudimentary, that there are details in which the line separating animals from human beings is barely perceptible.[13]

El Mercurio reiterated the theme three years later: "The form in which labor is constituted in agriculture is simply monstrous in our country; it is unworthy of a civilized country and an affront to Chilean landowners. . . . We are in the presence of an antisocial regime which sooner or later will cause violent reactions if the directing classes do not hasten to prevent them."[14]

Indicative of the growth of interest in the agricultural worker, the Radical party's program of 1912 for the first time advocated improvements for rural as well as industrial workers.[15] The following year the Catholic University sponsored the First Agrarian Social Week, a seminar designed to "orient and shape the consciences of those who direct, the patrones."[16] The speakers emphasized landowners' Christian duty to improve the material and moral condition of their workers but, as reflected in the following passage, there was little hint of concern about a possible breakdown of the traditional master-man relationship: "Given the state of dependence in which the field worker of Chile normally lives, and his rudimentary culture, one cannot expect the improvement of his material and moral condition through his own initiative. The masters, then, are those called upon to take the initiative in this chore in Chile, and they are the only ones whose intervention will always be effective, given the unrivalled influence they enjoy over their subordinates."[17] But the first Chilean university thesis on rural labor, finished the same year, presented a much less sanguine picture of the landowner's command. It predicted strikes and violence in the countryside as a result of the prevailing misery of the populace and the spread of socialist ideas.[18]

The most widely circulated tract on rural labor, in all probability, was the series of articles by muckraking journalist Tancredo Pinochet LeBrun which originally appeared in *La Opinión* of Santiago and in book form in 1916. Pinochet and a colleague visited the fundo of President Sanfuentes near Talca, disguised as peones looking for work, and experienced at first hand the reality of rural life. His impressions, conveyed in the form of letters to Sanfuentes, are summarized in the following passage:

> Your inquilino earns now, Excellency, about a third of what he did two generations ago. Do you understand that? Economically, there are no hopes for the subhuman of the fief. His destiny is fixed: his curve is downward, inflexibly descendant. Those beasts have suffered, have been hungry, have slept and eaten sprawled on the ground, without hope of saving enough so that their grandchildren might buy handkerchiefs or combs. During that same span of time, the Chilean agriculturist, the hacendado, has filled Santiago with palaces and automobiles, not as fruits of the talent with which they have run their haciendas but through the way they have exploited the slaves of the fief.[19]

Pinochet concluded with the following plea:

> The inquilino, resigned, submissive, has supported generations of slavery. All measures have been taken to avoid awakening the conscience of the human beast. But there are no architects capable, Excellency, of building walls to detain the flow of civilizing currents. And in this solemn moment, the act of supreme responsibility is your duty. You must hear the palpitations of the popular soul; you must hear clamors, supplications which later may become orders, impositions.[20]

Pinochet's warnings went unheeded by the directing groups, but his powers of prophecy were to be substantiated sooner than even he anticipated.

The Opening Round of Conflict

The earliest challenges to the autonomy of landowners in dealings with their workers arose out of the general social and political ferment of 1919–20. The first development was the appearance of a bill to regulate inquilino housing, introduced in Congress in 1919.[21] Of far greater consequence was the beginning in the same year of the campaign of rural unionization and attempts to improve working and living conditions by direct worker action—a move to extend the labor movement into the countryside. While the SNA and a wide spectrum of conservative and moderate opinion had for some time recognized the need to improve working conditions in agriculture, the SNA unalterably opposed these first attempts to force remedial action upon landowners. Although it rejected legislative solutions, the SNA nonetheless took actions in the twenties which indicated great landowner concern with new, unprecedented threats to their proprietary rights.

Landowners, shocked at the threats of rural social legislation, must have been profoundly astonished to find their loyal inquilinos taking matters into their own hands. Beginning late in 1919, rural Chile experienced the first partial breakdown of landowner control when, in isolated but widespread areas of the country, workers formed unions, petitioned for improvements, struck, and occasionally carried out acts of sabotage. Unemployed nitrate workers returning home from the north were often involved in these actions and the national labor federation (FOCh), currently growing more militant and radical, provided the organizational framework for the movement. The FOCh formed a Federal Council of Agricultural Workers in January 1921, and by the end of that year it had set up organizations between Coquimbo and Valdivia, most commonly near cities and towns. A convention of peasants of the province of Santiago was held in October 1921. The Labor Office recorded some fifty actual or attempted rural strikes throughout the country in 1921, and the FOCh threatened a general strike the same year in support of what it considered the right to organize and strike in the countryside.[22]

Landowners reacted to these developments with understandable alarm. From different parts of the country came reports that FOCh cadres were actively distributing "subversive" propaganda, promising the "abolition of property and distribution of the land," and "forcing" workers to organize.[23] The SNA was so concerned about potential violence and sabotage that it entertained a proposal to offer crop insurance to members.[24] Much more common but less publicized than strikes was the use of petitions or lists of grievances gathered by FOCh members on fundos and submitted to the Labor Office for its intervention. The issues were generally wages and perquisites, and inquilinos rather than afuerinos were the usual protagonists.[25]

The SNA responded to the disruption of landowner control in the countryside with appeals to President Alessandri for a crackdown on "subversive" activity. In a letter of May 1921, the SNA asked him to "recommend to the authorities that they strictly comply with laws protecting property and life and guaranteeing the functioning of the agricultural industry."[26] In his public reply, Alessandri reaffirmed property rights and condemned radical propaganda and any interference with the right to work. From the SNA's standpoint, however, Alessandri's answer was ambiguous and disappointing: he called on landowners to improve workers' conditions and failed to prohibit continuing organization of agricultural workers, stating only that he advised them not to organize in exactly the same manner as urban workers. In the absence of labor legislation there were no legal grounds for interfering, and Alessandri refused to do so—perhaps to demonstrate the need for passage of his pending labor bills.[27]

While Alessandri's response was thus unsatisfactory, its most onerous aspect was that he asked the Society to name a committee to discuss the "agrarian social question" with FOCh representatives. The SNA, of course, could not recognize the FOCh as spokesman for agricultural workers without tacitly affirming the existence of problems and the legitimacy of rural labor organization, and it flatly refused the invitation. On two separate occasions later in the year, however, SNA directors were subjected to humiliating experiences that demonstrated something of the new political realities; when they arrived for scheduled meetings with the president, they found Alessandri awaiting them in the company of FOCh officials. In each case, the SNA delegations refused to enter into discussions and left after delivering notes to Alessandri.[28] Overall, then, the Society obtained little satisfaction from Alessandri, whose word alone would probably have sufficed to restore order in the countryside. Therefore, landowners had to take matters into their own hands.

On the direct level, landowners met the threat of unionization and strikes with a combination of concessions and force, including blacklistings and dismissals of workers. The widespread firings of workers sparked a protest march outside of Santiago, at which police killed two FOCh members and injured several others.[29] Repressive measures were taken by individuals, by local committees of the Agrarian Union, and in many cases by the Labor Association, which was reported active in the countryside "suffocating and impeding strikes and counteracting the propaganda of subversive elements."[30] The SNA itself did not comment on the use of repressive tactics but did encourage the growth of the Agrarian Union and the Labor Association.

The SNA's public approach to the problem of rural agitation foreshadowed its later "policy of the good patrón," except that in the twenties improvements were to be voluntary rather than compulsory: "Improving one's economic and moral condition is a legitimate aspiration, and agricultural proprietors can do nothing but recognize this legitimacy and aid in its fulfillment. It is a necessity of the times, which forms an irresistible current. It is necessary to anticipate the demands that will come, and through a mutual reconciliation endeavor to unite the interests of worker and patrón for common ends."[31] If enlightened steps were taken, the SNA assured, "there will be no need to fear for the future of inquilinaje."[32]

The SNA recommended several kinds of measures. Company or professional unions, which the owner or his agents could manipulate, were encouraged as an antidote to the formation of industrial-type unions. *Boletín* articles on agricultural syndicates of the haciendas Callenque and Pullally, founded under the guidance of the League of Social Order and the Federation of Catholic Works, suggested that radicalism could be combatted by organized paternalism.[33] At the same time, the Society encouraged landowners and renters to standardize wages, perquisites, and working conditions on a local basis in order to eliminate exploitable inequalities. It also recommended such improvements as savings associations, schools, recreation centers and sports facilities such as soccer fields, better housing, producers' cooperatives that included inquilinos, conversion of the *pulpería* or fundo store into a consumers' cooperative, and distribution of seeds and implements to inquilinos in order to foster improvement of their diet. In 1923 the *Boletín* began to publish a section called "social works" to publicize means of improving workers' conditions, and the following year the SNA established an "agrarian welfare" department as a consulting service to members wishing to form white unions or initiate improvements. A medical doctor and social workers were later added to the department's staff.[34] It is impossible to know how widely the SNA's prescriptions were followed; McBride reported recent improvements in a minority of the fundos and the sprouting of soccer fields but suggested no connection with the SNA's campaign.[35]

Rural Chile was agitated intermittently through 1925; by that year, the Labor Office reported some 5,000 unionized agricultural workers.[36] Thereafter, primarily as a result of developments in national politics, calm was restored and inquilinaje granted a reprieve. Carlos Ibáñez, first as minister of the interior and later as president, systematically persecuted the FOCh, the Communist party, and other leftists. Without urban support, the rural unions collapsed. Ibáñez's extensive road-building program, combined with the definitive organization of the Carabinero Corps, greatly strengthened the government's ability to deal with future outbreaks of unrest in rural areas.

In matters of social and labor legislation affecting agriculture, the SNA in the twenties was no more ready to accept state intervention in traditionally autonomous matters than it was to concede workers the right to demand or negotiate instead of supplicating, hat in hand. The Asamblea de Agricultores had concluded that labor legislation "is neither necessary nor applicable in agriculture, nor would it yield any social improvement whatever for workers; on the contrary, its theoretical legal establishment would give rise to grave difficulties between patrones and workers, which could perturb social stability, agricultural savings, and crop yields."[37] The landowners' congress did show one glimmer of flexibility, however: while it rejected a bill to set standards for inquilino housing with a tax penalty for noncompliance, it was willing to accept such regulation if compliance were rewarded with tax reductions.[38]

The military intervention of 1924 abruptly changed the rules of the political game. Under military pressure, Congress enacted the basic social and labor laws that Alessandri had sponsored, which covered labor contracts, work accidents, arbitration and conciliation, unions, and social insurance (sickness, injury, and retirement) for wage earners and salaried employees.[39] Although various SNA directors privately expressed the desire to have these laws repealed, the SNA realistically accepted the 1924 legislation as a fait accompli and in the following years worked for the exemption of agriculture, at least from the laws' more onerous provisions. "Well inspired but impracticable" was the standard rhetoric in appealing for the suspension and "reform" of offending laws and regulations.[40] With minor exceptions, the SNA had no difficulty avoiding the application of social and labor legislation in agriculture because there existed no enforcement machinery through most of the twenties. A heightened threat of enforcement materialized in 1931, when the Ibáñez government promulgated a labor code containing revised texts of the 1924 laws. Creation of the Ministry of Labor in 1932 completed the machinery necessary to apply labor legislation in agriculture.

The 1930s: From Intransigence to Preemption

The SNA's initial response to threats in the countryside had been to appeal for executive intervention. Failing in that, it relied on the new grass roots landowner organizations to deal directly with the problem, while it began to preach a progressive brand of paternalism as the long-term solution. On the whole, the SNA rejected the legitimacy of unions and condemned the legislating of social change in agriculture. The only permissible and potentially effective means of changing the reality of peasant existence was through the voluntary efforts of landowners. In the thirties, however, increased pressure for rural reform and the SNA's adoption of the upper-class strategy dictated some flexibility in meeting the challenge to landowners' autonomy in labor relations.

Pressures for action against the rural status quo increased in part as a function of the growth of revolutionary and reformist political forces. The left saw unionization as an instrument for expanding its power at the expense of the oligarchy, while the center generally expressed the view that full citizenship rights should be extended to rural society. By the late thirties the left had spun off a number of pressure groups, such as the Liga Nacional de Defensa de los Campesinos Pobres and the Federación Nacional del Campesinado, which constantly lobbied in behalf of agricultural workers and smallholders and kept rural issues in the public eye. There were also several champions of the peasant in the Chamber of Deputies in the thirties. Foremost among them was Socialist Emilio Zapata, who used the congressional forum effectively to generate pressure for reform. Zapata's favorite political tactics were to demand labor inspections on the fundos of prominent politicians and to read into the congressional record the results of chemical analyses of food rations distributed as payment to agricultural workers.[41]

There was also an explosion of information and publicity about rural conditions from sources other than the left. The governmental statistical services carried out the first agricultural census in 1935-36, bringing to light information on varied aspects of rural life.[42] Both Catholic and lay schools of social service were established in the twenties and thirties, and their students' theses and reports generated volumes of information on rural as well as urban hygienic, nutritional, cultural, and housing conditions.[43] Law school theses probed the legal aspects of social legislation and unionization for agricultural workers.[44] The monthly *Acción Social* of the Ministry of Health and Social Welfare disseminated diverse kinds of data on social conditions, both urban and rural.[45] George McBride's book condemning the rural social structure was published in Spanish in 1938. These kinds of publicity and the political pressures exerted by the left generated even more information in the form of government-sponsored and private surveys. A government survey of several hundred rural families carried out in 1936, for example, found that wages were insufficient to support a single person adequately, and that, calculating the number of dependents per salary, agricultural labor was remunerated at impossibly low rates.[46] In almost every instance, the accumulation of information strengthened the case for reform.

Landowners also faced considerable pressure for remedial action from within the upper-class establishment. As a rule, working and living conditions on most fundos were objectively bad, presenting a convenient issue that the left constantly exploited for political advantage. Various political groups, such as the Conservative Youth and the Nazi party, called for substantive reforms in rural society, and a large segment of the right was willing to support at least moderate remedial measures. Elements of the Church were taking an active part in voluntary improvements projects, while by the end of the 1930s the Archbishop of Santiago, José María Caro, called publicly for better wages, improved working conditions, and unions for rural labor.[47] The upper-class rationale was aptly summarized in a government memorandum transmitting President Alessandri's sentiments: "Agriculturists by their example and deeds should silence the tendentious propaganda put out by certain media which desire only to undermine social stability." Such deeds moreover would contribute to a "perfect understanding and harmony between capital and the working classes—the solid base on which social peace rests."[48] The minister of agriculture, Fernando Möller, added a list of his own recommendations for landowners' actions in social improvement, including the expulsion of any members of agricultural societies who, "being able, have refused to cooperate in the efforts of social welfare."[49]

Not the least significant pressure for action in the rural sector derived from the existence of legislation and, by the thirties, of machinery for state involvement in labor relations and social welfare. After establishment of the Ministry of Labor in 1932, corps of inspectors, regional conciliation and arbitration boards, labor courts, and all the apparatus for implementation of the labor code were in place. Governments were constrained by law to grant legal status to unions, process collective labor petitions, enforce written contracts, investigate work accidents, and require employer and worker contributions to the social security systems in agriculture as in any other economic sector. Overall, the weight of both law and public administration by the thirties was on the side of bringing rural society under the umbrella of state regulation.[50]

Under Alessandri, then, the government began to apply the labor code in the countryside on a selective basis. As a result of insufficient funding the Labor Department lacked the personnel and vehicles to enforce labor law throughout rural Chile. However, within the limits of its ability, it did investigate reported violations of labor law and demand landowners' compliance when conditions warranted. The labor code also required the Ministry of Labor's mediation of all properly filed grievance petitions, whether the petitioning group was unionized or not. As Loveman's study reveals, the use of collective petitions was a very common practice in rural Chile in the thirties. It became a favorite tactic of the leftist parties, whose members helped draw up petitions and guide them through the legal process, receiving credit for any resultant successes while simultaneously developing a base of peasant support.[51]

Individual landowners often reacted indignantly to the intrusion of labor inspectors; Loveman reports numerous cases in which inspectors were physically driven from fundos and threatened with greater violence.[52] The SNA's institutional posture, however, was more moderate. In 1932, for example, the Society secured the Ministry of Labor's approval for a standard written contract and mailed out sample forms to its members, urging their compliance. It did so despite the fact that the use of written contracts invited the intervention of labor inspectors, since alleged contract violations could be investigated at any time. While it frequently supported landowners' complaints about the political motives and actions of individual labor inspectors, the SNA did not directly challenge the Labor Department's obligation and authority to investigate and mediate.[53] Thus it tacitly conceded the state's right to regulate labor relations in agriculture, while opposing specific provisions of labor and social welfare legislation.

A case in point is law 4054, on compulsory social insurance for wage earners. The SNA objected to this law on the grounds that employer contributions were too costly (3.5 to 5 percent of wages) and that the system did not deliver the services paid for outside the cities and towns.[54] The SNA's *Boletín* also had offered an interesting argument about paternalism in a 1927 editorial: "With the requirement of contributing to their workers' insurance fund falling upon all agriculturists, this circumstance will exempt them from the moral duty of aiding their dependents. In this manner . . . law 4054 . . . will harm those whom it is intended to help."[55] The most important of the Society's objections was its unstated fear that law 4054 would make agricultural wages subject to close scrutiny, since contributions were based on the total value of wages in cash, kind, and usage. With rural society already under observation, landowners wanted to offer no standing invitation for further investigation. The Society, then, fought the application of law 4054 in agriculture from its enactment in 1924. Even after social insurance began to be systematically applied in other sectors in the early thirties, the SNA continued to resist and succeeded in having the law suspended for further study several times through 1940.[56]

Unionization, the most feared challenge to landowners' authority, became a pressing issue in 1933 when the Ministry of Labor began granting legal status to all qualified agricultural unions that applied for it. The SNA first challenged the legality of agricultural unions under the labor code. By July 1933, both the Superior Labor Council and, more significantly, the Consejo de Defensa Fiscal had ruled against the Society's position and established the perfect legality of agricultural unions under various articles of the labor code. Subsequent interpretations by administrative or legal bodies consistently reached the same conclusion. The landowners' problem, then, was to overcome the legal right of agricultural workers to organize on the same terms as industrial labor.[57]

The SNA met the challenge with a series of public statements and with high pressure lobbying. As it had since the early twenties, the SNA argued that rural conditions were too different to allow union activities on the industrial model; above all, the vulnerability of agriculture to strikes at harvest time would jeopardize production and threaten the national welfare. *El Campesino* also claimed that unions would be nothing but "permanent foci of resistance and disorder within agricultural labors" and that the Ministry of Labor had acted from political motives "(1) to aid disruptive elements in winning over the peasant masses in their harvest of hate and discontent, and (2) to justify the maintenance of an infinity of employees and functionaries who have swelled the growing army of our bureaucracy."[58] Concurrently, the Society sent a series of protest notes to and held several interviews with President Alessandri and his minister of labor and called for a national convention of agriculturists to rally opposition to unionization. Reflecting a degree of diffidence, the SNA also carved out a bargaining position by drafting and submitting to the minister of labor a bill to legalize professional unions in agriculture as a substitute for current labor code provisions.[59]

At this time when the left and the labor movement were still relatively inactive in the countryside, the pressure generated by organized landowners clearly outweighed any that could be mustered for compliance with the labor code. Alessandri also undoubtedly recognized the danger to the political right inherent in rural unionization, as well as the potential for increased food prices in the cities, which might jeopardize the recently restored political stability. Therefore he ordered the suspension of legal inscription of agricultural unions in March 1933.[60] There was surprisingly little adverse public reaction to this landowner victory over the law, and perhaps for that reason the SNA dropped the matter of promoting legislation for professional unions. In failing to follow up on its initiative, however, the Society may have missed an opportunity to acquire workable preventive legislation capable of foreclosing the unionization issue for at least a few years.

The victory on unions carried a price—a series of government-sponsored rural reform bills. As suggested in chapter 6, Alessandri's agrarian reform bill was one quid pro quo. Another was a government minimum wage bill, drafted by the Superior Labor Council in 1934, which would apply specifically to rural as well as urban labor. This met the Society's determined resistance, largely because the prior establishment of written contracts and grievance procedures for agricultural workers might make minimum wages enforceable and thus drive up labor costs enormously. In one of its public statements, the SNA reverted to the following timeworn Darwinian argument for laissez-faire:

> In the case of our rustic peasant, the amount of his wage does not determine his standard of living. His temperate or vicious habits, his dedication to work or his laziness, his cultural level and sense of responsibility are what determine the use he makes of his resources. There is an enormous number of people who work in agriculture and live precariously in a state of misery . . . , but . . . in 90 percent of the cases the amount of their wages is not to blame for this situation, but rather in reality those people are victims of nothing more than their own unconsciousness.[61]

Jaime Larraín called a meeting of all societies and provincial assemblies for March 1935 to demonstrate producers' uniform opposition to minimum wage legislation; but in private, "fearing that this bill might become law," an ad hoc SNA committee studying the issue recommended working with the government by endorsing the concept and offering to help draft a separate bill suited to the "peculiarities" of agriculture.[62]

Amenable to the SNA's suggestion, Alessandri appointed a special commission on salaries, comprised largely of agricultural society members, to work under the minister of agriculture. After studying agricultural wages for a year, it finally drafted a minimum wage bill which, endorsed by the president, reached Congress in 1936.[63] This was the heart of Jaime Larraín's vaunted campaign for the "improvement of peasant life," through which the SNA hoped to identify itself and the landowners of Chile as the real champions of social justice for the rural masses. Following a flowery preamble professing the highest motives, the bill provided for the establishment of standards for wages and inquilino housing by comuna, with tax penalties for noncompliance. Standards would be set and enforced by voluntary local committees of landowners, and the Ministry of Labor would have no jurisdiction whatever. Theoretically, then, this measure would force landowners throughout the country to implement the reforms that the SNA had long been urging them to introduce voluntarily. Even though the bill was transparently impotent, the outcry from landowners forced the SNA to abandon it, leaving it to die an early and well-deserved death after only preliminary maneuvers in Congress.[64]

With the defeat of this attempt at internal regulation, neither the Society nor the government introduced further proposals for rural reform during the remainder of the Alessandri regime. In the face of growing negative publicity about rural conditions, however, the SNA did resort to considerable propaganda regarding landowners' alleged voluntary improvements. *El Campesino* often featured the activities of organizations such as the Unión Social de Agricultores, which was founded in 1936 as a branch of Catholic Action.[65] The Unión Social was designed to "foster greater unity and cooperation between the patrón and the agricultural worker" and thus to prevent the introduction of the class struggle in rural society.[66] Within a year of its founding, the Unión Social was reported to have twenty-three local chapters with 188 members, and to be serving 5,370 inquilino families in various material and spiritual ways.[67]

Rural Labor Under the Popular Front

Under the Popular Front government, the main social and economic issues which had engaged landowners since 1919 came to the fore. Although the rightist majority in the Senate assured the defeat of new agrarian reform legislation, unionization of agricultural workers required only an executive order and therefore became the most critical matter facing landowners between 1938 and 1940. This issue transcended the direct economic interests of landowners and agricultural workers; the larger question was the potential effect of agricultural unionization on national politics. Unions would provide the organizational basis for wresting the rural vote away from landowners and thus undermining the bastion of rightist electoral power. In 1939 and 1940 this scenario was more than a hypothetical possibility, for with the executive branch in Popular Front hands, only the right's slim majority in the Senate stood in the way of potentially serious reform. Moreover, the left-center alliance demonstrated increasing popularity during the Aguirre Cerda administration by winning each of the several congressional by-elections over the rightist opposition.[68] A relatively minor shift in rural voting patterns might give the Popular Front a congressional majority in the March 1941 general elections. Therefore the SNA did not fight the union battle alone but in close cooperation with the rightist parties and conservative Radicals who saw in agricultural unions the prospect of their demise.

The Popular Front victory in 1938, then, raised the distinct possibility that rural unionization would be resumed unless a new restraining order were forthcoming. While the Popular Front program did not specifically call for the right of agricultural workers to syndicate, it did emphasize agrarian reform and other kinds of benefits for the rural proletariat. There was no doubt about the views of the leftist parties and the CTCh, however: they openly advocated a vigorous policy of unionization and proselytization with the intention, in the Communist party's phrase, of "conquering the peasant masses for the movement of national liberation."[69] The left had made its first serious rural electoral effort in the 1938 presidential campaign, and after the victory it stood ready to take advantage of freer access to the agrarian population.[70] The key to its success was government support of the labor code.

Faced with a government partially under hostile control, heightened leftist interest in the rural population, and a position compromised by Larraín's prominent role in the Ross campaign, the SNA fully expected a revival of the rural union issue. It was so apprehensive that even before Aguirre Cerda's inauguration, it had quietly drawn up its own unionization bill to use as a fallback position if persuasion or threats should fail to sustain the Alessandri suspension. In contrast to 1933, when the SNA had offered to support professional unions as an alternative to the labor code, the 1938 situation was so grave that the Society was willing to concede a modified type of industrial union for agriculture.[71]

The SNA's fears were quickly realized; the new government immediately began registering agricultural unions in the Ministry of Labor. The Society's initial response was to eschew direct involvement, in view of its compromised position, while individual landowners, regional associations, *El Mercurio*, and other right-wing media protested energetically against the evils of unionization. However, an outbreak of rural strikes in Pirque, near Santiago, spurred the SNA to action.[72] Following a buildup of publicity in the press, Jaime Larraín and the presidents of seven other agricultural societies and provincial assemblies wrote to Aguirre Cerda on March 15, 1939, asking him to suspend further legalization of rural unions. In this mildly worded public letter, the societies pointed out the impracticability in agriculture of unions as prescribed by the labor code and assured the president that "union legislation based on the reality of the agrarian problem and which permits harmony between capital and labor will never be resisted by the developmental organizations which we represent."[73] *El Mercurio* presented additional reports of rural agitation, then appealed to His Excellency as a "progressive agriculturist who knows as few people do the Chilean agrarian problem."[74]

The government's first indirect response, an editorial in *La Nación*, rejected the landowners' appeal, and both the peasant organizations and the CTCh repudiated the landowners' initiative.[75] However, Aguirre Cerda responded in a public letter of March 20, citing his concern for "social harmony rather than conflict" and announcing his endorsement of unions for agricultural workers.[76] He proposed to chair personally a mixed commission of owners and labor to study agricultural unions and the whole gamut of rural social and economic problems, and he offered to suspend the inscription of new unions while the commission deliberated. In turn, as a guarantee against reprisals for union and political activity, the agricultural societies were to urge landowners not to dismiss workers during the suspension.[77] The landowner groups readily agreed to the president's terms, and on March 25, a Ministry of Labor decree suspended further legal unionization for the duration of the commission's existence.[78] This compromise, which was parlayed eventually into a landowner victory, was again a victory over Chilean law. However, one need only recall the SNA's arrogant refusal to meet with FOCh leaders in 1921 to recognize the degree to which landowners' power had eroded. In 1939 the SNA was overjoyed at the prospect of meeting with labor leaders as equals, to discuss and draft legislation on matters that only a few years ago were landowners' exclusive and autonomous domains.

For the landowners, perhaps for the entire right, the new suspension of rural unionization was the most crucial measure taken by the Popular Front government. The suppression of rural unions has commonly been interpreted as the key element in an implicit or explicit bargain between right and left which placed rural Chile out of bounds to the left, in exchange for withdrawal of rightist opposition to measures of urban reform, including price controls.[79] The left's initial endorsement of the presidential order, however, was merely a tactical concession to harmony within the Popular Front.[80] Subsequent events of 1939-40 clearly demonstrate that the left did not voluntarily renounce its intention of recruiting and organizing in the countryside. To understand the logic of the Popular Front's suspension of agricultural unionization and its later decisions affecting landowners, it is necessary to examine the position of the dominant force within the governing coalition, the Radical party.

The Radicals had never endorsed agricultural unions as their leftist allies had, nor rejected them as the Liberal and Conservative parties had.[81] The Radicals' silence on the issue reflected the party's social and ideological heterogeneity. Although by the thirties it was commonly identified as the party of the middle class, the Radical party still contained an important core of large landowners in the frontier area and the south. Among this group of moderate to very conservative Radicals were Aguirre Cerda himself, Cristóbal Sáenz, Víctor Möller, Humberto Alvarez, and other hacendados, some of them SNA members, who were philosophically closer to the Liberals or Conservatives than to their Marxist allies.[82] While they professed interest in social justice for rural workers, some of them were no more willing to see it accomplished by means of unions than were the agricultural societies; and from the beginning of the Popular Front government, Sáenz, Möller, and others worked with the SNA to prevent unionization.[83]

Although numerically small, the landowner element of the Radical party was well represented in Congress, in Aguirre Cerda's cabinets, and in the party leadership. The landowner group could easily have been outvoted, but the Radicals' endorsement of rural unions would obviously have caused problems with the president and might have driven the frontier-southern landowner wing out of the party and into the conservative opposition. Defection of that group would not only have strengthened the opposition in

Congress but would virtually have guaranteed a loss of some traditional Radical seats from that area in the 1941 elections.[84] The Radicals might have gambled on the Popular Front's gaining enough votes from a successful rural unionization drive to offset the loss of southern landowner support; but since the Radicals had no blue-collar labor apparatus of their own, they as a party would not profit directly from any Popular Front inroads in the popular vote. In fact, assuming that the Marxist parties gained strength from access to the rural masses, the Radical party stood to lose its dominant position within the Popular Front. Thus, from the viewpoint of narrow party and individual self-interest, the Radicals had nothing to gain by supporting rural unions.

A second weighty consideration for the Radicals was the expected impact of agricultural unionization on food prices. The flurry of strikes in early 1939 demonstrated that rural unions would press militantly for wage increases and improved working conditions. The resulting higher costs of food production would necessarily threaten the government's current campaign to roll back food prices and in the long run jeopardize the Radicals' commitment to the welfare of their predominantly urban constituency. Large increases in food costs would introduce an undesirable conflict between the Radicals' welfare and development objectives; in an inflationary setting, compensatory wage adjustments for the large and growing bureaucracy might threaten the government's ambitious plans for industrial development, launched in 1939 by the newly created CORFO. Finally, the experience of volatile popular responses to food price inflation in the past recommended against any measures that might cause a sudden rise in food costs. These potential consequences of agricultural unionization reinforced the Radicals' hesitation to support their Marxist allies' quest to organize the rural labor force.[85]

The Presidential Mixed Commission was constituted in April 1939 and spent several months deliberating. The SNA's basic position was summarized in a memorandum from the owners' representatives on the commission to Aguirre Cerda. It showed great flexibility and demonstrated how far the Society was willing to go in preemptive legislation. While rejecting unions, at least as prescribed in the labor code, the SNA now conceded that rural wages, housing, nutrition, and almost every other aspect of labor relations and social welfare should be regulated by law.[86] After numerous meetings and considerable acrimony, punctuated by the withdrawal of some labor representatives, the commission reported to the president two bills, which he endorsed and sent to Congress in November 1939. One of these was on unions, the other on minimum wages.

The unionization bill preserved the industrial format but retained some important safeguards for landowners, particularly the prohibition of federations and of strikes—the latter point reportedly included at the president's insistence over labor's strenuous objections.[87] The minimum wage bill was much more realistic and enforceable than that of 1936. Both bills were sidetracked in the Chamber of Deputies, however, due to opposition from left and right. Communists and Socialists initially resisted approving either bill while the possibility remained of applying the labor code. Their hopes were rekindled by occasional threats from within the administration to abrogate the presidential suspension of inscriptions and by a Supreme Court ruling of July 1940, which upheld the legality of agricultural unions under the labor code.[88] When reported out by the chamber's Committee on Legislation and Justice in October 1940, the union bill had been severely weakened by the conservatives and moderates.[89] *El Siglo* expressed the left's general reaction to the committee proceedings: "A rural union law passed by the current Chilean Congress would be the death sentence of the movement to organize agricultural workers." The Socialists responded by presenting their own bill which in effect called for implementation of existing law.[90]

On the right, there was no rush to enact the bills in any form so long as the possibility existed that divisions within the Popular Front might bring about its dissolution and reduce the general level of threat. Thus, although the agricultural societies, *El Mercurio*, and other interested parties endorsed the bills as presented to Congress, these proposals failed to move through the legislative process.[91] Finally, after revision and even further emasculation, the 1939 union bill emerged as law 8011 of 1947, which legalized but effectively prevented the formation of agricultural unions.[92]

The battle of union and wage legislation, however, was only part of the war. After its reluctant endorsement of Aguirre Cerda's suspension, the Communist party on April 2, 1939, publicly defied the president and launched a campaign to organize in the countryside without benefit of legal unions.[93] It immediately sent cadres into rural areas to proselytize, generate demand for agrarian reform, organize extralegal peasant associations, and encourage labor petitions and strikes for the betterment of conditions. The Socialists soon followed suit, as did the independent leftists, and in the next sixteen months rural Chile was disrupted as never before in a battle between left and right.

There is no way of accurately assessing the degree of mobilization and of landowner reaction. As we have seen, on one level there was a ground swell of demand for land nurtured and articulated by the left, both within and outside the government. Beyond that, there is ample evidence of massive disruption and some violence—of strikes and vigorous recruitment by workers and the leftist parties; and of firings, blacklistings, and intense organizational activity by landowners. The *Sesiones del Congreso* for 1939 and 1940 are replete with denunciations from both sides. Rightists denounced a coordinated strike on thirty-three fundos in the department of Caupolicán and a strike involving 3,000 agricultural workers in the department of Traiguén.[94] Leftist congressmen retaliated by filling the pages of the *Sesiones* with accusations of massive landowner retaliation, naming owners, fundos, and individual inquilinos evicted for suspicion of political activity.[95] The minister of labor reported in 1940 that "in the majority of the fundos of Longaví, workers have petitioned owners for economic improvement, housing, and food."[96] The Labor Department constantly received petitions and reports of strikes; rural workers filed 370 labor petitions in 1939 and 1940—21 percent of the total for that biennium.[97] *El Mercurio* reported the murder of a fundo administrator and arson of the fundo house by inquilinos fired for "communist" activity.[98] The minister of agriculture sent a hostile memorandum to the SNA in April 1940, denouncing the widespread, politically motivated firings, calling them "very nearly sabotage," and urging the Society to ask landowners to comply with the president's condition for suspending unionization. The SNA denied the allegations but complied with the request.[99]

The Communist party gave the following account of its activity for 1939 alone: 400 free unions organized with 60,000 members, intervention in over 200 labor petitions with good results, recruitment of 6,000 to 7,000 new party members in rural areas, and organization of various congresses and regional meetings of federated agricultural workers.[100] The Socialist party less specifically reported good results in organizing rural brigades.[101] After it began publication in August 1940, *El Siglo* of the Communist party daily carried a full page on rural conflicts. In several provinces and departments, the intendant or governor took the unprecedented step of intervening in widespread conflicts by convoking landowners and urging them to make immediate improvements to restore social peace.[102] In short, the fabric of rural society began to pull apart in 1939-40.

Landowners, Communists, and National Politics

While the battle raged in the fields of rural Chile, the political issues of rural unions and leftist political activity became subsumed within the general power struggle between right and left—particularly the struggle between the right and the Communist party. In announcing its rural campaign in April 1939, the Communist party had issued another challenge to the right and to its Popular Front allies: it called for the dissolution of the SNA on the grounds that it was trying to "block the revolutionary endeavor" and demanded the arrest of Jaime Larraín.[103] It repeated those demands several times over the next year and a half, and at Communist insistence the leadership of the Popular Front parties met to discuss the question of removing the SNA's charter.[104] Meanwhile the Communists spared no invective on the SNA, which *El Siglo* described as a "focal point of conspirators, speculators, and usurers, who defy the popular will, developing an agrarian policy of sabotage prejudicial to the national economy, . . . a reactionary organization at the service of imperialism and war, declared enemies of the working masses of the countryside."[105]

The SNA initially refrained from responding to these Communist attacks but did mount a campaign of pressure to close off the countryside to leftist proselytization and unionization. It consistently depicted all leftist activities in rural areas as "agitation" and warned of the negative consequences for social harmony, for production, and for the country in general; the Congreso de Agricultores of October 1939 placed very heavy emphasis on the issue of "agitation."[106] The right as a whole was committed to stopping leftist political and organizational activity in the country for the same reasons that it opposed legal unionization. Therefore the rightist parties and press used rural "agitation" as a major part of their campaign to isolate the Marxist parties, and particularly the Communists, from the mainstream of public opinion and from the Radicals. *El Mercurio*, for example, constantly called for repression of the left in the countryside. In a typically forceful statement, at the end of 1939 it demanded that the government "take all measures necessary to stop the agitation carried out in the fields by persons alien to agricultural labor, once and for all and in definitive form."[107]

As with the legal unionization issue, resolution of the matter of leftist penetration of the countryside lay with the Radical party. The Radicals had been challenged by both sides to take a stand, but they demurred until the SNA escalated the pressure by publishing a manifesto in April 1940 over the signatures of all board members and the presidents of all agricultural societies and provincial assemblies—among whom were several Radicals. The manifesto denounced the Communists for attacking the SNA and continued: "With false declarations of support for the regime, the Communists introduce their revolutionary preachings among the peasants and create an atmosphere incompatible with the mutual guarantees between capital and labor. . . . It is necessary . . . that public opinion know the firm intention of agriculturists to oppose the sovietization of the fields, which would mean the death of the nation itself."[108] The Communists immediately forced the issue. Denouncing the fact that Cristóbal Sáenz, current minister of foreign affairs, was among the signatories of the SNA manifesto, they called on the Radicals to explain such an unfraternal act and to define their position. Demonstrating their typical schizophrenia, the Radicals endorsed a Popular Front statement condemning the SNA's manifesto and the institution itself but independently confirmed their support of Sáenz's ministerial position.[109]

From that point forward, the momentum of conflict swung toward a solution favorable to landowners. While the SNA stepped up its activities, rightist forces launched an offensive to split the Popular Front by isolating the Communist party. With the issue drawn, "numerous personalities" of the Radical party joined the SNA to articulate their position in the conflict and to nudge the party toward a decision against leftist access to the rural masses.[110] The congress of agricultural societies held at Concepción in May 1940 called on the government to make a choice between the "legal" and the "revolutionary" approach to rural change.[111] In June 1940, the Communist party intensified its rural offensive in an effort to increase pressure on the Radicals.[112] The rightist congressional delegation and party leadership responded in August with a ten-point proposal to the government for reducing tensions in the country, which included liquidation of the Communist party and dissolution of the CTCh. Concurrently, Conservative deputy Sergio Fernández Larraín introduced a bill to outlaw the Communist party.[113]

The combination of the SNA's efforts, the general rightist offensive to split the Popular Front, and the accumulation of severe internal tensions within the governing alliance began to produce favorable results for landowners in August 1940. In a note of August 17, minister of the interior Guillermo Labarca cited the prevalence of "illegal strikes and the foment of public intranquility" and ordered the carabineros to exercise "strict vigilance over the activities of those professional agitators who artificially provoke social problems in our fields and industrial centers, inciting peasants and workers to initiate illegal movements against proprietors.[114] Despite the general frame of reference, the Labarca circular was clearly directed at Marxists in rural areas. *El Siglo* denounced it as "a tool utilized by the reactionaries to attack inquilinos who have shown a desire to form unions," while *El Campesino* reported that the measure "has awakened a profound gratification in agricultural circles and undoubtedly has contributed to improving the atmosphere of confidence that productive activities require."[115] Meanwhile the minister of agriculture, Fernando Möller, assured landowners: "I will not permit, for any reason, the disturbance of agricultural labors by strikes or political movements; if they occur, they will be repressed with the greatest severity, although those methods may produce resentment in some of our political allies."[116] These ministerial edicts were vigorously enforced by the carabineros, utilizing a method their director general labeled the "final judgment," which featured the physical eviction of striking agricultural workers and their families.[117]

Despite the government's crackdown on leftist rural activity, the March 1941 congressional election indicated the degree to which Marxist organizational and recruitment efforts had begun to challenge landowners' authority. Faced with continuing government repression, reported landowners' threats of reprisal, and the traditional constraints on free electoral choice, rural labor voted in large numbers for Marxist candidates. The Socialists and Communists combined captured almost 32 percent of the vote in selected rural comunas analyzed by Drake and, together with the Radicals, ran even with right-wing candidates. The Marxists' strong showing in rural areas contributed significantly to the 59 percent majority achieved by the Radicals and the left.[118] Although subsequent developments in national politics prevented the translation of the 1941 election results into reform, the incipient electoral revolt of the peasantry presaged the future demise of landowner domination of the rural vote and the revival of reformism in the 1960s.

The Popular Front years were a crucial juncture in the politics of reform in Chile. Although the Front had come to power with the announced intention of reforming rural society, its actions instead suffocated the rural mobilization nurtured by the Marxist parties. By upholding the 1933 ban on unionization and proscribing free political recruitment in the countryside, the left-center Popular Front essentially ratified the status quo as defined earlier by the progressive right under Alessandri. The dominant Radical party, with the initial agreement of the left, had decided to consolidate the gains of its urban constituency and postpone the extension of full citizenship rights and participation to agricultural workers. By 1940, then, Chilean democracy had become firmly entrenched in the cities and the mining enclaves; but the stability of the political system in subsequent years rested on a number of trade-offs and compromises—principally on the continued exclusion of the rural masses.

Notes

1. Affonso *et al., Movimiento campesino*; and esp. Loveman, *Struggle in the Countryside*.

2. Claudio Gay, *Historia física y política de Chile: Agricultura*, 2 vols. (Paris, 1862-65); McBride, *Land and Society*.

3. McBride, *Land and Society*, p. 148; Bauer, *Chilean Rural Society*, p. 145.

4. Bauer, *Chilean Rural Society*, pp. 50-57; McBride, *Land and Society*, pp. 3-14.

5. Bauer, "Chilean Rural Labor"; and Bauer, *Chilean Rural Society*, pp. 50-57.

6. Note that while the census distinguished between peón or gañán and afuerino, these categories more commonly are subsumed under the term peón (meaning unattached seasonal wage labor, regardless of ties with an inquilino household).

7. Cristóbal Kay, "The Development of the Chilean Hacienda System, 1850-1973," in Duncan and Rutledge, eds., *Land and Labour in Latin America*, pp. 103-39; Bauer, "Chilean Rural Labor."

8. Ramírez Necochea, *Historia del movimiento obrero. Antecedentes*, pp. 46-64; Izquierdo, *Sociedad de Agricultura*, pp. 109-58.

9. *BSNA*, 2 (1870-71), 343-47, 376-78, 386-92, 408-9; *ibid.*, 3 (1871-72), 181-90, 239-42. Marcial González, *Condición de los trabajadores rurales en Chile* (Santiago, 1876), contains three essays submitted in a competition sponsored by the Chilean committee for the 1875 International Exposition, along with the judges' comments. On the migration to Peru, see Watt Stewart, *El trabajador chileno y los ferrocarriles del Perú* (Santiago, 1939), pp. 5-48.

10. Horace Rumbold, *Reports by Her Majesty's Secretaries . . . on the Manufactures, Commerce, etc.* (London, 1876) p. 388.

11. For extensive bibliographies on the "social question," see Pike, *Chile and the United States*, pp. 343-47; and Morris, *Elites*, pp. 279-88.

12. Orrego Luco, *Casa Grande*, p. 55.

13. *BSNA*, 39 (1908), 74-75.

14. Quoted in *ibid.*, 42 (1911), 269.

15. Peter Snow, "The Radical Parties of Chile and Argentina" (unpublished dissertation in political science, University of Virginia, 1964), p. 71.

16. *Primera semana social agrícola* (Santiago, 1913), p. xii.

17. Carlos Reyes P., "La habitación del obrero agrícola," *Primera semana social agrícola*, p. 195.

18. Efraím Vásquez Jara, "El trabajador agrícola chileno ante la lei i ante la sociedad" (Memoria de Prueba, Universidad de Chile, 1913).

19. Tancredo Pinochet LeBrun, *Inquilinos en el fundo de Su Excelencia*, p. 56.

20. *Ibid.*, pp. 75, 78.

21. *MSNA* (1919), pp. 8-10.

22. Barría Serón, "Movimientos sociales, 1910-26," pp. 302-11; Affonso *et al.*, *Movimiento campesino*, pp. 15-24; Loveman, *Struggle in the Countryside*, pp. 134-41; Loveman, *Struggle in the Countryside: A Documentary Supplement* (Bloomington, Ind., 1976), pp. 7-26; *Federación Obrera*, Nov.-Dec. 1921; *Boletín de la Oficina del Trabajo*, año XII, no. 18 (1922), 264-73; *ibid.*, año XVI, no. 24 (1926), anexos.

23. *MSNA* (1921), pp. 3-4; *Revista Comercial*, año XXV, no. 1228 (Sept. 10, 1921), p. 48,907.

24. Minutes, Oct. 10, 1921, in *BSNA*, 53 (1922), 50.

25. Loveman, *Struggle in the Countryside*, pp. 134-41.

26. *MSNA* (1921), pp. 3-4; reprinted in Affonso *et al.*, *Movimiento campesino*, pp. 17-19.

27. *MSNA* (1921), pp. 5-8. Alessandri's response is reprinted in Affonso *et al.*, *Movimiento campesino*, pp. 20-23. Compare the interpretation in Loveman, *Struggle in the Countryside*, p. 136, which maintains that the president's response satisfied the SNA.

28. *MSNA* (1921), pp. 5-8.

29. Barría Serón, "Movimientos sociales, 1910-26," p. 311; Loveman, *Struggle in the Countryside*, pp. 134-41.

30. Minutes, July 21, 1924, in *BSNA*, 55 (1924), 524.

31. *El Agricultor*, 52 (1921), 1-2.

32. *Ibid.*, p. 2.

33. *BSNA*, 54 (1923), 556-59, 808-13.

34. *Ibid.*, 55 (1924), 541-43; Minutes, Apr. 28, 1930, in *ibid.*, 62 (1930), 390.
35. McBride, *Land and Society*, pp. 168-69.
36. Poblete Troncoso, *Organización sindical*, part I, anexo v.
37. *MSNA* (1919), pp. 8-9.
38. *Ibid.*, pp. 9-10.
39. Francisco Walker Linares, *Panorama del derecho social chileno* (Santiago, 1950), pp. 65-72; Thomas A. Pace, *Chilean Social Laws* (reprinted from *American Federationist*, n.d.), pp. 37-41; Morris, *Elites*, pp. 208-40.
40. *BSNA*, 59 (1927), 517; Minutes, Nov. 16, 1925, in *ibid.*, 56 (1925), 895. Almost every year the *MSNA* reported the SNA's participation in one or more commissions studying the "reform" of some aspect of the social or labor laws.
41. E.g., Cámara de Diputados, *Sesiones extraordinarias en 1933-34*, pp. 2938-39; Cámara de Diputados, *Sesiones ordinarias en 1939*, pp. 2816-17; Loveman, *Struggle in the Countryside*, pp. 150-64.
42. Dirección General de Estadística, *Agricultura, 1935-36: censo* (Santiago, 1938).
43. For a listing of the rural social studies of the thirties, see Ricardo Marín Molina, "Condiciones económico-sociales del campesino chileno" (Memoria de Prueba, Universidad de Chile, 1947), pp. 52-57, 163-65. One school of social work established during this period was the Escuela de Servicio Social de la Beneficencia. Several articles on rural social conditions appeared in the new journal *Revista de Asistencia Social*.
44. The following theses on rural labor were produced at the University of Chile's law school in the thirties: Alfredo Bowen Herrera, "Ensayo sobre el movimiento sindical y el sindicalismo agrícola" (1933); Raúl Fernández Correa, "Los obreros agrícolas ante el derecho social chileno" (1933); Carlos Lizana Cornejo, "La sindicalización campesina" (1939).
45. The section called "de la realidad social" occasionally published the findings of social workers on rural conditions, e.g., *Acción Social*, año VI, no. 65 (Dec. 1937), 55-56. Also Alfredo Bowen, "El derecho de asociación y nuestra realidad social agrícola," *ibid.*, año VII, no. 74 (Nov. 1938), 535-37.
46. Cited in Marshall Silva, "Lucha por la reforma agraria," pp. 97-99.
47. Drake, *Socialism and Populism*, p. 220; Oscar Larson and Carlos Valenzuela, *Respuesta a d. Rosendo Vidal G. y d. Carlos Aldunate E.* (Santiago, 1940). The SNA objected to the activities of another group of religious in Minutes, June 6, 1938, in *El C*, 70 (1938), 502.
48. Fernando Möller, Ministro de Agricultura, to the Agricultural Societies, Apr. 16, 1937 (Oficio no. 419), in *AN*, Min. de Agr., Oficios Remitidos Clasificados, 1937.
49. *Ibid.*
50. Walker Linares, *Panorama del derecho social*, pp. 72-75; Loveman, *Struggle in the Countryside*, p. 114; Loveman, *Documentary Supplement*, pp. 47-77.
51. Loveman, *Struggle in the Countryside*, pp. 72-112, 205-18. Note that under the new Ministry of Labor the Labor Office was replaced by an expanded Labor Department.
52. *Ibid.*, pp. 103-5, 142-43.
53. *MSNA* (1932), pp. 5-20; for one of many examples of the SNA supporting members' complaints, see Minutes, Nov. 22, 1937, in *El C*, 70 (1938), 70.
54. *BSNA*, 59 (1927), 517-19; Walker Linares, *Panorama del derecho social*, pp. 150-57; Pace, *Chilean Social Laws*, p. 38-41.
55. *BSNA*, 59 (1927), 518-19.

56. *El C*, 70 (1938), 381; *ibid.*, 73 (1941), 62; Walker Linares, *Panorama del derecho social*, pp. 52-53; Loveman, *Struggle in the Countryside*, pp. 85-87.

57. *MSNA* (1933), p. 57; Bowen Herrera, "Movimiento sindical," pp. 153-60; Affonso *et al.*, *Movimiento campesino*, pp. 24-26; Loveman, *Struggle in the Countryside*, pp. 114-18. Marín Molina, "Condiciones económico-sociales," pp. 138-39, summarizes the legal rulings through 1940. Cámara de Diputados, *Sesiones extraordinarias en 1932-33*, pp. 2615-16.

58. *El C*, 65 (1933), 299-301.

59. *MSNA* (1933), p. 57; Minutes, Mar. 27, 1933, in *El C*, 65 (1933), 290; Minutes, May 29, 1933, in *ibid.*, 392.

60. Loveman, *Struggle in the Countryside*, p. 118.

61. *El C*, 67 (1935), 1.

62. *MSNA* (1934), anexos, pp. 103-6.

63. *AN*, Min. de Agr., "Informes Comisión Salarios, 1936"; Zuaznábar de la Barra, "La Sociedad," pp. 38-43.

64. Cámara de Diputados, *Sesiones ordinarias en 1936*, 1, 34-36.

65. *El C*, 70 (1938), 10-11, 20.

66. *Estatutos de la Unión Social de Agricultores* (Santiago, 1936), p. 1.

67. Cámara de Senadores, *Sesiones ordinarias en 1938*, p. 1299.

68. Stevenson, *Chilean Popular Front*, pp. 105, 114-15, stresses that the right greatly feared a left-center victory in the 1941 elections. Note that a literacy requirement greatly limited the number of agricultural workers qualified to vote. However, landowners were apparently able to bend the literacy requirement, and the leftist parties could presumably do the same with the acquiescence of a friendly government. Beyond this, relatively small vote totals were required to win congressional elections in most rural districts.

69. Chacón Corona, *El problema agrario*, p. 32.

70. Varas, *Chacón*, pp. 107-8. The Socialist party in 1939 and 1940 published several pamphlets on rural matters, including *Cartilla sindical campesina* (Santiago, 1940).

71. Minutes, Dec. 12, 19, and 26, 1938, in *El C*, 71 (1939), 80-82.

72. *El Mercurio*, Mar. 14, 1939, pp. 3, 9; Minutes, Mar. 14, 1939, in *El C*, 71 (1939), 385.

73. *El Mercurio*, Mar. 16, 1939, p. 16; *El C*, 71 (1939), 122.

74. *El Mercurio*, Mar. 17, 1939, p. 3. Also see *El Mercurio* over the next ten days for additional information on rural conflict.

75. *La Nación*, Mar. 16, 1939, p. 3, cited in Affonso *et al.*, *Movimiento campesino*, pp. 33-35.

76. *El Mercurio*, Mar. 21, 1939, p. 11; *El C*, 71 (1939), 181.

77. *Ibid.*

78. Affonso *et al.*, *Movimiento campesino*, pp. 34-37. Santa Cruz Errázuriz, "Mejoramiento de los trabajadores," p. 83, says that over 100 rural unions received legal status before the suspension.

79. See Kaufman, *Politics of Land Reform*, pp. 25-26. Others have interpreted the suspension of rural unionization and other concessions to landowners as part of an arrangement between landowners and other elements of the bourgeoisie. E.g., Atilio Borón, "Notas sobre las raíces histórico-estructurales de la movilización política en Chile," *Foro International*, 16 (1975), 114-15. See also Loveman, *Struggle in the Countryside*, pp. 201-4. Loveman, in *Chile: The Legacy of Hispanic Capitalism* (New York, 1979), p. 258, calls the 1939 "arrangement" to suppress rural unions "the cornerstone in the edifice of Chilean formal democracy."

80. Varas, *Chacón*, p. 109.

81. Some sections of the Radical party did endorse rural unions, e.g., the Asamblea Radical of the Comuna of Retiro. Cámara de Diputados, *Sesiones ordinarias en 1939*, 2, 2808. At its national convention at La Serena in June 1939, the party took stands on several rural issues (agrarian reform, minimum wages, inquilino housing) but took no position on agricultural unions. *La Hora*, June 26, 1939, p. 2. On the Radical party during the Popular Front, see Durán Bernales, *El Partido Radical*, and Stevenson, *Chilean Popular Front*, pp. 94-112.

82. In an interview with *El C*, Sáenz uttered a statement that might have come from the mouth of Héctor Rodríguez de la Sotta: "Nature has created us unequal and the inequality imposed by higher laws must be accepted, without this signifying that the better endowed should not try to improve the standard of living of those who are physically, intellectually, and morally inferior." *El C*, 71 (1939), 2. See also Gabriel González Videla, *Memorias* (Santiago, 1975), 1, 213-18, for the views of the more moderate president of the Radical party at the 1939 party convention.

83. Sáenz was a prime mover behind the Congreso de Agricultores of October 1939. The Communist party accused Sáenz, Möller, and other Radical leaders of working with the right against their Marxist allies. *El Siglo*, Oct. 6, 1940, p. 8.

84. The tendency of conservative Radicals to bolt the party was quite pronounced both before and after the Popular Front. In addition to founding the Agrarian party in 1931, conservative party members withdrew in 1946 in protest against a Radical electoral alliance with the Communists, and formed the Democratic Radical party. Thus the threat of losing that wing of the party was quite real. Cortés and Fuentes, *Diccionario político*, pp. 411-12.

85. For discussion of the Radicals and rural unions in the 1940s, see ch. 8, under "Rural Reform in Eclipse."

86. *El Mercurio*, Apr. 25, 1939, p. 7.

87. Affonso *et al.*, *Movimiento campesino*, p. 39; *El Siglo*, Sept. 1, 1940, p. 9.

88. E.g., Labor Minister Juan Pradenas Muñoz threatened in Sept. 1940 to apply the labor code if Congress did not enact the government's bill within two weeks. *El Siglo*, Sept. 2, 1940, p. 7.

89. *El Siglo*, Oct. 17, 1940, p. 6; *ibid.*, Oct. 18, 1940, p. 7; *ibid.*, Oct. 26, 1940, pp. 5, 9; *ibid.*, Nov. 6, 1940, p. 1.

90. Cámara de Diputados, *Sesiones ordinarias en 1940*, 3, 2164-65.

91. *El Mercurio*, Aug. 1, 1940, p. 3; *ibid.*, Dec. 16, 1940, p. 25; Minutes, Aug. 19, 1940, in *El C*, 72 (1940), 606.

92. Affonso *et al.*, *Movimiento campesino*, pp. 49-55; Loveman, *Struggle in the Countryside*, pp. 124-29; also ch. 8, under "Rural Reform in Eclipse."

93. *El Mercurio*, Apr. 4, 1939, p. 3.

94. Cámara de Diputados, *Sesiones ordinarias en 1939*, pp. 2812-13; *El Mercurio*, Aug. 30, 1939, pp. 17, 19; *ibid.*, Nov. 30, 1939, p. 18; *ibid.*, Dec. 3, 1939, p. 33.

95. E.g., Senator Lafertte inserted some 1,000 names of workers allegedly fired, along with the names of the fundos and their owners, into the record. Cámara de Senadores, *Sesiones ordinarias en 1939*, pp. 800-809. Deputy Gaete cited 2,000 political firings in Cámara de Diputados, *Sesiones extraordinarias en 1939-40*, 2, 1401-9.

96. Minister of labor to minister of agriculture, no date, in *AN*, Min. de Agr., Trabajos Recibidos, 1940.

97. Loveman, *Struggle in the Countryside*, p. 130. See also Loveman, *El campesino chileno le escribe a Su Excelencia* (Santiago, 1971), section "Cartas a

Pedro Aguirre Cerda, 1938-41."

98. *El Mercurio*, May 15, 1940, p. 18; *ibid.*, May 16, 1940, p. 17.

99. *Ibid.*, Apr. 9, 1940, p. 3; Larraín to Möller (minister of agriculture), Apr. 8, 1940, in *AN*, Min. de Agr., Oficios Recibidos Sociedades Agrícolas, 1940.

100. Chacón Corona, *El problema agrario*, pp. 36-37.

101. Partido Socialista de Chile, *El Partido Socialista y su 6° Congreso Ordinario* (Santiago, 1940), unpaginated.

102. E.g., the governor of San Antonio, *El Mercurio*, Apr. 26, 1939, p. 18; the intendant of Arauco, *ibid.*, May 4, 1939, p. 24; the governor of Lontué, *ibid.*, Mar. 23, 1939, p. 17.

103. *El Mercurio*, Apr. 3, 1939, p. 22; *ibid.*, Apr. 4, 1939, p. 17.

104. Durán Bernales, *El Partido Radical*, pp. 98-100.

105. *El Siglo*, Sept. 6, 1940, p. 8.

106. *El C*, 71 (1939), unpaginated; *ibid.*, 635, 691-706.

107. *El Mercurio*, Nov. 30, 1939, p. 3.

108. Reprinted in *El C*, 72 (1940), 238-39 (p. 238 quoted).

109. *El Mercurio*, Apr. 23, 1940, p. 11; *ibid.*, Apr. 26, 1940, p. 19; *ibid.*, Apr. 30, 1940, p. 13; Stevenson, *Chilean Popular Front*, pp. 100-101.

110. Durán Bernales, *El Partido Radical*, pp. 98-100.

111. *El Mercurio*, May 19, 1940, p. 35.

112. Stevenson, *Chilean Popular Front*, p. 102. See also Super, "Popular Front Presidency," pp. 227-66.

113. Stevenson, *Chilean Popular Front,* pp. 103-4. Drake, *Socialism and Populism,* pp. 234-47, discusses Popular Front strategies and internal tensions, including Communist-Socialist rivalries.

114. Oficio no. 963, Aug. 17, 1940, in *El Mercurio*, Aug. 18, 1940, p. 27.

115. *El Siglo*, Aug. 31, 1940, p. 18; *El C*, 72 (1940), unpaginated.

116. *El Mercurio*, Aug. 21, 1940, p. 18.

117. Olavarría Bravo, *Chile entre dos Alessandri*, 1, 443-53.

118. Drake, *Socialism and Populism*, pp. 257-65.

8

Epilogue: Landowners and Politics, 1941–79

The Popular Front decision to confine reform to the cities offered landowners an extended respite from threats to their fundamental prerogatives. In the two decades following the collapse of the Popular Front, the SNA continued to be heavily engaged in pressure group politics but predominantly over issues of economic policy: price controls, import policy, taxation, and other measures bearing on agricultural producers' incomes. Although the primary rural social issues subsided in importance after the Popular Front, the forces at work between 1919 and 1940 had sown the seeds that eventually bore fruit in the reforms of the 1960s and '70s.

Most fundamentally, the protracted debate and extensive legislation of the twenties and thirties worsened the image of landowners and established both attitudes and principles that eroded the legitimacy of the hacienda system. The attitude developed that rural society as constituted in Chile was an embarrassing anachronism; even landowners admitted it by supporting preemptive reform against themselves. In the 1920s the principle was established that land reform was a legitimate function of the state and by the thirties that the state should regulate labor relations and social welfare in agriculture. After the extensive legislation of the period, many of landowners' traditional rights were no longer secured by law but by nonenforcement of law. Despite the virtual moratorium on rural reform in the 1940s and '50s, the images, the attitudes, and the principles remained to undermine landowners' ability to resist the renewal of pressure for change in the 1960s.

The continuity between the two periods of reform—1919 to 1940 and 1958 to 1973—is clear. The main rural issues of both reform cycles were the same, although the terms of the debate had shifted dramatically toward the left by the latter period. The SNA's approaches to resisting change likewise followed the patterns established in the first cycle of reform. As before, the SNA defended the status quo in the absence of demonstrably strong pressures and shifted to a preemptive, flexible stance when the demand for reform intensified. As under the Popular Front, when the threat of reform passed tolerable limits, the SNA reverted to a hard-line, anticommunist position. By the late 1960s, when landowners' political influence had waned significantly, the strain of corporatism that had existed in SNA strategy since the 1920s became more pronounced. After the election of Salvador Allende in 1970, the SNA virtually abandoned its efforts to resist within the framework of liberal democracy and adopted an antisystem corporatist strategy that culminated in *gremialismo* —a movement of mobilized functional groups which played a central role in overthrowing the Allende government.

This epilogue chapter, covering almost four very eventful and complex decades, offers an overview of organized landowners in politics through the 1970s. Renewal of the battle over agrarian reform in the 1960s and its intensification after 1970 directed scholars' attention to the SNA and its political role and spawned a substantial body of literature on landowners and politics in Chile. The following analysis draws heavily on these secondary sources, the press, published SNA materials, and the author's observations of the Chilean political scene over more than a decade. This chapter, then, makes no pretense of definitiveness, and its findings and interpretations will undoubtedly be subject to challenge and revision. Its purpose will be served if it portrays the evolving political role of landowners and the SNA and establishes the links between the rural issues in Chile's two cycles of reform in this century.

Rural Reform in Eclipse, 1941–58

For almost two decades after the breakup of the Popular Front in January 1941, developments in national politics spared landowners further threats of major social reform. The leftward movement of the electorate peaked in 1941; over the following two decades the right partially recovered its electoral strength, Radical fortunes fluctuated, and the left declined. The Conservative and Liberal parties together rarely held an absolute majority in Congress but, with the aid of conservative Radicals and the new Agrarian Labor party, the right wielded effective congressional veto power into the 1960s. Following Aguirre Cerda's death in 1941, moderate to conservative Radicals Juan Antonio Ríos (1942-46) and Gabriel González Videla (1946-52) occupied the presidency. Former strongman Carlos Ibáñez was elected to a second term (1952-58) with a populist program but soon turned to the right for support.[1]

A fundamental element in this new balance of political forces was the fragmentation and moderation of the left. After the Socialists left the Popular Front, their intense rivalry with the Communists precluded effective leftist cooperation for over a decade and weakened the national labor movement. The Socialist party, torn between socialist and populist tendencies, had begun to fragment in 1940 and suffered a precipitous decline in electoral strength through the following decade. The Communists continued to follow a course dictated largely by the international situation. With Russian entry into World War II, they resumed the tactic of cooperation with antifascist forces and remained relatively quiet through the war years. Only with the onset of the cold war and a change of administration in 1946 did the Communists revert to intense organizational and strike activity in rural as well as urban areas. In contrast to the Socialists', the Communists' electoral strength continued to grow until the party was outlawed in 1948. There followed a decade of defensive behavior, with self-preservation taking precedence over activism.

The Radical party also turned to the right following the collapse of the Popular Front. With accelerated inflation in the forties, the middle class's concern with bread and butter issues eclipsed its commitment to reform. The exercise of power further attenuated the Radicals' reformist orientation. Their control of the public administration provided the opportunity to satisfy middle-class aspirations through expanding and pampering the bureaucracy and opened avenues of upward mobility to ranking Radical politicians. After 1940, Radical administrations emphasized economic development, especially industrialization, over reform, and often governed with the aid of the right-wing Liberal party.[2]

In reaction to the Popular Front experience, by 1940 much of the right had reverted to the predepression hard line against reform. The national upper-class strategy of the thirties, adopted precisely to prevent reformers and revolutionaries from achieving power, lost some of its credibility and appeal after the 1938 election. Therefore a large segment of the right abandoned conciliation and concession, embracing anticommunism as the most effective, most immediate, and least costly antidote to reform. Reflecting this change, in 1941 Congress passed, but Aguirre Cerda vetoed, a bill outlawing the Communist party. In the cold war climate of 1948, following the Radicals' rightward turn, the right and center combined to proscribe the Communists. By this time a majority of the middle-class political establishment had joined the right in favoring selective repression over preemptive reform.[3]

Against this political backdrop, landowners had little reason for concern about threatening social legislation in the forties and fifties. The course of debate and action on the main rural issues of the Popular Front years—agrarian reform and unionization—illustrates the prevailing political conservatism of the period and the SNA's own reversion to a harder line on reform.

After peaking during the Popular Front years, agrarian reform declined as a political issue in the forties. In the context of urban priorities and accelerating inflation, governments were unwilling to make the investment necessary to sustain agrarian reform within the existing legal framework and were opposed to strengthening the basic 1935 law. The proscription of leftist activity in the countryside also reduced the grass roots pressure for land that had arisen between 1938 and 1940.

The SNA was content to witness the eclipse of agrarian reform as a political issue and as public policy. On one of the rare occasions when agrarian reform was debated in Congress, *El Campesino* curtly dismissed the concept as "contrary to the right of property."[4] Thus, with the SNA's complete acquiescence, Chile's first agrarian reform program lapsed into tokenism. The Caja de Colonización was unable to acquire additional Central Valley land after the mid-1940s and managed to settle only some 1,600 families in the two decades after the Popular Front. By 1960, parcels created by the Caja represented less than 2.5 percent of all rural properties and their owners less than one percent of the agricultural population.[5]

The political climate was also hostile to agricultural unions in the post-Popular Front years. The left was still effectively banned from the countryside, while the Radicals were unwilling to risk the political impact that unionization might have on food price inflation.

In response to this reduced pressure to allow unionization, the SNA announced its intention of opposing agricultural union legislation "by all means," explaining that it had endorsed the 1939 mixed commission union bill only under duress.[6] Meanwhile *El Campesino* editorialized, in a vein reminiscent of the twenties, that efforts to improve the rustics' "culture and morality" would be more effective than unions.[7] Pointing to a primary concern of the Radicals, it also warned that unionization would "create misery among the [urban] populace due to scarcity and the rising costs of agricultural production."[8]

After the 1939 mixed commission union bill had languished in Congress for seven years, political deals at the national level brought this issue back to the center stage. To obtain Communist electoral support in 1946, González Videla promised to rescind Aguirre Cerda's 1939 order suspending unionization, which was still in effect. However, needing Liberal votes to confirm his election in Congress (required when no presidential candidate obtained a majority of the popular vote), he later endorsed special restrictive legislation on rural unions. González Videla rescinded the suspension order in November 1946, and the Communists, abandoning their wartime policy of quiescence, again sent cadres into the countryside to organize unions, lead strikes, and generate demands for land. The result was a massive disruption of rural activity, reminiscent of the Popular Front years. Landowners retaliated directly with dismissals and blacklistings, and the SNA, in cooperation with the other agricultural entities, quickly marshaled its resources to denounce the "agitation" and prod Congress into action.[9]

Law 8811 of July 1947, considerably more stringent than the 1939 mixed commission bill, was clearly a victory for landowners and the right in general. While legalizing agricultural unions, the law set conditions on minimum size of the work force, length of continuous employment, and literacy, which made unionization virtually impossible on most rural properties. Moreover, the law prohibited strikes and immediately dissolved existing unions that failed to meet the new requirements.[10] In reality, law 8811 prohibited rural unionization as effectively as the 1933 and 1939 administrative suspensions had done. Reflecting landowners' satisfaction with the new law, *El Campesino* reported that "the danger of extending the labor struggle and social resistance to the fields has been reduced and conditioned by law 8811."[11]

As in 1939 and 1940, the Communists defied the law and intensified their campaign to organize and strike in the countryside. In response, the government cracked down on "subversion" while Congress enacted the 1948 "Law for the Permanent Defense of Democracy," which outlawed the Communist party and shackled the national labor movement.[12] Together, the unionization and anticommunist laws ratified the previous administrative suspensions of unions and the Labarca circular against "agitation," thus providing a foundation of legality for the continuance of landowner preeminence in the countryside and upper-class power in national politics.

In general, social and labor law appears to have been enforced somewhat more consistently, although still sporadically, in the forties and fifties. In 1945 the SNA established a "servicio de atención a las leyes sociales" to help members deal with the growing complexity of government regulation.[13] In the case of law 4054 on compulsory workers' insurance, the SNA's actions shifted from resisting the law's application in agriculture to opposing the periodic adjustments for inflation in employer contributions.[14] The only significant new social obligations applied to landowners during this period were a minimum wage law and new regulations on inquilino housing. Carlos Ibáñez enacted these measures at the outset of his term as decree-laws, apparently in return for Socialist support of his candidacy. Although the SNA objected strenuously to the measures, it had little recourse in dealing with the still-authoritarian president and relied on administrative delays and lax enforcement to blunt the impact of these decree-laws.[15]

The decline of agrarian reform and agricultural unionization as political issues gave the SNA a welcome respite from these major preoccupations of the thirties but did not diminish the Society's involvement in pressure group politics. Against the backdrop of accelerating inflation, urban-rural conflict between 1941 and 1958 centered on economic issues. The cost of living rose an average of nearly 20 percent annually in the forties and over 35 percent in the fifties, peaking at around 80 percent in 1955.[16] In view of the great impact of food prices on the cost of living, government efforts to control inflation inevitably focused on food. Beyond the concern for combatting inflation in general, additional considerations motivated the fight against inflation of food staples in particular. The connections between food price inflation and political instability and between food prices and malnutrition continued to be recognized in government circles. Growth of the urban population—from 52.4 percent of the country's total in 1940 to 65.3 percent in 1960—added weight to urban consumer demands for affordable food.[17] Finally, governments calculated that the provision of low-cost food staples for the urban populace would promote increased consumption of industrial products, thereby stimulating the national manufacturing sector.[18]

Two primary areas of policy engaged the SNA in constant battle with the Ríos, González Videla, and Ibáñez administrations. Price policy, the more pervasive issue, had direct and immediate repercussions on consumers as well as on producers and middlemen. Building upon the price control machinery of the thirties, later administrations established the Instituto de Economía Agrícola in 1942 and the Empresa de Comercio Agrícola a few years later. With greatly augmented powers and purviews, these agencies were more capable than their predecessors of setting prices by decree and of importing sufficient quantities of staples to reinforce the official prices through regulating the supply of grains, potatoes, and other staples. As Chilean agricultural production began to fall behind the level of domestic consumption in the forties, importation of staples—some of them available through the United States's surplus commodities program—became a major factor in governmental efforts to control food prices.[19]

Within the context of inflation, increased government expenditure, and budget deficits, another major question was whether to continue existing subsidies to agriculture or to divert government resources into urban services and industry. Direct governmental aid, directed primarily toward the large producer, included preferential railroad rates, cheap fertilizers, low tariffs on imported agricultural machinery, easy credit, and technical services. Low tax rates on agricultural land and income, denial of effective unionization, and lax application of labor and social welfare law constituted indirect subsidies for large producers.[20] Given the current national emphasis on development, landowners faced little pressure for tampering with existing subsidies directly linked to production; and the enactment of law 8811 in 1947 effectively killed the drive for unionization and stricter enforcement of labor and social welfare law in the countryside. The major challenge to landowners was to preserve the traditionally low level of taxation on agricultural land and income.

Under increasing pressure from varied urban constituencies, the governments of the forties and fifties sought to raise taxes and limit food price inflation to the extent possible without jeopardizing the already deficient level of agricultural production, and thus necessitating additional imports. The SNA response to the constant pressure against agricultural profits was to argue, and to substantiate with elaborate documentation, the position that agriculture was already squeezed between high taxes and low prices, and that the higher productivity required by the nation could only be achieved by policies to make agriculture more remunerative. It frequently charged that government policy was based on "demagogic criteria" that would destroy agriculture to satisfy other groups or interests.[21] In 1951, for example, *El Campesino* editorialized that any new burdens would crush an agricultural economy "already severely punished by unreasonable tax increases, a policy of restricted prices and inflated costs, by requisitions of products, and by threats of all kinds."[22] The SNA annually protested the official prices for wheat, milk, rice, and other staples in order to pressure for better prices the following year. It also hired more agricultural economists, who produced a growing volume of highly technical production cost studies and policy analyses to document the alleged low profit margins in agriculture. The country's agricultural associations met regularly to coordinate their actions, and in 1950 they established Acción Nacional Agraria, a suprainstitutional entity, to articulate the "national" agrarian view. Economic pressures spurred the establishment or revival of regional and national commodity producers' associations for cattle, wheat, milk, rice, fruit, and other products, and in 1953 the SNA seated representatives of these independent commodity associations in its council.[23]

The SNA record in protecting its constituents' economic interests in the 1940s and '50s was mixed. Despite some increases, agriculture still enjoyed the lowest taxation rate of any economic sector into the 1960s.[24] However, the SNA was unable to alter the policy of importing foodstuffs to regulate domestic prices. The overall effect of price policy is harder to gauge. The question turns on whether agricultural production could have responded to market incentives, or whether the rural property structure and distribution bottlenecks would have impeded greater productivity. While many economists conclude that price policy was discriminatory and retarded the growth of agricultural production, others argue with equal conviction that prices for agriculture were comparable to those for other sectors.[25] Regardless of whether price policy was actually discriminatory, one can hypothesize that agricultural price levels in the forties and fifties generally remained lower than they would have been without controls and price-depressing imports, with some impact on aggregate agricultural income.

While price and import policies may have affected the income generated by the agricultural sector as a whole, landowners' individual incomes were not adversely affected; in fact, one study concludes that real income for agricultural entrepreneurs actually rose by as much as 50 percent between 1940 and 1955.[26] With continued suppression of effective rural unionization, landowners were able to transfer any cost of negative price policy to their labor force, whose real income fell some 18 percent during the same period and continued to decline into the early sixties.[27] This redistribution of income within agriculture meant that rural workers, not landowners, bore whatever costs were involved in government's attempts to control food price inflation in the interest of the urban population.

While agricultural entrepreneurs prospered, the performance of the agricultural sector declined between 1940 and 1960. During this period, increases in agricultural production (2.03 percent per year) lagged behind population growth (2.23 percent per year), making Chile a net importer of food by the mid-forties and causing serious distortions in the country's balance of payments. Thus agriculture became a brake on development and a major cause of the economic stagnation of the fifties.[28] Despite the SNA's and many economists' claims that government policy was responsible for the worsening performance of agriculture, these developments confirmed to the urban public the "retrograde" image and further undermined landowners' credibility.[29]

Reflecting on the forties and fifties, one might wonder why landowners under SNA leadership made no serious effort to resolve the rural social and land questions while their political influence was still strong. Three mutually reinforcing answers suggest themselves. First, the SNA had learned in the thirties that Jaime Larraín's positions jeopardized national landowner unity—unity that was increasingly important to issues of common and immediate concern such as price and taxation policy. Second, along with the right, the SNA adopted the view that fighting "communism" was less costly and more effective in the short term, particularly in the cold war era, than preemptive reform. Finally, a 1953 *El Campesino* editorial alleged, and landowners may have believed, that discriminatory price policies "limit . . . the possibilities of bettering the standard of living of the rural population."[30] Thus after fighting the reformers to a standoff in 1940, the SNA acquiesced in the dominant national view that rural reform was too costly in an inflation-ridden, industrializing economy and that repressing the left was an effective antidote to reform. This failure to address the festering problems of the rural order undoubtedly weakened landowners' ability to withstand the onslaught of more radical reform in the sixties and seventies, when the opportunity for moderation had passed.

Alessandri and the Return to Preemption, 1958–64

The election of Jorge Alessandri in 1958 marked a crucial juncture for the Chilean upper classes. Ironically, while the right's own candidate had captured the presidency for the first time in thirty years, the primary message of the 1958 election was a renewed national sentiment for reform. The acceleration of inflation combined with economic stagnation during Ibáñez's term had sparked a new leftward movement of the electorate. Thus Alessandri won with the smallest plurality ever to elect a Chilean president, 31.6 percent, while the four left and center candidates garnered over two-thirds of the popular vote. Alessandri defeated Socialist Salvador Allende of the Marxist-dominated Popular Action Front (FRAP) by only 40,000 votes out of 1,235,000 cast. The narrow margin of victory raised questions about the administration's legitimacy, requiring Alessandri initially to govern as an independent and select primarily independent *técnicos* for his cabinets.[31]

Especially disturbing to the right was Allende's unexpectedly strong showing in rural districts; the long-feared collapse of landowner electoral control appeared imminent.[32] The strong leftist showing in the countryside reflected changes in rural society and national politics since the late 1940s. The decline of real wages and the increase of afuerinos in the rural labor force tended to undermine campesinos' remaining loyalty to the patrón. The "urbanization of the countryside" reinforced the decline of landowners' authority; as a result of the growth of provincial towns, improved rural transportation, increased government presence in the countryside, and the advent of the transistor radio, rural workers came increasingly into contact with the urban world, including its political representatives. Since 1952 the Catholic left had been active in the countryside, forming unions, building political bases and occasionally leading strikes in defiance of law 8811. Despite the ban on their activities, the Communists also had retained some rural presence.

The Ibáñez government had also helped induce the 1958 rural electoral revolt. First, an electoral reform replaced the easily controllable party ballot with the Australian ballot, allowing campesinos to vote with more freedom from coercion. Second, in 1958 Ibáñez honored a campaign promise to rescind the "Law for the Permanent Defense of Democracy," allowing the Communists to enter the presidential campaign. Competition between the FRAP and the reformist Christian Democratic Party (PDC, formerly the Falange) brought party cadres to ever remoter corners of rural Chile, yielding a harvest of votes for both groups.[33] *El Campesino's* understated commentary revealed landowners' concern about leftist inroads among agricultural workers: "In the recent campaign the rural masses showed dissatisfaction, which we must study and address courageously."[34]

The 1958 election provided the impetus for a shift in rightist strategy. Alessandri's narrow victory, Allende's strong showing, and the leftward swing of the rural vote indicated that the right's future success would depend on enhancing its appeal to a broader segment of the electorate in order to be competitive with the reformist parties. Further impetus for reform came from the Radicals, who, bending with the political winds, demanded reforms as the price of supporting Alessandri's government in Congress. The general radicalization of the electorate, combined with the tactical necessity of Radical congressional support, underlay the right's reversion to the flexibility that had characterized its response to the crisis years of the depression and the Socialist Republic. Thus even before the impact of the Cuban Revolution stimulated further growth of the left, the Alessandri government embarked on a course of moderate preemptive reform to shore up the waning political power of the upper classes.[35]

As in the thirties when the elites had turned to preemptive reform, landowners again were the segment most vulnerable to remedial action. The passage of time had only worsened and further institutionalized the negative landowner image, making the anachronistic agrarian structure increasingly difficult to defend. The declining performance of agriculture prompted several investigations—including an influential United Nations study in 1953—and set off a debate among Chilean and foreign economists that grew in intensity through the fifties. On one side were the monetarists, who argued that the problem of agricultural production was primarily the low rate of return dictated by discriminatory government policies. This, of course, was also the landowner view. On the other side were the structuralists, who revived and elaborated the views expounded by Moisés Poblete Troncoso in 1919. Without discounting entirely the evidence of negative government policy, the structuralists believed that agriculture, and by extension the entire economy, could only be improved by modifying the inefficient structure of rural property through agrarian reform. As the debate went on, the structuralist view won increasing public acceptance—perhaps in part because it justified and fortified the existing popular prejudice against landowners.[36]

From the time of his inauguration, Alessandri offered landowners the carrot and the stick. To overcome the stagnation of agriculture, he promised a development program and an end to price discrimination. At the same time, he referred to improving the condition of the rural worker and "tying him to the land he works."[37] Within Alessandri's first fifteen months in office, his administration made its first mild efforts at rural reform by issuing new regulations on worker housing and reorganizing the Caja de Colonización Agrícola to improve its efficiency.[38]

In the early 1960s, pressure for agrarian reform intensified as the impact of the Cuban Revolution spread through Latin America. The dramatic lesson of Cuba strengthened the case for preemptive reform, swelling the ranks of agrarian reform advocates throughout the hemisphere. The Economic Commission for Latin America, the International Labor Organization, and later, the Alliance for Progress endorsed agrarian reform as a method of achieving social justice and preventing revolution. Within Chile, the Catholic Church called more insistently for agrarian reform, and by 1960 the debate had engulfed the parties of the upper and middle classes. At a public forum in January 1960, representatives of the Conservative, Liberal, and Radical parties called in varying tones for land redistribution within the framework of a program to stimulate production.[39] By October 1960, Alessandri's minister of agriculture proposed an agrarian reform to "remedy existing defects in the distribution and exploitation of land."[40]

The SNA responded positively if not enthusiastically to the mounting sentiment for agrarian reform. It applauded Alessandri's modification of the Caja de Colonización, and in May 1960 *El Campesino* editorialized calmly that "agrarian reform constitutes a general movement that encompasses all countries: landowners do not fear it and will address it with profound responsibility and a modern spirit."[41] The SNA council set up a special committee on agrarian reform in early 1961.[42] The Society's emerging stance was reminiscent of Jaime Larraín's internal regulation approach to the problem of rural labor in the thirties. Larraín had attempted to isolate socially irresponsible landowners and direct punitive action toward them; in 1960, the criterion was efficiency in production. The SNA tactic was to depict the majority of landowners as efficient producers, and to welcome the application of reform to the inefficient minority. In the words of SNA president Guillermo Noguera Prieto: "We are the foremost partisans of this agrarian reform. We do not support inefficiency nor indolence and we view those guilty [of these faults] as true traitors to the agrarian cause."[43]

The congressional election of March 1961 galvanized the right to move from debate to legislation on agrarian reform. It confirmed in dramatic fashion the end of landowners' control of the rural vote and the heightened appeal of the left and the Christian Democrats. The Conservatives and Liberals together polled only 26.9 percent of the vote, dropping to less than a third of the seats in both chambers of Congress. The Radicals, now holding the balance of power in Congress and eyeing the presidency in 1964, demanded agrarian and other reforms as a condition for joining the right in a formal progovernment alliance. From their position of weakness, the rightist parties accepted the Radical proposal and a tripartite commission began work on an agrarian reform bill.[44]

The parties' bill bore some resemblance to the 1939 Socialist agrarian reform proposal and conformed to the SNA's criterion of preserving property of any size that produced efficiently. It would permit expropriation only of "abandoned or inefficiently worked" holdings and allow expropriated landowners to keep a reserve of eighty hectares of irrigated Central Valley land or its equivalent, in productive potential, in dry or inferior soils. In that sense it was more restrictive than law 5604 of 1935, which had made most large property subject to expropriation. Another feature of the bill, however, would provide vastly increased government leverage over rural property. It would allow deferred payments, in bonds adjusted to inflation and bearing 4 percent interest, on up to 80 percent of the value of expropriated property. Implementation of this provision required a constitutional amendment, which accompanied the bill. The parties' bill would also replace the Caja de Colonización Agrícola with new administrative bodies, principally the Corporación de la Reforma Agraria (CORA) and a rural development agency, the Instituto de Desarrollo Agropecuario (INDAP). Landowners' only guarantee against arbitrary interpretation or rigorous application of the criteria for inefficiency and abandonment was a provision for special tribunals where proprietors could appeal CORA expropriation decisions.[45] Overall, as with law 5604, the new bill would give government considerable discretion in the use of expropriation. Alessandri could be expected to employ it prudently; but, echoing landowners' fears of Alessandri's father's 1934 agrarian reform bill, several SNA directors pointed out that if the right's preemptive strategy failed and a reformist government were elected, agricultural property rights would be in grave jeopardy.[46]

Following the March election, the SNA had determined to draw up its own agrarian reform bill. After the parties assumed that role, the Society worked with them in an advisory capacity and received their draft legislation late in 1961. Debate within the Society focused on the constitutional amendment required to validate the bill. The council's committee on agrarian reform split, three directors endorsing the amendment and three rejecting it. The arguments against endorsement cited the potential for arbitrary interpretation of inefficiency and abandonment, the dangerous weakening of property rights in general, and the availability of alternate means to improve agricultural production. The report supporting the constitutional amendment centered on a classic argument for preemptive reform:

> This constitutional reform is oriented toward maintaining the rule of law in Chile, preventing social upheavals, and finding a just solution to the problem of recognizedly inefficient enterprises, which—whatever their number—serve as the basis for the dissolvent action of those who seek the total annihilation of the right of property and direct their unfounded criticisms against landowners in general. Nothing will be gained with an iron defense of all proprietors without exception. . . . Arrogance and incomprehension would be the best allies of subversion. Only vigilant and perceptive prudence, capable of reforming institutions when it is required, will permit maintenance of the legal tradition of our country, which has been achieved precisely by the opportuneness with which the citizenry has known how to react in the face of new problems posed by the circumstances of every epoch.[47]

The Society's full board of directors voted on the constitutional amendment on December 27, 1961. The outcome was a tie at twenty-one, with one abstention. As significant as the vote, however, was the failure to vote. Without exception, representatives of all the affiliated agricultural entities south of Ñuble province boycotted the meeting. Of a total of twenty qualified voters who did not attend, eleven were from southern societies or SNA provincial councils and four represented commodity associations whose operations centered in the frontier and lake districts. These associations had previously met, formed the Southern Agricultural Consortium (CAS), and rejected the parties' proposal.[48]

The 1961 vote underscored the continuing disagreement among landowners over defensive strategies. The regional elites of the frontier and south reiterated the hard line against concessions that they had articulated during the thirties. The disposition of the elected SNA directors, and of the provincial council and commodity association representatives from the core of central Chile, is not so easy to interpret. The CAS position may have convinced some directors that the restoration of gremio unity was more important than political flexibility. On the other hand, by the time of the SNA vote the Alliance for Progress had been launched, adding immeasurably to the rising tide of pressure for agrarian reform. Its offer of massive economic assistance to governments willing to undertake social reform may have seemed to improve the prospects of effective but moderate agrarian reform at minimal cost to landowners. Regardless of individuals' rationales, the council's tie vote indicated clearly that the right's agrarian reform plan had pushed the SNA—specifically its more flexible and moderate core area representatives—to the limits of acceptable landowner concession to the national upper-class strategy.[49]

The internal stress caused by the agrarian reform issue was reflected in several years of instability in the SNA leadership and frequent reversals in general orientation. The SNA simultaneously made vigorous efforts to win back the support of the southern wing by adopting harder lines on price policy and rural agitation and reforming its council to provide more effective regional representation.[50] Although common threats restored a degree of harmony within the gremio, the 1961 split left organized landowners weakened at a time when strength was essential.

The right-center coalition, meanwhile, had interpreted the SNA vote as failure to reject its agrarian reform bill and submitted it to Congress in early 1962. It emerged a few months later as law 15,020, and the enabling constitutional amendment passed in July 1963. As expected, the Alessandri government used its expanded powers over rural property judiciously and refrained altogether from expropriations. In less than two years, CORA acquired 60,000 hectares, most of it government-owned land, and settled only 1,066 peasant families.[51] Within the context of continent-wide mobilization and demand for revolutionary agrarian reform, these efforts were too transparently token to stem the radicalization of the Chilean electorate.

Land and Labor under the Christian Democrats, 1964–70

The failure of the right-center preemptive strategy became clear in a series of elections in 1964 and 1965. In the first of these, a congressional by-election in March 1964 in the rural province of Curicó, the candidate of the Conservative-Liberal-Radical "Democratic Alliance" finished behind a Socialist and slightly ahead of a Christian Democrat. Having billed this election as a national referendum on the Alessandri administration, the right dissolved the alliance, withdrew its support for the Radical candidate in the upcoming presidential election, and endorsed Eduardo Frei of the moderate wing of the Christian Democratic party to prevent the election of Salvador Allende, running again as the FRAP candidate. Frei was elected in September 1964 with the support of the right but with no commitment to it. The right suffered a further political decline in the congressional elections of March 1965; the combined Conservatives' and Liberals' share of the vote dropped to 12 percent and their congressional strength dwindled to 7 senators (out of 45) and 9 deputies (out of 147). The Radicals also lost dramatically, while the Christian Democrats gained an absolute majority in the Chamber of Deputies. With some of the Radicals tilting toward the left after 1965, the right for the first time was reduced to impotence in Congress.[52]

Landowners then found themselves in a precarious position. The Christian Democrats had offered a "revolution in liberty" to compete with the Marxist version of revolution. Central to that was the promise to create 100,000 new rural proprietors in six years. The PDC had no commitment to the landholding elites and little sympathy for them, and a large segment of the party held slight regard for capitalist private property.[53] Therefore the Frei administration had little hesitation in sacrificing landowners' remaining prerogatives in order to establish its "revolutionary" credentials in Chile and its "reformist" image abroad. Moreover, unlike the progressive right, the Christian Democrats were unwilling to let landowners reform themselves or even participate significantly in designing the reform process.

Landowners' fears of radical measures were quickly confirmed, as the PDC assaulted the rural order with new legislation and vigorous use of existing law. A 1965 law established parity between the rural and urban minimum wage, introduced the eight-hour work day in agriculture, and strengthened job security for rural labor. With increased resources and resolve, the Labor Department began an effective program to enforce labor law in the countryside. The Frei administration also employed the 1962 agrarian reform law vigorously, expropriating nearly 500 properties containing 8,000 inquilino families prior to the passage of the PDC agrarian reform law in 1967.[54]

After extensive intraparty debate, by October 1965 the administration had drafted the legislation that was to be the cornerstone of its agrarian policy. The bill on rural unions removed existing obstacles to organization and gave agricultural workers essentially the same rights as their industrial counterparts. In the PDC agrarian reform bill, which also reflected the views of the party's left wing, the most significant departure from the Alessandri law was that size replaced efficiency as the condition for landownership. By the terms of the PDC bill, any property larger than eighty basic irrigated hectares was subject to expropriation. An accompanying constitutional amendment would permit deferred indemnification for any expropriated property: 10 percent of assessed value would be paid in cash for efficiently exploited properties and between 1 and 5 percent for poorly exploited holdings. The ultimate nature of property in the reformed sector was vaguely defined, but the government would administer the expropriated holdings, or "*asentamientos*," for an indefinite transitional period. If enacted without major revision, this legislation clearly would open the way for an interested government to eliminate the traditional hacienda and even large modern capitalist farms.[55]

Along with these Christian Democratic initiatives, landowners faced two other threats: a massive mobilization of rural labor, and the government's attitude toward the campesinos' demands and actions. Both the PDC and the Marxists had built up large networks of rural committees and extralegal unions and federations which had carried out illegal strikes with increasing frequency in the early sixties. In the 1964 presidential campaign, both factions had mobilized their peasant organizations in fierce competition for the rural vote. With the seating of the Frei administration, then, rural labor was already highly organized and politicized. Both Christian Democratic and Marxist-led unions were ready to challenge the government's willingness to continue the traditional practice of defending landowners' proprietary rights by force.[56]

Considerable pressure came from within the government as well to withhold protection for landowners. The PDC left wing was strongly represented in the agrarian reform program, and two of its leading spokesmen, Jacques Chonchol and Rafael Moreno, headed INDAP and CORA, respectively. In 1965, some agrarian reform officials reportedly began to organize illegal unions and federations, lead protests and strikes, and encourage seizures of properties to dramatize demands for expropriation. Marxist organizers concurrently stimulated the breakdown of law and order in the countryside to challenge the government's authority and accelerate agrarian reform. The result was a mobilization of the rural masses that surpassed anything previously witnessed in Chile. The government, pledged to effect its revolution within the law, thus faced the choice of either ignoring that promise or using force on the peasantry, including its own supporters. In practice, it vacillated between repressing illegal rural activities and tolerating them. The significant thing for landowners was that while the state enforced their obligations, for the first time they could not rely upon it to uphold their proprietary rights.[57]

The drastic decline in rightist influence in government after 1964 placed the burden of landowner defense primarily on the SNA and its regional counterparts. The SNA initially turned to the insider approach to moderate the government's forthcoming agrarian reform and union legislation and to secure law enforcement in the countryside. In an attempt to regain its traditional access to the inner circles of government, the SNA council replaced President Víctor Braun Page with Luis Larraín Marín, a young man with credentials as a social progressive and contacts inside the PDC. After his election, Larraín obtained an interview with Frei and offered landowners' cooperation in formulating agrarian policy.[58]

For the first year of the Frei administration, then, and to a lesser degree for the following two, the SNA maintained a moderate official line and sustained a dialogue with the government. With the primary objective of retaining protection for efficient producers in the forthcoming PDC agrarian reform bill, the SNA virtually conceded the government's program of increasing benefits for rural labor, including unionization. Thus when the new minimum agrarian wage law passed in 1965, *El Campesino* instructed readers on how to comply, also recommending profit sharing in agricultural enterprises. The SNA position on the government's agricultural union bill was to accept it in general, while pushing for some restrictions on the right to strike; in a complete reversal of its earlier stand, in 1965 *El Campesino* announced that "no one can argue that the agricultural worker does not have the same right to organize as any other citizen of the country."[59] Recognizing the government's unwillingness to crack down on rural strikes, rather than raising the familiar and now futile cry of "agitation" the SNA acknowledged the existence of unions "at the margin of the law" and proposed to deal with their leaders in government-supervised ad hoc arbitration boards. Meanwhile the SNA's limited access to government and PDC circles allowed it some input into the formulation of agrarian reform legislation.[60]

However, the provisions of the government agrarian reform bill, unveiled in October 1965, revealed the failure of the SNA insider strategy. At that point, without entirely severing its lines of communication with government, the SNA shifted to a tougher stance. To gloss over differences within the gremio, the agricultural societies set up a Comando Coordinadora de Organizaciones Agrícolas to articulate the "national" view, and *El Campesino* inaugurated a "letters" section to publish the hard-line views of individual landowners. By identifying agrarian reform with Communism, the SNA sought to separate Frei and the moderates from the PDC left, who controlled the agrarian reform machinery, and to enlist the support of urban groups. In its public statements, the SNA made three basic allegations: that the collectivist nature of the asentamiento mocked peasants' desires for private property; that high agrarian reform officials were Marxist sympathizers; and that the costs of agrarian reform—declining food production and maintenance of a large, inefficient new bureaucracy to administer the reformed sector—were too great for Chile to bear. Meanwhile the SNA leadership continued to work for modification of the PDC bill in Congress.[61]

When the PDC agrarian reform and union bills finally emerged virtually unchanged from Congress in 1967, Luis Larraín resigned and Hugo Zepeda Barros was elected SNA president. In his inaugural speech, Zepeda acknowledged the SNA's defeat, accepted the new legal conditions of land ownership, and emphasized the futility of future lobbying from a position of weakness. Zepeda rejected further deals with "politicians" and implicitly criticized the SNA's strategy of cooperating with the progressive right in 1961 and attempting under Frei to moderate PDC legislation: "Nothing was corrected; there were only promises that today are mere words that no one remembers."[62] In mapping out future strategy, Zepeda urged a return to building up an agrarian bloc based on strength of numbers and intersocietal unity: "The best support for the agrarian sector lies in the strength of the gremio"; from a strong base, "the gremios can always turn to the various political factions to find support for their just aspirations."[63]

During the remainder of the Frei administration, the SNA mounted a rearguard action to slow and discredit agrarian reform. Concurrently, as an SNA *Memoria* reported, landowners turned to "reordering and revitalizing their bases and organizations."[64] As in other times of political crisis, such as the post-World War I mobilization, the depression, and the Popular Front years, the SNA again called on landowners to fortify the gremio for defense. Although not generically different, the SNA's gremio orientation of the late sixties was more intense and effective than at any earlier time. With the eclipse of the right and the uncertain prospects for its recovery, it was clear that further reliance on the formal political system of parties and elections was infeasible. The state's erratic enforcement of landowners' rights, moreover, made tight organization and coordinated action at the grass roots more critical than ever. From the SNA's institutional viewpoint as well, a new direction seemed advisable. Since the 1961 agrarian reform debate, and despite the SNA's attempts to decentralize, landowners in the frontier and south looked to the CAS as their spokesman. This had left the SNA with a rival for national agrarian leadership, diminished prestige, and reduced power.

Combined with the greater need to strengthen the gremio was the emergence of increased opportunity to do so. An important development that tended to reduce regional as well as social divisions among landowners was the decline of the traditional large estate. Agrarian reform had reduced many of the large, highly assessed holdings to eighty hectares by 1970; even more had been subdivided—legally until 1966, illegally thereafter—and sold or transferred to relatives to avoid agrarian reform. The result was the rapid growth of medium-sized units in the heartland of the hacienda and throughout the country. As its own membership began to reflect the changes in land tenure—as its members were reduced to eighty hectares or less and as new medium proprietors joined the institution—the Society responded to their needs while continuing to defend large landowners against agrarian reform.[65]

For these owners of medium-sized property, defending the traditional large estate was not the primary issue in the late sixties. After the PDC rural labor legislation and the growth of rural unions, landowners were no longer able to transfer the cost of the continuing urban-oriented price policy to their work force, as they had done in the forties and fifties. To those without a large estate to defend, the more important issues were economic: prices, agricultural minimum wage, import policy, costs of credit and fertilizer—the same primary concerns of landowners in the frontier and lake areas. In addition to its continual lobbying on these economic issues, the SNA also responded to landowners' pressing need for modernization and efficiency in production. It launched a productivity campaign, expanded its technical and commercial services, and, through

El Campesino and special publications and seminars, familiarized landowners with the fundamentals of business administration as applied to the modern capitalist farm, or "*empresa agrícola*." The adoption of this technocratic line and the growing influence in the SNA's council of younger agronomists, agricultural engineers, and economists tended to disassociate the SNA somewhat from the stereotypical large landowner and to facilitate its accommodation with other segments of rural society.[66]

A second development which aided the SNA's attempt to strengthen the gremio was the Christian Democrats' creation of two new kinds of rural organizations. Seeking improved welfare for small proprietors, INDAP created campesino cooperatives in both the reformed and the traditional minifundio sectors which by 1970 brought together some 40,000 small producers. It also organized some 60,000 smallholders into local and provincial committees, united under the rubric of the Confederación Nacional de Pequeños Agricultores de Chile. These newly organized small proprietors shared some common ground, in areas of costs and prices, with larger landowners.[67] Equally important for the SNA were employers' unions, created by the 1967 agricultural union law and subsequently organized with SNA aid. By 1970 there were nearly 10,000 members organized in local syndicates, provincial federations, and a Confederación Nacional de Sindicatos de Empleadores Agrícolas de Chile (CONSEMACH). This represented approximately a third of the number of large and medium agricultural properties in the country.[68]

While attempting to expand its own membership, the SNA also fostered and strengthened alliances with other associations in order to forge the broadest possible bloc of rural interests. In this endeavor the SNA borrowed the modern organizational techniques of labor unions. It established training programs for leaders of rural organizations and emphasized the importance of contact with the grass roots: "We must always remember that only through continuous contact and exchange of ideas will we be able to represent our bases authentically, and that with their support the intermediary organizations become the social vehicle that achieves due consideration and respect from the state."[69]

By the end of the Frei administration, the PDC reforms and the SNA's organizational efforts had laid the basis for a more broadly based and vigorous agrarian gremio. In 1969 the Society elected a former president of CONSEMACH, Benjamín Matte Guzmán, as its new president. In early 1970, at what *El Campesino* correctly called a "historic" meeting, the SNA, CAS, and CONSEMACH met in Temuco with the leadership of the Confederación de Pequeños Agricultores and agreed upon a plan to defend their common interests. To consolidate its relations with the new organizations, the SNA expanded its council from 86 to 140 seats to incorporate representatives of the cooperatives, smallholders' confederation, and employers' unions; for propaganda purposes, it also offered representation to agricultural workers' unions. While larger landowners still dominated the SNA, the Society made constant efforts to exploit the emerging common ground among all agricultural landholders and producers by muting its public defense of the large estate and emphasizing issues, such as prices, taxes, credit, and property rights, which affected the whole spectrum of rural entrepreneurs. As a result of these developments, the SNA by 1970 could legitimately claim to represent a far broader segment of the agrarian population than ever before.[70] Its potential for effective political action was enhanced commensurately.

Overall, the Christian Democratic government made a substantial beginning in the transformation of rural society. Much of the rural labor force finally had attained the protection of the state, the benefits of nearly half a century of social legislation, and improved standards of living, while by 1970 some 140,000 workers were organized in five national federations. The change in land tenure was less impressive: rather than the 100,000 new landowners promised, only 29,000 rural families had acquired land—and the majority of them still remained in CORA-administered asentamientos without individual land titles. Some 1,300 large holdings had been expropriated, leaving between 3,000 and 4,000 properties over eighty basic hectares in the country. Almost 20 percent of the country's irrigated land and 12 percent of its dry farm land had passed into the reformed sector.[71]

Measured against its own goals, the "revolution in liberty" was at best a qualified success. Judged by its benefit for the political future of the Christian Democrats, it was a failure. The PDC tactic of mobilizing the masses through base organizations, in competition with the Marxists, raised expectations of greater reward than the PDC could or would deliver. The growth of mass organizations and the PDC's lack of firm commitment to capitalist private property frightened the upper and comfortable middle classes, and the cost of reform programs seemed to threaten the standard of living of the working and salaried middle classes. Reforms in the rural sector were at the core of the political failure of the PDC administration. While landowners lost some of their land and the certainty of state protection for their traditional rights, and while the urban population shared the financial cost of rural reforms, the vast majority of the mobilized peasantry still had not received its promised land. This generalized discontent was projected into the 1969 congressional and 1970 presidential elections.

The Unidad Popular Years, 1970–73

Buoyed by a substantial recuperation of its voting strength in the 1969 congressional election and determined to stand firm against further structural reform, the right fielded its own candidate in the 1970 presidential election. Ex-president Jorge Alessandri, running as a conservative independent, faced Salvador Allende of the Unidad Popular coalition (UP, the former FRAP with additional non-Marxist components) and Christian Democrat Radomiro Tomic. Although Alessandri led in the pre-election polls, Allende achieved a narrow plurality in the popular vote. After two tense months, Congress confirmed Allende's victory in November 1970. Allende's election launched Chile on the road toward socialism and presaged an accleration of change in rural society.[72]

After the UP victory, the terms of the agrarian reform issue shifted again to the left. With the rapid elimination of the large estate no longer in question, debate within the government centered on the nature of agricultural property during the transition to socialism.[73] While landowner organizations had enjoyed limited access to the Frei administration and even less influence on its policies, they had virtually no direct means of influencing UP policy. The SNA's initial memorandum to Allende revealed the deterioration of landowners' bargaining terms; only nine years after its hesitant endorsement of agrarian reform against inefficient landowners, the SNA was now reduced to pleading with a hostile government to respect the integrity of small and medium farms—those with eighty hectares or less.[74]

Lacking the congressional majority needed for a new law, the Allende administration proved very adept at maximizing every legal recourse at its disposal to speed up agrarian reform. In all areas of the economy it employed decree-laws from the Socialist Republic that provided wide powers of "requisition." In land, it also used article 171 of the 1967 agrarian reform law, which provided for the dispatch of government "interventors" to administer agricultural properties afflicted by labor disputes. Once installed, the interventor could administer the property so as to bankrupt it and thus make it liable to expropriation or foreclosure to state banking institutions. The government used this tactic so extensively that it soon ran out of politically reliable interventors.[75]

Even more threatening to landowners was the rise of "hypermobilization" in the countryside and the government's refusal to contain it by force. Elements of the governing coalition consistently pressed the administration through words and actions to accelerate the establishment of socialism. The Movement of the Revolutionary Left (MIR), a revolutionary faction to the left of the UP, was particularly active in fomenting direct campesino action. From December 1970, the Chilean countryside, especially in the south, was torn as never before by land invasions, strikes, and disruptions of production. The state's virtually complete withdrawal of protection for property rights threatened not only the unexpropriated landowners but also those previously reduced to the eighty-hectare reserve. In short, effective guarantees for private agrarian property disappeared.[76]

Like the right in general, the SNA leadership had been shocked at

Allende's victory. In the absence of any viable alternative, it initially maintained an open if not cordial dialogue with the new administration. Landowner spokesmen paid the customary courtesy call on the president-elect, and Allende's minister of agriculture opened the annual Temuco agricultural fair in November. In December 1970, the SNA president and a group of directors visited Cuba to investigate the prospects of trade in agricultural products and received a personal tour of Cuban agricultural facilities from Fidel Castro.[77] Although these developments unfolded in an atmosphere of tense normality, *El Campesino* warned that "while assuming this open attitude toward the government, the gremio leaders are not fooling themselves. They are aware that profound changes are coming, some of which will be painful."[78]

Relations with the government became increasingly strained in early 1971 as the UP accelerated the pace of agrarian reform and refused to crack down systematically on violence and illegal land seizures. SNA and other society leaders held several more meetings with Allende to ask for law enforcement. In one instance the president responded that he would use the "moral force" of the government, rather than physical force, to restore order.[79] It quickly became clear, however, that persuasion would not deter UP plans for rapid elimination of all large holdings. As violence, land seizures, interventions, and expropriations increased, the SNA opposition stiffened. In October 1971, Allende canceled his appearance at the opening of the International Fair of Santiago (formerly the SNA livestock exposition) after receiving an advance copy of SNA president Matte's speech. In a letter to Matte, Allende called the language of the speech "unacceptable" and its allegations "absolutely unfounded." He also condemned Manuel Valdés, president of CONSEMACH, for submitting a memorandum on agricultural problems directly to the minister of defense.[80] After this rebuff, the SNA abandoned its one-sided attempt at dialogue.

Throughout the following year, the chaos in agrarian reform intensified. Most remaining holdings over eighty hectares were formally expropriated or otherwise brought under state or direct campesino control. Under strong internal pressure to abolish all private property in land, the government, through narrow interpretation of the law, denied reserves to 90 percent of all landowners legally expropriated and reduced the reserves of many others to forty hectares. Not only large landowners but also a segment of the peasantry found reason for dissatisfaction with UP policy. Recipients of individual land titles under Frei came under fire as a kulak-like privileged class in the countryside. While the government reached no firm decision about the definitive form of property in the reformed sector, it discontinued the asentamientos and began establishing Centros de Reforma Agraria (CERAs). These transitional entities resembled the asentamientos

Table 17
Expropriations under the Frei and Allende Governments

	Number of Properties	Total Area (millions of hectares)
Frei (1965-70)	1,319	3.4
1971	1,378	2.6
1972	2,062[a]	2.8
1973 (to Sept.)	1,050	1.2
Total under Allende	4,490	6.6
Total, 1965-Sept. 1973	5,809	10.0

[a]Includes Jan.-Oct. 1972 only; expropriations in Nov. and Dec. 1972 are included in 1973 total.
SOURCE: Chonchol, "La reforma agraria en Chile," p. 610.

but were larger, more democratic, and, because of their collective operation, were also easier for the SNA and the opposition parties to depict as de facto state farms. As a result, the CERAs were unpopular among campesinos who aspired to individual parcels, and the UP often had to establish less rigid "peasant committees" to administer expropriated properties. Meanwhile police protection for the remaining private landowners continued to be largely withheld.[81]

The SNA and its members resisted UP policy on several fronts. As individuals, members worked within the rightist parties and Congress; some, including former president Benjamín Matte, joined the extremist Patria y Libertad; many, under the rubric of CONSEMACH, formed self-defense groups to offer physical resistance to land occupations and disruptions of production and to retake occupied properties. Aided by the SNA's legal department and the College of Lawyers, landowners also clogged the courts with appeals and suits to delay legal transfer of their land to the state.[82] Others gave up and joined the exodus from Chile.

The SNA's institutional position after the breakdown of dialogue with Allende was based on the unstated premise that the government would have to be radically altered or removed, constitutionally or violently, before the completion of its six-year term.[83] SNA strategy was to create public consciousness of the government's illegitimacy and the negative effects of its policies. Simultaneously, the Society played a leading role in building a multiclass network of groups to act as a countervailing force against the organized working class and to take direct action against the government.

In the area of public opinion, *El Campesino* publicized the illegal land seizures, the interventions and requisitions, the expropriations, and the violence in the countryside. The production decline that the SNA had alleged in the late 1960s had become a palpable reality under the UP, and *El Campesino* constantly stressed the hardship that this caused for the urban populace. It also exploited campesino dissatisfaction with UP policy, championing their resistance to the CERAs and demands for individual property titles.[84] Radio Agricultura played a prominent role in the SNA's public opinion campaign. When a government-ordered closure threatened its financial solvency, the SNA sold "liberty bonds" to keep it on the air. Its director was arrested and the station closed on several occasions on charges of subversion and other violations. Radio Agricultura was seen as either the "voice of liberty" or the chief "inciter to sedition," according to one's perspective.[85]

By 1972 the SNA's resistance to the UP was subsumed within the broader front of upper-class opposition. The Allende administration united the upper classes as never before. In contrast to the Frei government's concentration of structural reform in the rural sector, the UP reforms were both more radical and more generalized. Fulfilling his campaign promises, Allende moved to nationalize copper, banking, communications, and large and medium industry, and to extend existing controls over business in the private sector. After an initial period of shock and disarray, the business elites began to react by strengthening and expanding their organizations to confront a government which had marked them for eventual extinction.[86] *El Campesino* observed in 1972: "The previous indifference with which other sectors of the country witnessed the abuses committed on landowners has ended. This sacrifice of the rural sector has permitted the whole country to realize clearly that risking our courage is the price of survival."[87]

In contrast to the movement that gave birth to the Confederación de la Producción y del Comercio in 1934, the antigovernment mobilization beginning in 1971 extended far beyond the economic elites to encompass large elements of the middle class and even segments of the peasantry and the "aristocracy of labor." UP policies posed both real and imaginary threats to all these groups. The relative status and income advantages of the salaried middle class vis-à-vis labor were eroded by abolition of the legal distinctions between white- and blue-collar workers and by various UP policies favoring labor. The standard of living of the middle class and privileged sectors of the working class, such as the copper miners, was also jeopardized in an economy of hyperinflation and shortages of consumer goods. Moreover, the UP administration posed explicit or implicit threats to the independence and income of professionals, small entrepreneurs, and non-UP bureaucrats, while the military feared the prospect of armed people's militias. Much of the peasantry saw its aspirations for a private plot of land threatened by the collectivist tendencies of agrarian reform under Allende. Driven by these real and imagined threats to their status, income, or existence, much of the middle class, some of the peasantry, and a fraction of the working class joined forces with the elites to fight the common enemy.[88]

One face of this alliance was political collaboration between the upper- and middle-class parties, particularly the National party (the fused Conservatives and Liberals) and the Christian Democrats. Together, these parties held a majority in Congress, controlled the judiciary, and still exercised influence within the bureaucracy. However, given the vast power vested in the executive and Allende's creative use of existing machinery—including discretionary law enforcement—the parties alone were incapable of stalling the revolution. In the words of a rightist spokesman, the parties "were not prepared for a frontal attack on Marxism. Obviously a good speech, a declaration, a bill, or a law can have considerable effect in a state of law. But since we found ourselves living under the law of the jungle, it was necessary to find another means of facing the problem."[89] That other means was "gremialismo."

The gremio movement that arose to challenge Allende and the UP has been called "the mass line of the bourgeoisie."[90] Gremialismo had a vague ideology—more of a mystique—that asserted the primacy of the gremio as the legitimate form and expression of human activity by function rather than by class. It stressed private property and enterprise, called for social solidarity in place of class struggle, and, as a student gremio leader put it, felt that "problems should be solved with technical rather than political criteria."[91] Faced with a hostile state that they could no longer control, the gremios rejected "politics" and existing political institutions as illegitimate. In the view of the SNA president, gremialismo offered an alternative to "an institutionality rendered sterile by formalisms, compromises, and also by a neutralization derived from electoral eventualities, so subject to changes and vices. . . . [The gremios are] a power distinct from the traditional structure. The gremios seek direct dealings with those representatives of the government who may merit their confidence."[92] Thus gremialismo was essentially a means of resistance that borrowed the left and PDC tactic of mass mobilization and applied it to generate a counterforce competitive in numbers and organization with the pro-Allende working class. It provided an ostensibly nonpartisan framework for action which could mobilize hundreds of thousands of people for demonstrations and strikes. By 1972 the gremios had become, and saw themselves as, a kind of "parallel power" alongside the government—similar to Lenin's concept of the worker soviets under the Kerensky government.[93]

The gremio movement was based on the unification of existing economic, professional, and other functional interest groups and the creation of new ones. It brought organizations of the business elites, peasants, professionals, medium and small entrepreneurs, and even a few labor unions together with noneconomic functional groups such as women, students, and neighborhood councils (*juntas de vecinos*). After tentative beginnings late in the Frei administration, the organizational consolidation accelerated in 1971 when the Confederación de la Producción y del Comercio, consisting of large businessmen and landowners, joined the confederations of retail merchants and small industrialists and artisans in the Frente Nacional de la Actividad Privada (National Front of Private Enterprise). In parallel fashion the various professional associations—lawyers, agronomists, accountants, doctors, engineers, librarians, and others—merged their 70,000 members into the Confederación Unida de Profesionales de Chile in 1971. The following year the Comando Nacional de Defensa Gremial was formed to coordinate the activities of the varied groups that had mobilized in resistance to the UP government. By 1973 over a thousand gremios were allied in the grass roots antigovernment movement.[94]

Along with the SOFOFA and other elite groups, the SNA played a central role in the gremio movement. Having turned earlier to perfecting its own gremio organization to fight the Christian Democrats, the SNA offered a model for the other sectors more recently galvanized to action against the UP government. In its own assessment, the SNA "has been in the vanguard, not to shout its presence nor give [the movement] a particular character, but to save Chile."[95] The participation of the SNA and most other elite associations was relatively low-key; while their financial resources, organizational strength, and influence formed the core of the movement, the most visible leadership was selected from more middle-class groups untainted by previous association with the big landowner and business organizations. With Jaime Guzmán, a Catholic University student, León Vilarín of the truckers' association, and Rafael Cumsille of the retail merchants' confederation articulating the gremio viewpoint, the SNA through its media portrayed those spokesmen as "the authentic expression of the provinces, isolated and held back for years by the insatiability and voracity of centralism; expression of the man of the middle class who, isolated in the city, bears his frustration and inarticulateness in solitude."[96]

The gremio movement, supported by the opposition media, conducted an escalating campaign of publicity, mass demonstrations, and work stoppages which culminated in two "employers' strikes." The first, in October 1972, grew out of a strike by the national truck owners' association protesting UP plans for nationalizing transportation in Aysén province. Coordinated and supported by the Comando Nacional de Defensa Gremial, the shutdown quickly spread to encompass most production, distribution, and professional activities in the private sector, including agriculture, where both the SNA and its affiliates and the PDC-led campesino organizations supported the strike. This surprising and awesome display of gremio power ended only with Allende's incorporation of military officers into his cabinet.[97]

The second strike, in August 1973, assumed the same general form but pursued a different objective. The opposition had failed in the March 1973 congressional election in its bid to obtain the two-thirds majority necessary to impeach the president. Now, following the frustration of its strategy for a "constitutional coup," the opposition turned to the gremios as a means of attacking the government. The second employers' strike paralyzed the economy, revealed the impotence of the government, and convinced the wavering military that only its intervention could restore order and prevent a protracted civil war. When it came on September 11, as Armand Mattelart has observed, "the coup of the generals . . . [was] in reality the coup of the gremios."[98]

Rural Society under Military Rule

Developments since the coup still await the impartial analysis that can come only with the passage of time and subsidence of polemics. Moreover, while the main thrusts of the military's policies are fairly clear, the suppression of free inquiry and expression in Chile has made reliable information on the motivations and results of particular policies and programs both difficult to obtain and suspect. As a case in point, the nine years of rural reform under the Christian Democrats and the UP were observed and recorded by scholars and functionaries, Chilean and foreign, left and right, and freely communicated to a curious world. Developments under the military have been quieter but equally significant; yet one must rely for information primarily on official reports, a muzzled press, and an academic community that survives by asking few hard questions.[99] Therefore the following pages attempt only a preliminary overview of the junta's main agrarian policies during its first six years—the equivalent of a presidential term under the 1925 constitution—and an assessment of the SNA's role in the political process under the military.

One indisputable point is that the SNA effusively welcomed the coup that it had helped to generate: "The *patria* has triumphed. Joy invades the hearts of all free and democratic Chileans, in all of which there is one desire—to press forward with national reconstruction."[100] Under the junta, the SNA quickly recovered the access to and influence in government that it had lost in 1964. The Chilean military, unlike the Peruvian or the

Brazilian, had not received specialized training to prepare its officer corps to run the country.[101] Upon assuming control, moreover, the military encountered a bureaucracy headed by UP appointees whom it systematically persecuted in its holy war to extirpate the "cancer of Marxism." Thus the military turned to the private sector for advice and personnel.

From the outset, the junta relied on the SNA for technical advice and general policy orientation and later recruited its civilian agricultural personnel from within the Society's ranks. In 1976 SNA secretary general Sergio Romero Pizarro became subsecretary of agriculture, the top civilian post in the agricultural bureaucracy. In 1978 the junta selected former SNA president Alfonso Márquez de la Plata as the first civilian minister of agriculture since 1973. The SNA reciprocated in 1979 by electing as its president Germán Riesco Zañartu, former director of the Oficina de Planificación Agrícola under the military.[102] SNA involvement in government extended beyond the level of top personnel. Beginning in 1977, a private SNA-established foundation assumed the administration of several of the government's agricultural schools, in a corporatist arrangement resembling that of the nineteenth century.[103]

The close linkage between the SNA and government gave the Society a preponderant role in the formulation and execution of agricultural policy; in fact, the SNA's influence appeared virtually as strong as it had been prior to the advent of mass politics in 1919. The important and highly visible role of the SNA and some other elite economic associations under the junta foreshadowed the corporatist nature of the new institutional order which the military set out to establish in Chile. The chairman of the junta-appointed commission charged with writing a new constitution indicated in a 1976 statement a greater formal role for functional groups: "The new fundamental text . . . will give special importance to the intermediate organisms of society, such as the professional and technical colleges, gremio, feminine, and youth organizations, et cetera, which have an undisputed right to intervene in the great decisions which affect the destinies of the country."[104] And the constitution, approved in a controversial plebiscite on September 11, 1980, did contain several provisions confirming the privileged position of the SNA and its counterparts in the new institutional order.[105]

The junta's agrarian policy unfolded within the framework of a general economic and social policy featuring the application of classical economics, as taught by Milton Friedman, to a country long accustomed to extensive state control. In addition to returning most of the enterprises expropriated under the UP to private hands, the junta stripped back the bulk of the tariffs, exchange and price controls, and production subsidies that had accrued since the depression and launched an austerity program to control the runaway inflation. A major objective of these policies was to make private enterprise more efficient by forcing Chile to produce goods in which it enjoys a competitive advantage in the international marketplace. The reorientation of the economy was largely financed by foreign capital and subsidized by severe repression of the labor movement, resulting in low wages and the absence of strikes. This shock treatment produced mixed economic results after six years: inflation was brought down to manageable levels, the quality and variety of exports was up, but the industrial sector, which had relied on heavy tariff protection, had suffered from foreign competition. The social cost of the junta's policies was reflected in extremely high unemployment, redistribution of national income in favor of the upper classes, and reduced standards of living for the working and middle classes.[106]

The SNA supported the junta's economic policies in general, with numerous specific reservations: "We have repeatedly declared our support for the principles of the social economy of the marketplace which the Supreme Government advocates. We believe that they are a powerful tool that will permit the country to emerge from the economic and social prostration into which the Marxist dictatorship plunged it. However, we repeat with equal emphasis that the agricultural sector, due to its special characteristics, turns on factors very different from those that affect other activities."[107] Such radical changes as the lifting of price supports and controls and elimination of most tariffs on agricultural products proceeded with the SNA's tacit or explicit support. Nonetheless, as the foregoing quotation indicates, the SNA did not always prevail when its views clashed with those of the junta's general economic advisors. Thus the Society continued—in respectful tones—its traditional lobbying on a range of economic issues.

The overall impact of junta policy in the rural sector varied by social group and region. Given the SNA's preponderant role in policy formulation, it is not surprising that the greatest benefits were reaped by the modern producers of the core area, who possessed the capital, expertise, and climate to grow specialized export crops, especially out-of-season fruits for Northern Hemisphere consumption. These entrepreneurs, primarily those possessing the basic eighty-hectare reserve or more, received subsidized credit earmarked for export producers, and they were largely responsible for the success of the junta's program to promote agricultural exports. On the other hand, landowners in the frontier and the south who produced primarily for the domestic market did not benefit, and perhaps suffered, from the imposition of free market agriculture. The contraction of purchasing power and the competition of foreign commodities in the Chilean market had contributed since 1973 to a decline in the production of traditional crops, such as cattle, wheat, and most vegetables. Most adversely affected by the junta's policies were the middle and lower strata of rural society, those least equipped for free market competition. Moreover, they lost the support provided by the two previous administrations and the basic rights and welfare gained over the preceding nine years. For the lower strata of rural society especially, a decade of hope and real gains in income and living standards was reversed.[108]

During the PDC and UP administrations, the traditional repression of rural labor had given way to an impressive ground swell of organization under government auspices. New legislation and enforcement of labor law in the countryside had improved working conditions and increased the real income of rural labor. But, in its zeal to persecute Marxists and fortify private enterprise, the junta destroyed the Chilean labor movement built up over the previous hundred years. In the countryside, unions were purged, placed under government control, or disbanded altogether. Strikes were forbidden and the benefits provided by labor law put into abeyance. Once again the patrón rather than the state dictated the terms of work, and the "*sol a sol*" workday and low wages made their return with a drastic erosion of living standards for rural workers. The junta's 1979 "Plan Laboral," a blueprint for a new labor-relations system featuring the open shop, employer participation, and other traits of white unions, was to apply in agriculture as well as in industry. The SNA's enthusiastic support for this plan, contrasting with the opposition of even junta-appointed labor leaders, suggested that its effects in the countryside would resemble those of the 1947 law which legalized but effectively prohibited unions in agriculture.[109]

When the military took over, Chile had experienced almost a decade of land expropriation on a grand scale. Because relatively little land had been legally transferred into private hands, CORA in 1973 controlled some 60 percent of all irrigated land and 32 percent of the remaining arable land in Chile—almost 10 million hectares in all. Inheriting this vast amount of land, administered as CERAs and other transitional entities, the junta automatically became arbiter of the future configuration of rural society. After initially suspending expropriations and guaranteeing all reserves up to forty hectares, the junta embarked on a program of "consolidation" of agrarian reform. Land determined to have been illegally expropriated was returned to previous owners; in 1,512 cases, the entire estate was turned back regardless of size. Legally expropriated landowners left with less than eighty hectares were invited to reconstitute the basic reserve, in exchange for waiving all claims to future government compensation. By the end of 1977, these two processes had consumed approximately 30 percent of CORA's land. Another large portion of CORA's holdings, judged unsuitable for subdivision and assignment to peasants, was sold in large units to individual buyers. Also by the end of 1977, the government had assigned approximately one-third of CORA's land to some 40,000 campesinos in the form of family agriculture units. Reversing the previous orientation toward collectivism, the junta distributed parcels as private property with no restrictions on alienation. Given the amount of land remaining to CORA after 1977, one can project that the total number of families receiving parcels will not far exceed half the number Eduardo Frei promised in 1964.[110]

The process of "consolidation," while delivering the private plots desired by most campesinos, made a mockery of agrarian reform in almost every other way. As a result of large-scale restitution of private property, thousands of former beneficiaries were deprived of any claim to a plot. And with the breakup of the CERAs into manageable family units, the excess population not selected to receive parcels joined the landless and often the unemployed. The procedures for selecting recipients of land reportedly were subject to serious abuses, resulting in the assignment of plots to urban elements and other strangers to the land in question. Thus the beneficiaries of agrarian reform represented the privileged few among the mass of rural workers and impoverished minifundistas never affected directly by agrarian reform.[111]

The new class of family farmers, along with the vastly greater number of minifundistas, was adversely affected by government austerity and the establishment of a free market economy. The junta cut back on credit, agricultural extension, aid to cooperatives, and a variety of services previously directed toward small producers, with the result that many reverted to subsistence production and suffered the consequent contraction of income. The dean of the University of Chile's school of agronomy, a man unsympathetic to agrarian reform, has written of the junta's "consolidation": "Agrarian policy has aristocratic tendencies because it benefits only the elites and because the great masses of farmers are not instructed in the advantages and difficulties of the social economy of the marketplace."[112] As a result of these economic travails, increasing numbers of agrarian reform beneficiaries failed to meet their mortgage payments and were forced to lease or sell their land. One estimate is that, by the end of 1977, up to 25 percent of beneficiaries in some provinces had sold, while others had leased, their plots to neighboring landowners and become sharecroppers on their own land.[113] For these unfortunates, agrarian reform not only failed to provide a better life but ended in their complete disillusionment.

Abandoning its erstwhile anti-UP allies from the lower ranks of the agrarian gremio, the SNA tacitly and sometimes explicitly supported the government's "consolidation" of agrarian reform. In response to a 1977 pastoral letter from the Chilean bishops addressing the "crisis" among small and medium landowners, the SNA articulated a Darwinian view that could have come directly from the 1919 Asamblea de Agricultores' report on proposed land legislation: "Without the spirit of struggle and discipline in work, the new proprietors will march unalterably toward failure. This situation cannot be attributed to the system but to the natural result of the selection process, by virtue of which only those who try their best succeed and the rest fail."[114] At the SNA's urging, the government in 1978 amended the 1967 agrarian reform law to eliminate the eighty-basic-hectare limit on land exempt from expropriation in order to legitimize and guarantee the restored large holdings and those created through purchase of land from the reformed sector. The same decree authorized corporate ownership for agricultural enterprises.[115] At the end of 1978, the government symbolically culminated its counterreform and ended Chile's second cycle of agrarian reform by abolishing CORA. A man with close ties to the SNA was chosen to head the new Office of Agrarian Normalization, the agency charged with liquidating all remaining state-owned agricultural land.[116]

After six years of military rule, then, Chilean rural society had undergone profound change. When the military assumed power, landowners' most basic interests—property rights and control over their labor force—had been under intense attack for almost a decade, and a new rural order was taking shape. The violent overthrow of the UP government in 1973 abruptly halted the revolution in the countryside. Then, reversing the trends under the previous three administrations, the junta proceeded to restore landowners' traditional rights and much of their property; and by eradicating liberal democracy, it removed the intermittent threat of reform under which landowners had lived since 1919. The impact of a decade of reform was still visible in the altered property structure and the somewhat modernized production units in the agricultural sector. However, the most notable feature of rural Chile after six years of counterrevolution was the survival, perhaps even the strengthening, of the traditional order in the countryside.

Landowners and Politics: Summary and Conclusions

As this chapter has indicated, the main political issues affecting landowners after 1940 were the same as those initially identified, extensively debated, and tentatively resolved during Chile's first cycle of reform beginning in 1919. In response to pressure from both left and right, mechanisms had been established in the thirties to protect the urban consumer against uncontrolled food price inflation. Concurrently, moderate but potentially effective agrarian reform legislation was passed, and the initial steps were taken to extend the protection of labor and social welfare law to agricultural workers. Led by the SNA, landowners opposed the more extreme threats to their interests, but by the 1930s they generally viewed moderate reform as an acceptable cost for maintaining their own fundamental prerogatives and the preeminence of the national upper class.

In the climate of moderation that ensued following the collapse of the Popular Front, landowners' fear of rural social reform abated, while the struggle with urban interests over economic policy intensified. The SNA fought to retain existing subsidies, secure adequate government investment, and obtain favorable price and import policies for agriculture in the face of increasing competition for scarce economic resources from industry and the urban middle and working classes. Meanwhile, the financial demise of the agrarian reform program and the legalization of the repression of rural labor left the large estate and the rural social structure intact. By 1960, however, the deteriorating condition of agricultural labor, the urbanization of the countryside, the deficient performance of the agricultural sector, and the influence of the Cuban Revolution reopened the attack on the rural status quo. Nurtured by Marxists and Christian Democrats and aided by electoral reforms, rural labor emerged as a new political force, free of landowners' control and increasingly disposed to radical action in pursuit of revolutionary change in the countryside. These developments challenged landowners' interests and prerogatives to a degree that far exceeded the threats of the thirties.

As earlier, the organized landowners' struggle to preserve their rights and privileges demonstrated adaptability, determination, and resilience. The SNA's approaches to resisting reform after 1940 were essentially those adopted in response to the advent of mass politics. During the forties and fifties, when economic issues were paramount, the SNA had joined the majority of the political right in adopting a firm antireformist position, reminiscent of its pre-1930s stances. However, in the face of increased pressure for reform after 1958, the SNA joined the rightist majority in reverting to the flexible, preemptive tactics adopted in response to the crisis of the depression and the Socialist Republic. Thus, as under Jaime Larraín thirty years before, the SNA worked to identify itself as the champion of responsible, practicable rural reform and hesitantly endorsed the Alessandri agrarian reform in an attempt to stem the tide of rural mobilization and political radicalization.

However, like Arturo Alessandri's preemptive measures of the thirties, his son's moderate reforms were insufficient to contain the leftward movement of the Chilean electorate in the 1960s. After the election of the Christian Democrats, the selective withdrawal of physical protection of landowners' legal rights, and the passage of new agrarian reform and unionization laws, the SNA shifted from its progressive stance to the more rigid basic defensive tactics that it had used successfully against the Popular Front government—strengthening the gremio and engaging the "Marxist" adversary on various fronts. In contrast to 1941, however, in 1970 an unfriendly government was replaced by an implacably hostile one. Having earlier conceded the Christian Democratic reforms, the SNA after 1970 faced the real threat that its members' remaining property and its own raison d'être would disappear. Lacking influence and the ability to defend its constituency under the Allende administration, the SNA embraced a strident antisystem corporatism that developed into gremialismo and turned its power toward overthrowing the UP government and Chilean democracy.

Active participation in the overthrow of a government and a political system, although a radical departure from the SNA's usual tactics, was not inconsistent with landowners' historic pattern of resistance to reform. Indeed, the SNA's actions and attitudes during the first cycle of reform reveal that landowners—like most of the elites—had adapted only reluctantly and tentatively to the imperfect liberal democracy that emerged in Chile after the collapse of oligarchic hegemony. The development and persistence of rightist antidemocratic ideologies—especially varieties of corporatism—revealed the failure of the 1925 constitution to gain complete acceptance among the upper classes and segments of the middle classes. The SNA itself indicated the conditional nature of its adherence to Chilean democracy in occasional statements, both official and casual, while at the practical level it consistently pressured for functional representation in the public administration as a means of thwarting reformist legislation produced by competitive mass politics. The Popular Front period further revealed the SNA's and the right's qualified acceptance of liberal democracy: after failing to prevent the election of the center-left alliance, they subsequently attempted to redefine the parameters of the political system in order to eliminate two new and threatening political forces—rural labor and the Communist party.

As indicated by SNA statements and actions between 1919 and 1940, organized landowners' adherence to the rules of constitutional democracy was contingent on the successful defense of their interests at an acceptable cost. By the 1930s, a majority within the SNA had adopted the view that tactical concessions, both token and substantive, were an acceptable price to pay for the prevention of structural reform. However, when reform first threatened to pass acceptable limits under the Popular Front, the SNA had quickly revealed its unwillingness to accept the full consequences of political democracy. In the 1960s, under mounting pressure for change, the SNA's preemptive strategy failed and the Christian Democratic reforms ensued. The 1967 agrarian reform and unionization laws severely circumscribed landowners' traditional rights over property and labor, leaving them without further concessions to offer in defense of their own and the broader upper-class interests; the limits of acceptable cost had been reached and, for many landowners, exceeded. When faced after 1970 with mobilized rural masses and a government unable or unwilling to protect landowners' remaining legal rights, the SNA responded in a manner consistent with its fifty years' experience in resisting reform. Having exhausted all effective means of defense within the existing institutional order, the landowners abandoned their severely strained allegiance to the Chilean political system and embraced the common Latin American elite response to the challenge of reform—the destruction of liberal democracy.

Notes

1. The general analysis of the 1941-58 period is based largely on: Gil, *Political System*, pp. 88-297; Drake, *Socialism and Populism*, pp. 242-306; Olavarría Bravo, *Chile entre dos Alessandri*, vol. 2; Ricardo Cruz-Coke, *Geografía electoral de Chile* (Santiago, 1952); González Videla, *Memorias*, vols. 1-2; Ernst Halperin, *Nationalism and Communism in Chile* (Cambridge, Mass., 1965), pp. 1-59, 118-35; Peter Snow, *El radicalismo chileno: historia y doctrina del Partido Radical* (Buenos Aires, 1972), pp. 89-141.

2. On the political behavior of the middle classes during the period of Radical ascendancy, see James Petras, *Politics and Social Forces in Chilean Development* (Berkeley, Cal., 1970), pp. 123-57; Claudio Véliz, "Obstacles to Reform in Latin America Today," *The World Today*, 19, no. 1 (Jan. 1963), 18-29; Frederick B. Pike, "Aspects of Class Relations in Chile, 1850-1960," *Hispanic American Historical Review*, 43 (1963), 14-33.

3. For insight into the debate within the Conservative party, see Orrego Vicuña, ed., *Horacio Walker y su tiempo*. The Conservative party formally split in 1949 over social orientation and the best means of fighting communism. Cortés and Fuentes, *Diccionario político*, p. 117.

4. *El C*, 84 (July 1952), 33. Note that with vol. 78 (1946), page numbering in *El C* went to a single-issue basis. Thus the month is noted in all citations after 1945.

5. CIDA, *Tenencia de la tierra*, pp. 248-53.

6. *El C*, 77 (1945), 179, 197-98; Loveman, *Documentary Supplement*, pp. 103-16.

7. *El C*, 76 (1944), 385.

8. *Ibid.*, p. 206.

9. Loveman, *Struggle in the Countryside*, pp. 170-73. Details of the SNA's efforts to amend the bill are found in Jean Carrière, "Landowners and the Rural Unionization Question in Chile, 1920-48," *Boletín de Estudios Latinoamericanos y del Caribe*, no. 22 (June 1977), 34-52.

10. Loveman, *Struggle in the Countryside*, pp. 120-32; Loveman, *Documentary Supplement*, pp. 138-58.

11. *El C*, 79 (July 1947), 5.

12. Loveman, *Struggle in the Countryside*, pp. 170-73; Drake, *Socialism and Populism*, pp. 283-90. Note that the U.S. government strongly supported repressing the Communists.

13. *El C*, 77 (1945), 705.

14. *Ibid.*, 80 (Feb. 1948), 8-10, for example.

15. *Ibid.*, 85 (Apr. 1953), 7; *ibid.* (Oct. 1953), 49-50; Loveman, *Struggle in the Countryside*, pp. 83-85, 93-95; Loveman, *Documentary Supplement*, pp. 77-79.

16. See ch. 5, n. 1, for a survey of the literature on Chilean inflation history; for 1950-70, see Vittorio Corbo Lioi, *Inflation in Developing Countries: An Econometric Study of Chilean Inflation* (Amsterdam, 1974).

17. CIDA, *Tenencia de la tierra*, p. 12.

18. Mamalakis, "Public Policy and Sectoral Development," in Mamalakis and Reynolds, eds., *Essays on the Chilean Economy*, pp. 3-11, 169-71. On general economic policy during this period, see Ricardo Ffrench-Davis, *Políticas económicas en Chile: 1952-1970* (Santiago, 1973); Mamalakis, *Growth and Structure of the Chilean Economy*, pp. 89-365; Pinto Santa Cruz, *Chile, un caso*, pp. 107-98. Also, Herman Finer, *The Chilean Development Corporation* (Montreal, 1947).

19. Mamalakis, "Public Policy and Sectoral Development," pp. 3-11; Kurt Ulrich B., *Algunos aspectos del control del comercio en la agricultura chilena, 1950-58* (Santiago, 1964). The SNA often denounced the "dumping" of surplus wheat and other commodities. *El C*, 88 (Aug. 1956), 12-14; *ibid.*, 89 (Aug. 1957), 5.

20. CIDA, *Tenencia de la tierra*, pp. 173-79, 235-47; Ffrench-Davis, *Políticas económicas*, pp. 153-85; Universidad de Chile, Instituto de Economía, *La tributación agrícola en Chile, 1940-1958. Algunas implicaciones económicas del sistema tributario chileno* (Santiago, 1960).

21. *El C*, 84 (June 1952), 5.

22. *Ibid.*, 83 (June 1951), 5.

23. *El C*, 83 (Oct. 1951), 5-11; *ibid.*, 84 (Jan. 1952), 5; *ibid.* (Feb. 1952), 5, 42-45; *ibid.* (Sept. 1952), 5; *ibid.*, 85 (Oct. 1953), 49. Note that Kaufman, *Politics of Land Reform*, p. 151, reports that the commodity associations attained seats in the SNA council in the 1960s.

24. CIDA, *Tenencia de la tierra*, pp. 235-41.

25. On the structuralist-monetarist debate, see David Feliz, "An Alternative View of the 'Monetarist-Structuralist' Controversy," in Albert O. Hirschman, ed., *Latin American Issues: Essays and Comments* (New York, 1961), pp. 81-93. Mamalakis, "Public Policy and Sectoral Development," pp. 117-48, argues the case for discriminatory price policy, while CIDA, *Tenencia de la tierra*, pp. 206-10, 244-46, examines the major arguments and embraces the structuralist position. See also Jeanine Swift, *Agrarian Reform in Chile: An Economic Study* (Lexington, Mass., 1971), pp. 12-17.

26. Mamalakis, "Public Policy and Sectoral Development," pp. 117-48; also Swift, *Agrarian Reform*, pp. 14-15.

27. Mamalakis, "Public Policy and Sectoral Development," pp. 117-48; Loveman, *Chile*, p. 262; Swift, *Agrarian Reform*, pp. 9-11; and for Latin America in general, Rodolfo Stavenhagen, "Seven Fallacies about Latin America," in James Petras and Maurice Zeitlin, eds., *Latin America: Reform or Revolution?* (Greenwich, Conn., 1968), p. 29.

28. Studies of Chilean agricultural development in the forties and fifties include: Economic Commission for Latin America/Food and Agricultural Organization, *Análisis de algunos factores que obstaculizan el incremento de la producción agropecuario* (Santiago, 1953); Pierre R. Crosson, *Agricultural Development and Productivity: Lessons from the Chilean Experience* (Baltimore, 1970); Roberto Echeverría, *The Effect of Agricultural Price Policies on Intersectoral Income Transfers* (Ithaca, N.Y., 1969); Marto A. Ballesteros, "Desarrollo agrícola chileno,

1910-1955," *Cuadernos Económicos* (Universidad Católica de Chile), 2, no. 5 (Jan.-Apr. 1965), 7-40; and Mamalakis, "Public Policy and Sectoral Development," pp. 117-48.

29. See ch. 2, p. 37, for discussion of the "retrograde" image in the sixties. Also *El C*, 99 (Nov. 1967), 39; and Loveman, *Struggle in the Countryside*, pp. 197-200.

30. *El C*, 85 (Jan. 1953), 11.

31. On the 1958 election, see Gil, *Political System*, pp. 227-33.

32. Petras, *Politics and Social Forces*, pp. 263-83, analyzes the 1958 and 1964 male rural vote for Allende.

33. Andrés Pascal, *Relaciones de poder en una localidad rural* (Santiago, 1968), uses the term "urbanization of the countryside." See also Loveman, *Struggle in the Countryside*, pp. 189-201; Petras, *Politics and Social Forces*, pp. 256-72; Kaufman, *Politics of Land Reform*, pp. 26-30. On the early Catholic rural labor movement, see Henry A. Landsberger and Fernando Canitrot M., *Iglesia, intelectuales, y campesinos* (Santiago, 1967), and Oscar Domínguez C., *El campesino chileno y la acción católica rural* (Madrid, 1961).

34. *El C*, 90 (Oct. 1958), 15.

35. Kaufman, *Politics of Land Reform*, pp. 49-51. Other moderate or token Alessandri reforms included housing and minimum wage measures.

36. See above, n. 25.

37. *El C*, 90 (Oct. 1958), 7-8.

38. CIDA, *Tenencia de la tierra*, pp. 252-53; William C. Thiesenhusen, *Chile's Experiments in Agrarian Reform* (Madison, Wis., 1966), pp. 34-36.

39. *El C*, 92 (Jan. 1960), 11-12. On Catholic agrarian reform programs, see Thiesenhusen, *Chile's Experiments in Agrarian Reform*.

40. *El C*, 92 (Oct. 1960), 23.

41. *Ibid.* (Apr. 1960), 5; *ibid.* (Mar. 1960), 5.

42. *Ibid.* 93 (May 1961), 7-8.

43. *Ibid.* 92 (Oct. 1960), 13.

44. Gil, *Political System*, pp. 234-37; Kaufman, *Politics of Land Reform*, pp. 51-53.

45. James Becket, "Land Reform in Chile," *Journal of Inter-American Studies*, 5 (1963), 177-211; Loveman, *Struggle in the Countryside*, pp. 225-40. Note that the concept of eighty basic irrigated hectares, originally defined in the 1962 agrarian reform law, was incorporated into the Christian Democratic law of 1967; thus forthcoming references to "eighty hectares" should be understood as eighty basic Central Valley irrigated hectares or their equivalent on other soils.

46. *El C*, 94 (Jan. 1962), 8-17.

47. *Ibid.* (quote, pp. 10-11).

48. *Ibid.*, pp. 8-17; Constantine Menges, *Chile's Landowners Associations and Agrarian Reform Politics* (Santa Monica, Cal., 1968).

49. Kaufman, *Politics of Land Reform*, pp. 61-66, 73-76, argues the role of political experience in determining the right's and the SNA's flexibility on agrarian reform.

50. *El C*, 94 (Apr. 1962), 6-7, 18-19; *ibid.*, 95 (Jan. 1963), 6.

51. Loveman, *Struggle in the Countryside*, pp. 235-40; Swift, *Agrarian Reform*, pp. 34-35.

52. Gil, *Political System*, pp. 242-43, 298-311. See also Gil and Charles J. Parrish, *The Chilean Presidential Election of September 4, 1964* (Washington, D.C.,

1965); Parrish, Arpad von Lazar, and Jorge Tapia-Videla, *The Chilean Congressional Elections of March 7, 1965: An Analysis* (Washington, D.C., 1965).

53. The literature on the Christian Democrats and the Frei administration is abundant. For a detailed account, see Arturo Olavarría Bravo, *Chile bajo la democracia cristiana*, 6 vols. (Santiago, 1966-71). Broader analyses of the political system during the Frei government include: Petras, *Politics and Social Forces*; Ben Burnett, *Political Groups in Chile: The Dialogue between Order and Change* (Austin, Tex., 1970); and Norbert Lechner, *La democracia en Chile* (Buenos Aires, 1970), pp. 86-158.

54. Loveman, *Struggle in the Countryside*, pp. 240-56; Loveman, *Documentary Supplement*, pp. 161-74.

55. Kaufman, *Politics of Land Reform*, pp. 79-113; Loveman, *Struggle in the Countryside*, pp. 259-71.

56. Petras, *Politics and Social Forces*, pp. 219-30.

57. Kaufman, *Politics of Land Reform*, pp. 114-44; Loveman, *Struggle in the Countryside*, pp. 257-59. James Petras and Hugo Zemelman Merino, *Peasants in Revolt: A Chilean Case Study, 1965-1971*, tr. Thomas Flory (Austin, Tex., 1972), focuses on a hacienda illegally seized in 1965 and the development of its occupants' political consciousness.

58. *El C*, 97 (Apr. 1965), 4; *ibid.* (June 1965), 4; Kaufman, *Politics of Land Reform*, pp. 151-54.

59. *El C*, 97 (Sept. 1965), 6-7; *ibid.* (May 1965), 3.

60. *Ibid.* (July 1965), 9-10, 15; *ibid.* (Sept. 1965), 6-7.

61. Kaufman, *Politics of Land Reform*, pp. 162-66, 221-86, discusses urban reactions to agrarian reform. *El C* for the years 1965 through 1968 is full of statements of these themes. E.g., 97 (Nov. 1965), 28-33; *ibid.* (Dec. 1965), 20-27; *ibid.*, 98 (Feb. 1966), 28-31; *ibid.* (Apr. 1966), 18-23; *ibid.* (Nov. 1966), 16-21; *ibid.*, 99 (Feb. 1968), 4-5, 16-19; *ibid.* (Mar. 1968), 4-5, 42-47. (Note that for unexplained reasons *El C* for both 1967 and 1968 appeared as vol. 99.) Theodore H. Moran, *Multinational Corporations and the Politics of Dependence: Copper in Chile* (Princeton, N.J., 1974), pp. 198-218, examines the right's use of Frei's copper "Chileanization" bill to obstruct passage of the PDC agrarian reform bill.

62. *El C*, 99 (July 1967), 17.

63. *Ibid.*

64. *Ibid.*, 101 (Apr. 1970), 20.

65. See Loveman, *Struggle in the Countryside*, pp. 251, 315; César Soto, "Crisis y violencia en la sociedad chilena," in Enrique Gomáriz *et al.*, *Chile bajo la junta (economía y sociedad en la dictadura militar chilena)* (Madrid, 1976), pp. 306-7; Wayne Ringlien, "Economic Effects of Chilean National Expropriation Policy on the Private Commercial Farm Sector, 1964-69" (unpublished dissertation in economics, University of Maryland, 1971); Jacques Chonchol, "La reforma agraria en Chile," *Trimestre Económico*, 43, no. 3 (July-Sept. 1976), 607; Cristóbal Kay, "Chile: evaluación del program de reforma agraria de la Unidad Popular," *Desarrollo Económico*, 15, no. 57 (Apr.-June 1975), 87-88.

66. Ringlien, "Economic Effects"; Kaufman, *Politics of Land Reform*, p. 151; Sergio Gómez, *Los empresarios agrícolas* (Santiago, 1972), pp. 53-66. Gómez reports incidents such as the landowner blockage of the Central Highway in April 1968, protesting the official wheat price, which indicate increased militance of economically pressed landowners, as well as the SNA's ability to exploit this new mood. The SNA pushed its productivity campaign through cooperation with the

new Centro de Estudios para Empresas Agrícolas of the Universidad Católica and the Instituto Chileno de Administración Racional de Empresas (ICARE).

67. Loveman, *Struggle in the Countryside*, pp. 275-76; Solon Barraclough and José A. Fernández, coordinators, *Diagnóstico de la reforma agraria chilena* (Mexico City, 1974), pp. 184-89.

68. Gómez, *Empresarios agrícolas*, pp. 33-51, 66-68. The criterion for "medium" property was that it employ a minimum of four full-time workers. Note that CONSEMACH typically employed more radical tactics than did the SNA; e.g., in 1969 some 300 members assembled in Melipilla to retake occupied fundos.

69. *El C*, 100 (Apr. 1969), 14-15; *ibid.*, 101 (Sept. 1970), 24-25.

70. *Ibid.*, 100 (June 1969), 21; *ibid.*, 101 (Feb. 1970), 14-15; *ibid.* (June 1970), 32-35. The SNA's council prior to this reform is analyzed in Arriagada, *Oligarquía patronal chilena*, pp. 154-63.

71. Loveman, *Struggle in the Countryside*, pp. 271-73, 290, 319; Barraclough and Fernández, *Diagnóstico de la reforma agraria*, pp. 36-39, 71, 176-77.

72. The literature on the 1970 election and the UP administration is vast and still growing. For bibliography, consult the *Handbook of Latin American Studies* for each year since 1970, or Lee H. Williams, Jr., *The Allende Years: A Union List of Chilean Imprints, 1970-1973, in Selected North American Libraries* (Boston, 1977). Arturo and J. Samuel Valenzuela review the early literature in "Visions of Chile," *Latin American Research Review*, 10, no. 3 (Fall 1975), 155-75. The following section relies on numerous studies, including: Stefan de Vlyder, *Allende's Chile: The Political Economy of the Rise and Fall of the Unidad Popular* (Cambridge, Eng., 1976); Paul E. Sigmund, *The Overthrow of Allende and the Politics of Chile, 1964-1976* (Pittsburgh, 1977); Arturo and J. Samuel Valenzuela, eds., *Chile: Politics and Society* (New Brunswick, N.J., 1976); Philip O'Brien, ed., *Allende's Chile* (New York, 1976); Ian Roxborough, Philip O'Brien, and Jackie Roddick, *Chile: The State and Revolution* (New York, 1977); Federico Gil, Ricardo Lagos E., and Henry Landsberger, eds., *Chile at the Turning Point: Lessons of the Socialist Years, 1970-1973* (Philadelphia, 1979); and Arturo Valenzuela, *The Breakdown of Democratic Regimes: Chile* (Baltimore, 1978).

73. Barraclough and Fernández, *Diagnóstico de la reforma agraria*, pp. 18-20, 25-35; de Vlyder, *Allende's Chile*, pp. 176-78; Loveman, *Struggle in the Countryside*, pp. 283-84.

74. *El C*, 101 (Nov. 1970), 13.

75. Barraclough and Fernández, *Diagnóstico de la reforma agraria*, pp. 40-41; Loveman, *Struggle in the Countryside*, pp. 281-83.

76. Kyle Steenland, *Agrarian Reform under Allende: Peasant Revolt in the South* (Albuquerque, N.M., 1977); Norman Gall, "The Agrarian Revolt in Cautín. Pt. 1: Chile's Mapuches; Pt. 2: Land Reform and the MIR," *American Universities Field Staff Reports*, West Coast South America Series, 19, nos. 4 & 5 (1972); Henry A. Landsberger and Tim McDaniel apply the term "hypermobilization" primarily in the urban context, in "Hypermobilization in Chile, 1970-73," *World Politics*, 28 (1976), 502-41. The number of illegal occupations of fundos increased from 9 in 1967, to 148 in 1969, to 1,278 in 1971. Barraclough and Fernández, *Diagnóstico de la reforma agraria*, pp. 195-98.

77. *El C*, 101 (Nov. 1970), 13; *ibid.* (Dec. 1970), 27; *ibid.*, 102 (Jan. 1971), 14-17.

78. *Ibid.*, 101 (Dec. 1970), 19.

79. *Ibid.*, 102 (Jan. 1971), 4.

80. *Ibid.* (Nov. 1971), 18-23 (quote from p. 23).

81. Steenland, *Agrarian Reform under Allende*; Loveman, *Struggle in the Countryside*, pp. 281-301, 320; David Baytelman, "Problems of Collective Land Exploitation in Chilean Agriculture," in Gil, Lagos, and Landsberger, eds., *Chile at the Turning Point*, pp. 121-59; Choncol, "La reforma agraria en Chile," pp. 611-14.

82. *El C*, 103 (July 1972), 3.

83. For an incisive summary of the varying opposition views and strategies, see Ian Roxborough, "Reversing the Revolution: The Chilean Opposition to Allende," in O'Brien, ed., *Allende's Chile*, pp. 192-216.

84. See *El C*, 103-4 (1972-73); e.g., 104 (June 1973), 24-61. Barraclough and Fernández, *Diagnóstico de la reforma agraria*, pp. 213-18, summarizes the overall strategy of the "agrarian bourgeoisie," including the use of Radio Agricultura. Also Baytelman, "Problems of Collective Land Exploitation," pp. 133-45.

85. *El C*, 103 (June 1972), 12; *ibid.*, 104 (Oct. 1973), 7; Armand Mattelart, "El gremialismo y la linea de masa de la burguesía chilena," in Gomáriz *et al.*, *Chile bajo la junta*, p. 100.

86. Barbara Stallings, *Class Conflict and Economic Development in Chile, 1958-1973* (Stanford, Cal., 1978), compares the political strategies and actions of the economic elites, esp. the SOFOFA, during Chile's last three civilian administrations.

87. *El C*, 103 (June 1972), 23.

88. Roxborough, "Reversing the Revolution"; Roxborough, O'Brien, and Roddick, *Chile: The State and Revolution*, pp. 103-21; Cristóbal Kay, "Chile: The Making of a Coup d'Etat," *Science and Society*, 39 (1975), 3-25.

89. Jorge Fontaine (president of the Confederación de la Producción y del Comercio), quoted in Mattelart, "El gremialismo," p. 114.

90. *Ibid.*, from the article's title. This section on gremialismo and its actions is based primarily on the Mattelart article; on Patricio García F., *Los gremios patronales* (Santiago, 1973); and Stallings, *Class Conflict*, pp. 39-40, 137-51. Drake, "Corporatism and Functionalism," provides historical background as well as coverage of the movement itself. *El C* also featured constant coverage of the gremio movement, including a major article following the Oct. 1972 "employers' " strike (103 [Nov. 1972], 18-53).

91. Jaime Guzmán, interview printed in *El C*, 103 (Dec. 1972), 110.

92. *El C*, 103 (Nov. 1972), 6.

93. The original version of Armand Mattelart's article makes the Lenin comparison explicit: "La bourgeoisie à l'école de Lénine: Le 'grémialisme' et la ligne de masse de la bourgeoisie chilienne," *Politique Aujourd'hui*, 1-2 (Jan.-Feb. 1974), 23-46.

94. García suggests the beginnings of a tighter alliance among the business elites by 1969. García, *Gremios patronales*, pp. 69-73; also Stallings, *Class Conflict*, pp. 111-20. The professionals reorganized in 1972, forming the Confederación de Colegios Profesionales.

95. *El C*, 103 (Nov. 1972), 7.

96. *Ibid.*, p. 9.

97. García, *Gremios patronales*, provides detailed coverage of the 1972 strike; see also *El C*, 102 (Nov. 1972), 18-53.

98. Mattelart, "El gremialismo," p. 116. Valenzuela concurs: "The breakdown of Chilean democracy was more the result of countermobilization against perceived

threats than excessive mobilization of sectors demanding their due." (*Breakdown of Democratic Regimes*, p. 79.) Valenzuela, *ibid.*, pp. 77-106, offers valuable analysis of developments leading to the coup; and Alain Touraine, *Vida y muerte del Chile popular*, tr. Aurelio Garzón del Camino (Mexico City, 1974), gives incisive personal observations of the immediate background to Sept. 11. See also Roxborough, O'Brien, and Roddick, *Chile: The State and Revolution*, pp. 117-21.

99. Most of the literature on Chile since Sept. 11, 1973, focuses on regime terror and human rights violations—certainly the most dramatic aspects of the military's rule. Reliable studies of most other aspects of the post-Allende years are notable for their scarcity. In addition to the works cited in the notes, this section draws on the press and on the brief analyses that have appeared as postscripts to most books on the UP government written after 1973. Of the Chilean press, I have relied particularly on *El Mercurio* (proregime) and the Catholic monthly *Mensaje* (tolerated opposition), as well as the news weekly *Ercilla*. Alan Angell's annual articles in *Current History* provide good summaries, and antiregime journals such as *Chile Informativo* (Mexico City) and *Chile-América* (Rome) offer considerable useful information.

100. *El C*, 104 (Oct. 1973), 7.

101. For a brief comparison of the Peruvian and Brazilian militaries' training and capacity for governing with those of the Chilean armed forces, see Robert Kaufman, *Transition to Stable Authoritarian-Corporate Regimes: The Chilean Case?* (Beverly Hills, Cal., 1976), pp. 42-47.

102. *El C*, 107 (Aug. 1976), 10-11; *ibid.*, 109 (May 1978), 17; *ibid.*, 110 (Apr. 1979), 14.

103. *Ibid.*, 108 (May 1977), 4-5; *ibid.*, 109 (Feb.-Mar. 1978), 4.

104. Enrique Ortúzar Escobar, "La nueva institucionalidad chilena," *Cuadernos del Instituto de Ciencia Política* (Universidad Católica de Chile), no. 1 (1976), 18. Drake, "Corporatism and Functionalism," pp. 114-16, examines corporatist tendencies under the junta.

105. *Today: The Journal of Political News and Analysis*, 3, no. 3 (Sept. 26, 1980), p. 11. I wish to thank Professor Jerry Knudson of Temple University for kindly offering me a copy of the draft constitution.

106. Domingue Hachette, *Aspectos macroeconómicos de la economía chilena: 1973-1976* (Santiago, 1977); Oscar Catalán and Jorge Arrate, "Chile: la política del régimen militar y las nuevas formas del desarrollo en América Latina," *Boletín de Estudios Latinoamericanos y del Caribe*, no. 25 (Dec. 1978), 51-71; Víctor Villanueva, *Modelo contrarrevolucionario chileno* (Lima, 1976), pp. 140-54. *Investigación Económica* (Universidad Nacional Autónoma de Mexico), 36, no. 2 (Apr.-June 1977) is an issue devoted to a series of articles, primarily by Chilean exiles (Pedro Vuskovic *et al.*), collectively titled "La política económica en Chile de 1970 a 1977." The Oficina de Planificación Nacional (ODEPLAN) reported economic conditions in its *Informe económico mensual*. The military's guiding principles and long-range plans for economic development are expressed in: Junta de Gobierno, *Declaración de principios del gobierno de Chile* (Santiago, 1974); ODEPLAN, *Eficiencia económica para el desarrollo social: plan nacional indicativo de desarrollo, 1976-1981* (Santiago, 1976); and ODEPLAN, *Estrategia nacional de desarrollo económico y social: políticas de largo plazo* (Santiago, 1977). For bibliographies, see: Servicio de Extensión de Cultura Chilena, *Bibliografía de la política económica de la Junta de Gobierno de Chile, 1973-76* (Santiago, 1977); and Pío García and Carmen Gloria Olave, "Chile: economía y política económica; bibliografía analítica de publicaciones desde el golpe de estado," *Investigación*

Económica, 36, no. 2 (Apr.-June 1977), 309-41, which covers the UP years as well as the junta.

107. *El C*, 107 (Oct. 1976), 2.

108. This and the following analysis of change in the agrarian sector are based primarily on Joseph Collins's brief *Agrarian Reform and Counter-Reform in Chile* (San Francisco, 1979); Raúl Miranda S., "La política agraria de la Junta Militar: antecedentes y perspectivas," *Investigación Económica*, 36, no. 2 (Apr.-June 1977), 147-81; José Garrido Rojas, "Comentarios sobre la reforma agraria (septiembre 1973-diciembre 1977)," in *El C*, 109 (June 1978), 18-25; David Stanfield, "The Chilean Agrarian Reform, 1975," University of Wisconsin, Land Tenure Center, *Newsletter*, no. 52 (Apr.-June 1976), 1-13; Soto, "Crisis y violencia," pp. 305-18; Luis Quiros-Varela, "Agrarian Policies in Chile: Stagnation, Reform and Counter-Reform in the Countryside" (unpublished dissertation in political science, University of North Carolina, Chapel Hill, 1979), pp. 281-339.

109. Elías Sánchez C., "Plan laboral y reacciones," *Mensaje*, 28, no. 277 (Mar.-Apr. 1979), 101-4 and 172; Jaime Ruiz Tagle, "El nuevo plan laboral: ¿libertad o liberalismo?" *Mensaje*, 28, no. 281 (Aug. 1979), 433-37; *El C*, 110 (Jan. 1979); ODEPLAN, *Estrategia nacional de desarrollo*, pp. 61-64, sets forth the principles of the junta's labor policy. O.Valenzuela, "Condiciones de vida de los campesinos," *Mensaje*, 26, no. 260 (July 1977), 354-58, summarizes a study of rural conditions which the article's author did under contract to the U.S. Agency for International Development.

110. Collins, *Agrarian Reform and Counter-Reform*; Garrido Rojas, "Comentarios sobre la reforma agraria"; Hugo Villela, "Autoritarismo y tenencia de la tierra: Chile 1973-1976," *Revista Mexicana de Sociología*, 41, no. 1 (Jan.-Mar. 1979), 205-41; José Bengoa, "La evolución de la tenencia de la tierra y las clases sociales agrarias en Chile," *Investigación Económica*, 38, no. 147 (Jan.-Mar. 1979), 127-58, traces the changes in land tenure and class structure from the early 1960s to the late 1970s.

111. Collins, *Agrarian Reform and Counter-Reform*, pp. 6-8.

112. Garrido Rojas, "Comentarios sobre la reforma agraria," p. 25.

113. *Ibid.*, p. 23. O. Valenzuela, "Condiciones de vida," p. 358, writes that minifundistas as well as new recipients of plots by 1977 were suffering "a frank deterioration in their living conditions."

114. *El C*, 108 (July 1977), 5.

115. *Ibid.*, 109 (June 1978), 10-11; *ibid.* (July 1978), 3.

116. *Ibid.*, (Dec. 1978), 7; *ibid.*, 110 (Jan. 1979), 6. The head of the new government agency was former president of the SNA-founded Corporación de Desarrollo Social para el Sector Rural—a private rural educational organization.

Appendixes

Appendix 1

SNA Members as Political Participants: Incidence of National Office-Holding during Members' Lifetimes, Selected Years

Year	Total Number Members[a]	Number Congressmen (only)	Number Ministers (only)	Number Both	Total Number Participants	Percent Participation
1873	231	103	1	28	132	57.1
1885	193	65	0	24	89	46.1
1895	267	68	1	26	95	35.6
1901	373	71	5	39	115	30.8
1909	693	94	6	36	136	19.6
1918	782	112	4	52	168	21.5
1924	1,094	110	4	62	176	16.1
1928	1,777	116	9	51	176	9.9
1933	1,464	95	14	40	149	10.2
1936	2,378	107	16	36	159	6.7

[a]This number includes only individual members, and eliminates companies and other corporate SNA members.
SOURCE: *MSNA* (years indicated); Valencia Avaria, *Anales de la República*, vols. 1, 2.

Appendix 2

SNA Members as Members of the Club de la Unión, Selected Years

Year	Number SNA Members[a]	Number in Club de la Unión	Percent
1895	267	137	51.3
1918	782	431	55.1
1933	1,464	371	25.3

[a]Includes individual members only.
SOURCE: *MSNA* (1895, 1918, 1933); *Memoria del Club de la Unión*, 1895, 1918, 1933.

Appendix 3

SNA Directors as Political Participants: Incidence of National Office-Holding during Directors' Lifetimes, Selected Years

Year	Total Number Directors	Number Congress-men (only)	Number Ministers (only)	Number Both	Total Number Partici-pants	Percent Participa-tion
1873	17	9	0	5	14	82.4
1885	17	7	0	3	10	58.8
1895	17	5	0	2	7	41.2
1901	22	5	0	5	10	45.5
1909	22	5	0	8	13	59.1
1918	22	5	1	8	14	63.6
1924	30	5	1	9	15	50.0
1928	30	8	1	10	19	63.3
1933	37[a]	13	1	8	22	59.5
1940	45	9	4	6	19	42.2

[a]Excludes bureaucrat appointees to the board for 1933 and 1940.
SOURCE: *MSNA* (years indicated); Valencia Avaria, *Anales de la República*, vols. 1, 2.

Appendix 4

SNA Directors as Members of the Club de la Unión, Selected Years

Year	Number Directors	Number in Club de la Unión	Percent
1895	17	14	82.4
1918	22	21	95.5
1933	37	32	86.5

SOURCE: *MSNA* (1895, 1918, 1933); *Memoria del Club de la Unión*, 1895, 1918, 1933.

Appendix 5

SNA Directors with Minimum of Ten Years Tenure, 1869–1940

Name and Years as Director	Length of Tenure[a]	National Office[b]	Party[c]	B.D.[d]	Profession	Nonagricultural Economic Interests
Domingo Bezanilla B. 1869–77, 1878–85	15	D		Yes		Commerce, banking, industry
Juan Domingo Dávila Larraín 1869–88	19	D	L	No	Lawyer	
Vincente Dávila Larraín 1870–85, 1889–93	19	D, M	L	No		
Ramón Barros Luco 1871–89, 1891–93, 1901–10	29	S, D, M, P	L	Yes	Lawyer	Industry
Pedro Lucio Cuadra Luque 1871–82	11	S, D, M	L	Yes	Mining engineer, university professor	Banking, commerce, industry
Félix Echeverría Valdés 1871–72, 1873–76, 1877–85	12	D	L	Yes	Lawyer	
Rafael Larraín Moxó 1871–91	20	S, D	C	Yes	Agronomist	Banking
Lauro Barros Valdés 1872–91	19	S, D, M	L	Yes		
Nathan Miers Cox 1872–97	25	S	C	Yes		
Matías Ovalle Errázuriz 1873–89	16	D, M		Yes		Mining, utilities
Lisímaco Jara-Quemada Vargas 1874–99	25		C	No		

Appendix 5 (cont.)

SNA Directors with Minimum of Ten Years Tenure, 1869–1940

Name and Years as Director	Length of Tenure[a]	National Office[b]	Party[c]	B.D.[d]	Profession	Nonagricultural Economic Interests
Juan de Dios Morandé 1874–99	25	D		No		
Martín Drouilly 1875–85	10			No		
Macario Ossa Cerda 1877–87	10	D	C	Yes		Banking
Manuel J. Domínguez Cerda 1879–93	14		C	Yes		Newspaper, commerce
Raimundo Larraín Covarrubias 1879–80, 1885–93, 1901–16	24		C	Yes		
Salvador Izquierdo Sanfuentes 1883–93, 1909–17, 1929–40	30			Yes	Agricultural engineer	Commerce, industry
Raimundo Valdés Cuevas 1887–1905	18		C	Yes		
Ascanio Bascuñán Santa María 1889–93, 1906–17	15	S, D, M	R	Yes	Engineer	Railroads, industry
Francisco de Borja Valdés Cuevas 1889–91, 1899–1913	16	D, M	I	Yes		Banking
Daniel Ortúzar Cuevas 1891–1905	14	D	C	No		
Andrés Respaldiza Valdivieso 1891–1917	26			Yes	Agricultural engineer	

Diego Vial Guzmán 1895–97, 1901–2, 1914–26	15			No		
Joaquín Echenique Gandarillas 1897–1920	23	S, D	C	Yes	Engineer, publisher	Newspaper, industry
Ambrosio García Huidobro 1897–1909	12			No		
Luis Larraín Prieto 1897–1930	33	D, M	C	Yes		Industry
Pedro Ruiz-Tagle García Huidobro 1897–1925	28			Yes		Utilities
Rafael Tagle Jordan 1897–1913	16			No		
Julio 2° Zegers 1897–1913	16	D		No		
Alejandro Huneeus G.H. 1901–20	19	D, M	C	Yes	Lawyer	Newspaper
Mauricio Mena Larraín 1904–6, 1908–40	34	D	C	Yes	Lawyer	
Ramón Cruz Montt 1905–38	33			Yes		
Exequiel Fernández I. 1906–18	12	D		No		
Eliodoro Yáñez 1908–22	14	S, D, M	L	Yes	University professor, publisher	Newspaper
Enrique Matte Eyzaguirre 1910–18, 1930–32	10			No		

Appendix 5 (cont.)

SNA Directors with Minimum of Ten Years Tenure, 1869-1940

Name and Years as Director	Length of Tenure[a]	National Office[b]	Party[c]	B.D.[d]	Profession	Nonagricultural Economic Interests
Juan de Dios Rodríguez C. 1912-30	18			Yes		
Jorge Silva Somarriva 1912-16, 1926-36	14	D, M	C	Yes		Industry
Francisco Encina 1913-21, 1931-38	15	D	N	Yes	Lawyer	Commerce, industry
Alberto Tagle Ruiz 1913-27	14		C	Yes	Lawyer	Banking
Carlos V. Risopatrón 1915-25	10	D	C	Yes		
Alberto Correa Valenzuela 1916-29	13			No		
Alberto Valdivieso 1916-38	22			No		
Guillermo Barros Jara 1917-29, 1930-31	13	S, M	L	Yes	Lawyer	Commerce, banking
Luis Correa Vergara 1918-40	22	M		Yes		Industry
Francisco Garcés Gana 1918-38	20	D, M	L	Yes	Lawyer	Banking, commerce, industry
Máximo Valdés Fontecilla 1918-1940	22	D, M	I	Yes		Banking, commerce, industry

Carlos Briones Luco 1921-34	13	D	R	Yes	Engineer, military	Mining
Maximiliano Ibáñez 1921-33	12	D, M	L	Yes	Lawyer, university professor	Newspaper
Miguel Letelier Espínola 1921-40	19	D, M	L	Yes	Engineer	Industry, commerce
Arturo Lyon Peña 1921-38	17	S, D	C	Yes	Lawyer	Newspaper, banking
Pedro Opazo 1921-24, 1925-33	11	S, D, M	LD	Yes		
Miguel Covarrubias Valdés 1925-40	15			Yes	Engineer	Industry
Jaime Larraín García-Moreno 1929-40	11	D, S	C	Yes	Lawyer, agronomist	
J. Florencio Valdés Ossa 1930-40	10			Yes	Engineer	Mining

[a]Some directors listed as terminating in 1940 actually continued to serve after that date, but their participation was not traced beyond 1940.
[b]D = Deputy; S = Senator; M = Minister; P = President.
[c]C = Conservative; L = Liberal; N = National; R = Radical; I = Independent; LD = Liberal Democratic.
[d]Listed in Biographical Dictionary.

SOURCE: *MSNA* (1869-1940); Pedro Pablo Figueroa, *Diccionario biográfico de Chile*; Virgilio Figueroa, *Diccionario histórico y biográfico de Chile; Diccionario biográfico de Chile*, 1st and 3rd eds.

Appendix 6

SNA Members in Congress, Selected Years

Year	Congress	Deputies		SNA	Senators		SNA
		Total	SNA	Percent	Total	SNA	Percent
1873	17th, 1873-76	97	28	28.9	20	9	45.0
1885	21st, 1885-88	114	22	19.3	40	11	27.5
1895	24th, 1894-97	94	21	22.3	32	11	34.4
1901	26th, 1900-1903	94	26	27.7	32	11	34.4
1909	29th, 1909-12	95	21	22.1	32	8	25.0
1918	32nd, 1918-21	118	26	22.0	37	14	37.8
1924	34th, 1924	118	23	19.5	37	14	37.8
1928	35th, 1926-30	132	27	20.5	45	12	26.7
1933	37th, 1933-37	143	17	11.9	45	11	24.4
1936	37th, 1933-37	143	23	16.1	45	15	33.3

SOURCE: *MSNA* (year indicated); Valencia Avaria, *Anales de la República*, vols. 1, 2.

Appendix 7

Wholesale Agricultural Price Index 1879-1940 (1940 = 100)[a]

Year	Index	Year	Index	Year	Index
1879	3.7	1899	9.8	1920	45.1
1880	4.1	1900	11.6	1921	39.6
1881	4.7	1901	9.7	1922	41.6
1882	4.1	1902	11.4	1923	43.5
1883	5.5	1903	11.9	1924	44.4
1884	5.4	1904	12.4	1925	55.1
1885	5.7	1905	13.6	1926	48.0
1886	5.9	1906	13.1	1927	43.3
1887	5.5	1907	17.6	1928	52.1
1888	6.5	1908	20.7	1929	53.0
1889	6.9	1909	20.6	1930	40.1
1890	6.2	1910	21.9	1931	32.5
1891	6.7	1911	22.8	1932	50.4
1892	7.5	1912	21.7	1933	66.2
1893	8.3	1913	22.6	1934	63.3
1894	8.9	1914	24.6	1935	70.0
1895	7.8	1915	33.8	1936	89.2
1896	7.5	1916	27.6	1937	112.0
1897	8.2	1917	36.1	1938	100.5
1898	8.0	1918	33.2	1939	90.2
		1919	36.5	1940	100.0

[a]This is a weighted index based on wheat, barley, beans, lentils, corn, potatoes, wool, and livestock. It is presented here to provide a general overview of the inflation of agricultural prices. It is not accurate for short-term fluctuations. For specific prices and short-term price patterns, see: Bauer, *Chilean Rural Society*, pp. 233-34; *Sinópsis estadístico, 1918*, p. 118; *Sinópsis estadístico, 1925*, p. 117; and *Anuario estadístico, año 1942. Comercio interior y comunicaciones*, p. 46.

SOURCE: Adolfo Latorre Subercaseaux, "Relación entre el circulante y los precios en Chile" (Memoria de Prueba, Universidad Católica de Chile, 1958).

Bibliography

I. Manuscript Sources: Archivo Nacional *(AN)*

Archivo del Ministerio de Agricultura. Oficios, 1924-40.
Archivo del Ministerio de Fomento. Oficios, 1927-30.
Archivo del Ministerio de Hacienda. Vols. 894, 956, 1004, 1135, 1228, 1333, 1431, 1546, 1730.
Archivo del Ministerio de Industria y Obras Públicas. Vols. 2640, 2849.
Archivo del Ministerio de Relaciones Exteriores, Culto y Colonización. Vol. 204.

II. Interviews

Jaime Larraín García-Moreno. Santiago. Dec. 6, 1968.
Gerardo Larraín Valdés. Santiago. Aug. 3, 1976.

III. Bibliographic Aids and Reference Works

Anguita, Ricardo. *Leyes promulgadas en Chile desde 1810 hasta el primero de junio de 1913*. 5 vols. Santiago, 1912-13.

Anuario de la prensa chilena. Santiago, annual.

Cariola, Carmen, and Osvaldo Sunkel. "Chile." In Roberto Cortés Conde and Stanley J. Stein, eds. *Latin America: A Guide to Economic History, 1830-1930*. Berkeley, Cal., 1977.

Corporación de Fomento de la Producción. *Geografía económica de Chile*. Texto refundido. Santiago, 1965.

Cortés, Lía, and Jordi Fuentes. *Diccionario político de Chile (1810-1966)*. Santiago, 1967.

Diccionario biográfico de Chile. 1st and 3rd eds. Santiago, 1936, 1940.

Espinoza, Enrique. *Jeografía descriptiva de la República de Chile*. 4th ed. Santiago, 1897.

Figueroa, Pedro Pablo. *Diccionario biográfico de Chile*. 4th ed. 3 vols. Santiago, 1897-1901.

Figueroa, Virgilio. *Diccionario histórico y biográfico de Chile*. 5 vols. Santiago, 1925-31.

García, Pío, and Carmen Gloria Olave. "Chile: economía y política económica;

bibliografía analítica de publicaciones desde el golpe de estado." *Investigación Económica*, 36, no. 2 (Apr.-June 1977), 309-41.

Handbook of Latin American Studies. vols. 1-40. Variable place of publication, 1935-78.

Riso-Patrón, Luis. *Diccionario geográfico de Chile*. Santiago, 1928.

Servicio de Extensión de Cultura Chilena. *Bibliografía de la política económica de la Junta de Gobierno de Chile, 1973-76*. Santiago, 1977.

Ugarte Vial, Jorge, ed. *Historia e índice de las leyes*. Vols. 2 and 3. Santiago, 1950.

University of Wisconsin, Land Tenure Center. *Agrarian Reform in Latin America: An Annotated Bibliography*. Madison, Wis., 1974.

Valencia Avaria, Luis. *Anales de la República*. 2 vols. Santiago, 1951.

Williams, Lee H., Jr. *The Allende Years: A Union List of Chilean Imprints, 1970-1973, in Selected North American Libraries*. Boston, 1977.

IV. Government Publications

A. STATISTICS, CENSUSES, TAX ROLLS

Dirección General de Estadística. *Agricultura, 1929*. Santiago, 1930.

______. *Agricultura, 1935-36: censo*. Santiago, 1938.

______. *Anuario agropecuario, 1934-35*. Santiago, 1936.

______. *Anuario estadístico de la República de Chile*. Santiago, 1869-1930, 1942. (To 1915, published by Oficina Central de Estadística.)

______. Estadística chilena. Santiago, 1931-40.

______. *Resultados del x censo de la población efectuado el 27 de noviembre de 1930*. Vol. 1. Santiago, 1931.

______. *Sinópsis estadístico de Chile* (title varies slightly). Santiago, 1919, 1925, 1933.

Dirección General de Impuestos Internos. *Rol de avalúos: tasación general practicada el año 1928*. 63 vols. Valparaíso, 1929.

Impuesto agrícola: rol de contribuyentes. Santiago, 1874.

Indice de propietarios rurales i valor de la propiedad rural según los roles de avalúos comunales. Santiago, 1908.

B. OTHER OFFICIAL PUBLICATIONS

Boletín de las leyes y decretos del gobierno. Santiago, 1897, 1898, 1918-40.

Caja de Colonización Agrícola. *Memoria, años 1939-40*. Santiago, 1942.

______. *Hacia una nueva vida por la colonización*. Santiago, 1941.

______. *Tierra Chilena*. 1939-40.

Congreso Nacional, Cámara de Diputados. *Sesiones ordinarias*. 1888, 1896, 1897, 1900-1909, 1918-40.

______. *Sesiones extraordinarias*. 1895/96, 1900/1901, 1905/6, 1910/11, 1918/19-1940/41.

______. Cámara de Senadores. *Sesiones ordinarias*. 1905-7, 1918-40.

______. *Sesiones extraordinarias*. 1905/6, 1906/7, 1918/19-1940/41.

Diario Oficial. 1919-20.

Junta de Gobierno. *Declaración de principios del gobierno de Chile*. Santiago, 1974.
Lei de presupuestos de entradas y gastos ordinarios de la administración pública de Chile para el año 1896. Santiago, 1896.
Ministerio de Agricultura. *Memoria*. 1924-40.
Ministerio de Fomento. *Memoria*. 1927-30.
Ministerio de Hacienda. *Memoria*. 1869-87.
Ministerio de Industria y Obras Públicas. *Memoria*. 1887-1924.
______. *Asociación de Viticultores*. Santiago, 1895.
Ministerio de Salud Pública y Bienestar Social. *Acción Social*. Año III-VIII (1935-40).
Oficina de Planificación Nacional (ODEPLAN). *Eficiencia económica para el desarrollo social, 1976-81*. Santiago, 1976.
______. *Estrategia nacional de desarrollo económico y social: políticas de largo plazo*. Santiago, 1977.
Oficina del Trabajo. *Boletín*. Año I-XVI (1911-26).
Santiago. Dirección General de Subsistencias, *Memoria, año 1928*. Santiago, 1929.

V. Periodicals

A. NEWSPAPERS

El Alba (Santiago). 1905.
El Chileno (Santiago). 1905.
Federación Obrera (Santiago). 1921.
El Ferrocarril (Santiago). 1888, 1905.
El Mercurio (Antofagasta). 1922.
El Mercurio (Santiago). 1900-1940, 1967-79.
El Mercurio (Valparaíso). 1882.
La Nación (Santiago). 1939-40.
El Siglo (Santiago). 1940.

B. JOURNALS AND MAGAZINES

Current History (Philadelphia). 1967-79.
Ercilla (Santiago). 1967-79.
Mensaje (Santiago). 1973-79.
Revista Chilena (Santiago). 1917-19.
Revista Comercial (Valparaíso). 1921.
Revista de Asistencia Social (Santiago). 1935-38.
Revista Económica (Santiago). 1886-88.
Today: The Journal of Political News and Analysis (Brunswick, Ohio). 1980.

VI. The Sociedad Nacional de Agricultura

A. ARCHIVAL MATERIALS

"Actas de las Sesiones del Consejo Directivo." 1869-1940.

"Nómina de Socios." (Archivo, Sección Socios).

B. PUBLICATIONS

El Agricultor. Vols. 48-52 (1917-22).

Boletín de la Sociedad Nacional de Agricultura. Vols. 1-47 (1869-1916), 53-65 (1922-33).

El Campesino. Vols. 65-110 (1933-79).

Congreso Regional Agrario de Concepción. Santiago, 1925.

Estatutos de la SNA. Santiago, 1930.

Memoria de la Sociedad Nacional de Agricultura. 1870-1940.

La SNA en las provincias: labor de la delegación de la SNA en su jira por el sur del país. Santiago, 1924.

VII. Other Chilean Voluntary Associations

Asociación del Trabajo. *Boletín*. Año I-V (1925-29).

Centro Industrial y Agrícola. *Revista*. Vols. 2-3 (1900-1903).

Club de la Unión. *Memoria*. 1895, 1918, 1933.

Sociedad Agrícola y Ganadera de Osorno. *Agricultura Austral*. Año VI (1939).

Sociedad de Fomento Fabril. *Boletín*. Vols. 1-57 (1883-1940).

______. *Memoria*. 1883-1940.

Unión Social de Agricultores. *Estatutos*. Santiago, 1936.

VIII. Chilean University Theses[1]

Barría Serón, Jorge. "Los movimientos sociales de Chile desde 1910 hasta 1926." 1960.

______. "Los movimientos sociales de principios del siglo xx." Facultad de Filosofía y Educación, 1953.

Bowen Herrera, Alfredo. "Ensayo sobre el movimiento sindical y el sindicalismo agrícola." 1933.

Donoso Vergara, Guillermo. "Estudio histórico-económico de la producción y comercio de granos." 1938.

Edwards Hurtado, Fernando. "Estudios sobre política de colonización interior." 1939.

Espinoza Ferrari, Germán. "Realizaciones económicas y sociales de la ley no. 5604 sobre colonización agrícola nacional." 1940.

Fernández Correa, Raúl. "Los obreros agrícolas ante el derecho social chileno." 1933.

Finkelstein Rosolie, León. "La agricultura y los organismos de fomento." 1945.

Fuenzalida Ríos, Rodolfo. "El latifundio y el problema de la división de la tierra." 1939.

[1]All are Memorias de Prueba for the Facultad de Ciencias Jurídicas y Sociales, Universidad de Chile, except as otherwise noted.

García, Víctor. "El problema de la colonización." 1936.
Gómez T., Jorge. "La Junta de Exportación Agrícola." 1944.
Labarca Letelier, René. "Subproducción agrícola y sistema de propiedad ante la estadística chilena." 1943.
Latorre Subercaseaux, Adolfo. "Relación entre el circulante y los precios en Chile." Universidad Católica de Chile, 1958.
Lizana Cornejo, Carlos. "La sindicalización campesina." 1939.
Long, Eduardo. "La propiedad en la ley sobre colonización agrícola." 1937.
Macchiavello Varas, Constantino. "Contribución al estudio de nuestro problema de la carestía de la vida frente al problema de las subsistencias." 1933.
Manquilef Vargas, Adela. "El Ministerio de Agricultura y la política agraria." 1951.
Marín Molina, Ricardo. "Condiciones económico-sociales del campesino chileno." 1947.
Marshall Silva, Jorge. "La lucha por la reforma agraria." 1941.
Santa Cruz Errázuriz, Gonzalo. "El mejoramiento de los trabajadores agrícolas y la sindicalización campesina." 1941.
Talesnik Rabinovich, Gregorio. "Intervencionismo del estado y control de precios por el mismo: estudio especial del Comisariato General de Subsistencias y Precios." 1940.
Torres Moncada, Inés. "Alimentación de las clases populares." 1938.
Trivelli F., Hugo. "Expansión y estructura agrarias en Chile." 1941.
Undurraga Villegas, Emilio. "De la Junta de Exportación Agrícola." 1940.
Vásquez Jara, Efraím. "El trabajador agrícola chileno ante la lei i ante la sociedad." Facultad de Leyes i Ciencias Políticas, 1913.
Waiser P., Myriam, Carlos Muñoz L., and Eduardo Irazabal L. "La clase hacendada en Chile durante el siglo xix." Escuela de Sociología, 1967.
Zuaznábar de la Barra, Rafael. "La Sociedad Nacional de Agricultura." 1947.

IX. Books, Pamphlets, Articles, and Dissertations.[2]

Adams, Mildred, ed. *Latin America: Evolution or Explosion?* New York, 1963.
Adie, Robert F., and Guy E. Poitras. *Latin America: The Politics of Immobility*. Englewood Cliffs, N.J., 1974.
Affonso, Almino, *et al. Movimiento campesino chileno*. Santiago, 1970.
Aguirre Cerda, Pedro. *El problema agrario*. Paris, 1929.
Alessandri Palma, Arturo. *Recuerdos de gobierno*. 3 vols. Santiago, 1967.
Alexander, Robert J. *Arturo Alessandri: A Biography*. 2 vols. Ann Arbor, Mich., 1977.
Allende, Salvador. *Realidad médico-social chilena*. Santiago, 1939.
Alvarez Andrews, Oscar. *Historia del desarrollo industrial de Chile*. Santiago, 1936.
Angell, Alan. *Politics and the Labour Movement in Chile*. London, 1972.
Arriagada, Genaro. *La oligarquía patronal chilena*. Santiago, 1970.

[2]This section is limited to works cited in the text.

Asamblea de Agricultores de la Comuna de San José. Valdivia, 1925.

Ballesteros, Marto A. "Desarrollo agrícola chileno, 1910-1955." *Cuadernos Económicos* (Universidad Católica de Chile), 2, no. 5 (Jan.-Apr. 1965), 7-40.

Balmori, Diana, and Robert Oppenheimer. "Family Clusters: Generational Nucleation in Nineteenth-Century Argentina and Chile." *Comparative Studies in Society and History*, 21 (1979), 231-61.

Baraona, Rafael, Ximena Aranda, and Roberto Santana. *Valle de Putaendo: estudio de estructura agraria.* Santiago, 1960.

Barraclough, Solon, and José A. Fernández, coordinators. *Diagnóstico de la reforma agraria chilena.* Mexico City, 1974.

Barría Serón, Jorge. *El movimiento obrero en Chile.* Santiago, 1971.

Barros Lezaeta, Luis, and Ximena Vergara Johnson. *El modo de ser aristocrático: el caso de la oligarquía chilena hacia 1900.* Santiago, 1978.

Bauer, Arnold J. "Chilean Rural Labor in the Nineteenth Century." *American Historical Review*, 76 (1971), 1059-83.

______. *Chilean Rural Society from the Spanish Conquest to 1930.* Cambridge, Eng., 1975.

______. "The Hacienda el Huique in the Agrarian Structure of Nineteenth Century Chile." *Agricultural History*, 28 (1972), 455-70.

______, and Ann Hagerman Johnson. "Land and Labour in Rural Chile, 1850-1935." In Kenneth Duncan and Ian Rutledge, eds. *Land and Labour in Latin America: Essays on the Development of Agrarian Capitalism in the Nineteenth and Twentieth Centuries.* Cambridge, Eng., 1977.

Beals, Carleton. *Latin America: World in Revolution.* New York, 1963.

Becket, James. "Land Reform in Chile." *Journal of Inter-American Studies*, 5 (1963), 177-211.

Bengoa, José. "La evolución de la tenencia de la tierra y las clases sociales agrarias en Chile." *Investigación Económica*, 38, no. 147 (Jan.-Mar. 1979), 127-58.

Bennett, Peter D. *Government's Role in Retail Marketing of Food Products in Chile.* Austin, Tex., 1968.

Blest Gana, Alberto. *Martín Rivas.* 8th ed. Santiago, 1961.

Borde, Jean, and Mario Góngora. *Evolución de la propiedad rural en el Valle del Puangue.* 2 vols. Santiago, 1956.

Borón, Atilio. "Notas sobre las raíces histórico-estructurales de la movilización política en Chile." *Foro Internacional*, 16 (1975), 64-121.

Burnett, Ben. *Political Groups in Chile: The Dialogue between Order and Change.* Austin, Tex., 1970.

Cabero, Alberto. *Recuerdos de don Pedro Aguirre Cerda.* 2nd ed. Santiago, 1948.

Canessa Ibarra, Ismael. "Salario y medicina social." *Acción Social*, año VII, no. 75 (Dec. 1938-Jan. 1939), 14-16.

Carmagnani, Marcello. *Sviluppo industriale e sottosviluppo economico: il caso cileno (1860-1920).* Turin, 1971.

Carrière, Jean. "Landowners and the Rural Unionization Question in Chile, 1920-48." *Boletín de Estudios Latinoamericanos y del Caribe*, no. 22 (June 1977), 34-52.

Catalán, Oscar, and Jorge Arrate. "Chile: la política del régimen militar y las nuevas formas del desarrollo en América Latina." *Boletín de Estudios Latinoamericanos y del Caribe*, no. 25 (Dec. 1978), 51-71.

Cea Egaña, José Luis. *La representación funcional en la historia constitucional de Chile*. Santiago, 1976.

Centro de Estudios Socio-Económicos. "Estudio: imágen de la agricultura en Chile." Loose leaf. 3 vols. Santiago, 1966.

Chacón Corona, Juan. *El problema agrario y el Partido Comunista. Informe ante el XI Congreso Nacional del Partido Comunista de Chile, 1939*. Santiago, 1940.

Chaporro, Leoncio. *Anotaciones críticas sobre el cultivo de la tierra en Chile*. Santiago, 1939.

______. *Colonización y reforma agraria: hacia una distribución mas justa de la tierra en Chile*. Santiago, 1932.

Chonchol, Jacques. "Poder y reforma agraria en la experiencia chilena." *Cuadernos de la Realidad Nacional* (June 1970), pp. 50-87.

______. "La reforma agraria en Chile." *Trimestre Económico*, 43, no. 3 (July-Sept. 1976), 599-623.

Collins, Joseph. *Agrarian Reform and Counter-Reform in Chile*. San Francisco, 1979.

Comité Interamericano de Desarrollo Agrícola (CIDA). *Chile: tenencia de la tierra y desarrollo socio-económico del sector agrícola*. Santiago, 1966.

Concha, Malaquías. *El programa de la Democracia*. 2nd ed. Santiago, 1905.

Convención Nacional de la Producción y del Comercio 1967-1968. Santiago, 1968.

Corbo Lioi, Vittorio. *Inflation in Developing Countries: An Econometric Study of Chilean Inflation*. Amsterdam, 1974.

Correa Prieto, Luis. *El Presidente Ibáñez*. Santiago, 1962.

Correa Vergara, Luis. *Agricultura chilena*. 2 vols. Santiago, 1938.

Couyoumdjian, Ricardo. "El mercado del salitre durante la primera guerra mundial y la postguerra, 1914-1921. Notas para su estudio." *Historia*, 12 (1974-75), 13-55.

Crosson, Pierre R. *Agricultural Development and Productivity: Lessons from the Chilean Experience*. Baltimore, 1970.

Cruz-Coke, Ricardo. *Geografía electoral de Chile*. Santiago, 1952.

Cruz-Coke Lassabe, Eduardo. *Pensamiento de Cruz-Coke*. Santiago, 1974.

Davis, Tom E. "Eight Decades of Inflation in Chile, 1879-1959: A Political Interpretation." *Journal of Political Economy*, 71 (1963), 389-97.

de León, César A. "Las capas medias en la sociedad chilena del siglo xix." *Anales de la Universidad de Chile*, año CXXII (1964), 51-95.

de Vylder, Stefan. *Allende's Chile: The Political Economy of the Rise and Fall of the Unidad Popular*. Cambridge, Eng., 1976.

Domínguez C., Oscar. *El campesino chileno y la acción católica rural*. Madrid, 1961.

Donoso, Ricardo. *Alessandri, agitador y demoledor*. Mexico City, 1952.

Donoso Letelier, Crescente. "Notas sobre el orígen, acatamiento y desgaste del régimen presidencial, 1925-1973." *Historia*, 13 (1976), 271-352.

Dragoni, Carlo, and Etienne Burnet. "L'alimentation populaire au Chile; première enquête générale de 1935." *Revista Chilena de Higiene y Medicina Preventiva*, 1, nos. 10-12 (Oct.-Dec. 1938), 407-611.

Drake, Paul W. "Corporatism and Functionalism in Modern Chilean Politics." *Journal of Latin American Studies*, 10 (1978), 83-116.

______. "The Political Responses of the Chilean Upper Class to the Great Depression and the Threat of Socialism, 1931-33." In Frederic Cople Jaher, ed., *The Rich, the Well Born, and the Powerful*. Urbana, Ill., 1973.

______. *Socialism and Populism in Chile, 1932-52*. Urbana, Ill., 1978.

Drouilly, Martín, and Pedro Lucio Cuadra. *Ensayo sobre el estado económico de la agricultura en Chile*. Santiago, 1878.

Durán Bernales, Florencio. *El Partido Radical*. Santiago, 1958.

Echaíz, René León. *Evolución histórica de los partidos políticos chilenos*. 2nd ed. Buenos Aires, 1971.

Echeverría, Roberto. *The Effect of Agricultural Price Policies on Intersectoral Income Transfers*. Ithaca, N.Y., 1969.

Economic Commission for Latin America/Food and Agricultural Organization. *Análisis de algunos factores que obstaculizan el incremento de la producción agropecuaria*. Santiago, 1953.

Edwards Matte, Guillermo. *El Club de la Unión en sus ochenta años, 1864-1944*. Santiago, 1944.

Edwards Vives, Alberto. *La fronda aristocrática*. 6th ed. Santiago, 1966.

______, and Eduardo Frei Montalva. *Historia de los partidos políticos chilenos*. Santiago, 1949.

Ellsworth, P. T. *Chile: An Economy in Transition*. New York, 1945.

Encina, Francisco. "Nuestra situación agraria." *Revista Chilena*, año III, tomo IX, no. 27 (Nov. 1919), 212-13.

______, *et al*. "La subdivisión de la propiedad rural en Chile en 1919." *Mapocho*, tomo V, vol. 13 (1966), 20-29.

Espinoza, Roberto. *Cuestiones financieras de Chile*. Santiago, 1909.

Eyzaguirre, Jaime. *Chile durante el gobierno de Errázuriz Echaurren, 1896-1901*. Santiago, 1957.

Feliz, David. "An Alternative View of the 'Monetarist-Structuralist' Controversy." In Albert O. Hirschman, ed., *Latin American Issues: Essays and Comments*. New York, 1961.

Fetter, Frank W. *Monetary Inflation in Chile*. Princeton, N.J., 1931.

Ffrench-Davis, Ricardo. *Políticas económicas en Chile: 1952-1970*. Santiago, 1973.

Finer, Herman. *The Chilean Development Corporation*. Montreal, 1947.

Gall, Norman. "The Agrarian Revolt in Cautín. Pt. 1: Chile's Mapuches; Pt. 2: Land Reform and the MIR." *American Universities Field Staff Reports*, West Coast South America Series, 19, nos. 4 & 5 (1972).

García F., Patricio. *Los gremios patronales*. Santiago, 1973.

Gay, Claudio. *Historia física y política de Chile: Agricultura*. 2 vols. Paris, 1862-65.

Gibbs, Guillermo. *La tierra y el inquilinaje*. Santiago, 1890.

Gil, Federico. *The Political System of Chile*. Boston, 1966.

______, Ricardo Lagos E., and Henry A. Landsberger, eds. *Chile at the Turning*

Point: Lessons of the Socialist Years, 1970-1973. Philadelphia, 1979.

______, and Charles J. Parrish. *The Chilean Presidential Election of September 4, 1964*. Washington, D.C., 1965.

Gomáriz, Enrique, *et al. Chile bajo la junta (economía y sociedad en la dictadura militar chilena)*. Madrid, 1976.

Gómez, Sergio. *Los empresarios agrícolas*. Santiago, 1972.

Góngora, Mario. *Encomenderos y estancieros*. Santiago, 1970.

______. *Orígen de los inquilinos de Chile central*. Santiago, 1960.

González, Marcial. *Condición de los trabajadores rurales en Chile*. Santiago, 1876.

______. *Estudios económicos*. Santiago, 1889.

González, Pedro Luis. *50 años de labor de la Sociedad de Fomento Fabril*. Santiago, 1933.

González Videla, Gabriel. *Memorias*. 2 vols. Santiago, 1975.

Graham, Richard, "Political Power and Landownership in Nineteenth Century Latin America." In Graham and Peter H. Smith, eds., *New Approaches to Latin American History*. Austin, Tex., 1974.

Grayson, George. "The Chilean Christian Democratic Party: Genesis and Development." Unpublished dissertation in political science, Johns Hopkins University, 1967.

Grunwald, Joseph. "The 'Structuralist' School on Price Stability and Development: The Chilean Case." In Albert O. Hirschman, ed., *Latin American Issues: Essays and Comments*. New York, 1961.

Guilisasti Tagle, Sergio. *Partidos políticos chilenos*. 2nd ed. Santiago, 1964.

Hachette, Domingue. *Aspectos macroeconómicos de la economía chilena: 1973-1976*. Santiago, 1977.

Hakim, Peter, and Giorgio Solimano. *Development, Reform, and Malnutrition in Chile*. Cambridge, Mass., 1978.

Halperin, Ernst. *Nationalism and Communism in Chile*. Cambridge, Mass., 1965.

Haring, C. H. "Chile Moves Left." *Foreign Affairs*, 17 (1938-39), 618-24.

Heise González, Julio. "El caciquismo político en el Período Parlamentario (1891-1925)." In Neville Blanc Renard, ed., *Homenaje al Profesor Guillermo Feliú Cruz*. Santiago, 1973.

______. *La constitución de 1925 y las nuevas tendencias político-sociales*. Santiago, 1951.

______. *Historia de Chile: El Período Parlamentario, 1861-1925*. Santiago, 1974.

Hernández, Silvia. "The Andean Passes between Chile and Argentina: A Study in Historical Geography." Unpublished master's thesis in geography, University of California, Berkeley, 1970.

______. "Transformaciones tecnológicas en la agricultura de Chile central. Siglo xix." *Cuadernos del Centro de Estudios Socioeconómicos*, no. 3 (1966), 1-31.

Hirschman, Albert O. *Journeys toward Progress: Studies of Economic Policy-Making in Latin America*. New York, 1963.

Hofstadter, Richard. *The Age of Reform: From Bryan to F.D.R.* New York, 1956.

Hurtado Ruiz-Tagle, Carlos. *Concentración de población y desarrollo económico: el caso chileno*. Santiago, 1966.

Infante Barros, Marta. *Testigos del treinta y ocho*. Santiago, 1972.

International Labour Office. *Household Income and Expenditure Statistics* (no. 1, 1950-65). Geneva, 1967.

Izquierdo Fernández, Gonzalo. *Un estudio de ideologías chilenas: la Sociedad de Agricultura en el siglo xix*. Santiago, 1968.

______. "Octubre de 1905. Un episodio en la historia social chilena." *Historia*, 13 (1976), 55-96.

Jobet, Julio César. *Ensayo crítico del desarrollo económico-social de Chile*. Santiago, 1955.

Johnson, John J. *Political Change in Latin America: The Emergence of the Middle Sectors*. Stanford, Cal., 1958.

Kaempffer Villagrán, Guillermo. *Así sucedió 1850-1925. Sangrientos episodios de la lucha obrera en Chile*. Santiago, n.d.

Kaufman, Robert R. *The Politics of Land Reform in Chile, 1950-1970*. Cambridge, Mass., 1972.

______. *Transition to Stable Authoritarian-Corporate Regimes: The Chilean Case?* Beverly Hills, Cal., 1976.

Kay, Cristóbal. "Chile: evaluación del programa de reforma agraria de la Unidad Popular." *Desarrollo Económico*, 15, no. 57 (Apr.-June 1975), 85-110.

______. "Chile: The Making of a Coup d'Etat." *Science and Scoiety*, 39 (1975), 3-25.

______. "The Development of the Chilean Hacienda System, 1850-1973." In Kenneth Duncan and Ian Rutledge, eds. *Land and Labour in Latin America: Essays on the Development of Agrarian Capitalism in the Nineteenth and Twentieth Centuries*. Cambridge, Eng., 1977.

Keller, Carlos. *La eterna crisis chilena*. Santiago, 1931.

______. *Un país al garete*. Santiago, 1932.

Kirsch, Henry. *Industrial Development in a Traditional Society: The Conflict between Entrepreneurship and Modernization in Chile*. Gainesville, Fla., 1977.

Lagos, L. Aníbal. *Los ferrocarriles transandinos como instrumentos de confraternidad y expansión económica internacional*. Santiago, 1931.

Lagos Valenzuela, Tulio. *Bosquejo histórico del movimiento obrero en Chile*. Santiago, 1941.

Landsberger, Henry A., and Fernando Canitrot M. *Iglesia, intelectuales, y campesinos*. Santiago, 1967.

______, and Tim McDaniel. "Hypermobilization in Chile, 1970-73." *World Politics*, 28 (1976), 502-41.

Larraín García-Moreno, Jaime. *Mejoramiento de la vida campesina*. Santiago, 1936.

______. *Orientación de nuestra política agraria*. Santiago, 1932.

Larson, Oscar, and Carlos Valenzuela. *Respuesta a d. Rosendo Vidal G. y d. Carlos Aldunate E.* Santiago, 1940.

Lechner, Norbert. *La democracia en Chile*. Buenos Aires, 1970.

Loveman, Brian. *El campesino chileno le escribe a Su Excelencia*. Santiago, 1971.

______. *Chile: The Legacy of Hispanic Capitalism*. New York, 1979.

______. *Struggle in the Countryside: A Documentary Supplement*. Bloomington, Ind., 1976.

______. *Struggle in the Countryside: Politics and Rural Labor in Chile, 1919-1973*. Bloomington, Ind., 1976.

MacEóin, Gary. *Latin America, the Eleventh Hour*. New York, 1962.

Maier, Joseph, and Richard W. Weatherhead, eds. *Politics of Change in Latin America*. New York, 1964.

Malloy, James M., ed. *Authoritarianism and Corporatism in Latin America*. Pittsburgh, 1977.

Mamalakis, Markos. *The Growth and Structure of the Chilean Economy: From Independence to Allende*. New Haven, Conn., 1976.

______, and Clark W. Reynolds. *Essays on the Chilean Economy*. Homewood, Ill., 1965.

Mander, John. *The Unrevolutionary Society: The Power of Latin American Conservatism in a Changing World*. New York, 1969.

Manns, Patricio. *Las grandes masacres*. Santiago, 1972.

______. *Revolución de la escuadra*. Valparaíso, 1972.

Mardones Restat, Jorge. "El problema de la alimentación en Chile." *Revista de Medicina y Alimentación*, 1 (1935), 367-78.

______, and Ricardo Cox. *La alimentación en Chile. Estudios del Consejo Nacional de la Alimentación*. Santiago, 1942.

Marín Vicuña, Santiago. *La valorización territorial de la república*. Santiago, 1918.

Martner, Daniel. *Historia de Chile: historia económica*. Vol. 1. Santiago, 1929.

Mattelart, Armand. "La bourgeoisie à l'école de Lénine: Le 'gremialisme' et la ligne de masse de la bourgeoisie chilienne." *Politique Aujourd'hui*, 1-2 (Jan.-Feb. 1974), 23-46.

______, Carmen Castillo, and Leonardo Castillo. *La ideología de la dominación en una sociedad dependiente. La respuesta ideológica de la clase dominante chilena al reformismo*. Buenos Aires, 1970.

Matthei, Adolfo. *La agricultura en Chile y la política agraria chilena*. Santiago, 1939.

______. *Política agraria chilena*. Padre Las Casas, Chile, 1935.

McBride, George M. *Chile: Land and Society*. Baltimore, 1936.

Menges, Constantine. *Chile's Landowners Associations and Agrarian Reform Politics*. Santa Monica, Cal., 1968.

______. "Public Policy and Organized Business in Chile: A Preliminary Analysis." *Journal of International Affairs*, 20 (1966), 343-65.

Miranda S., Raúl. "La política agraria de la Junta Militar: antecedentes y perspectivas." *Investigación Económica*, 36, no. 2 (Apr.-June 1977), 147-81.

Montero Moreno, René. *La verdad sobre Ibáñez*. Buenos Aires, 1953.

Moran, Theodore H. *Multinational Corporations and the Politics of Dependence: Copper in Chile*. Princeton, N.J., 1974.

Morris, James O. *Elites, Intellectuals, and Consensus: A Study of the Social Question and the Industrial Relations System in Chile*. Ithaca, N.Y., 1966.

Nunn, Frederick M. *Chilean Politics, 1920-1931: The Honorable Mission of the Armed Forces*. Albuquerque, N.M., 1970.

______. *The Military in Chilean History. Essays on Civil-Military Relations, 1810-1973*. Albuquerque, N.M., 1976.

O'Brien, Philip, ed. *Allende's Chile*. New York, 1976.

Olavarría Bravo, Arturo. *Chile bajo la democracia cristiana*. 6 vols. Santiago, 1966-71.

______. *Chile entre dos Alessandri; memorias políticas*. 4 vols. Santiago, 1962.

______. *La cuestión social en Chile*. Santiago, 1923.

Orrego Luco, Luis. *Casa Grande*. 3rd ed. Santiago, 1934.

Orrego Vicuña, Claudio, ed. *Horacio Walker y su tiempo*. Santiago, 1976.

Ortúzar Escobar, Enrique. "La nueva institucionalidad chilena." *Cuadernos del Instituto de Ciencia Política* (Universidad Católica de Chile), no. 1 (1976).

Pace, Thomas A. *Chilean Social Laws*. Reprinted from *American Federationist*, n.d.

Pan American Union. *Constitution of the Republic of Chile, 1925*. Washington, D.C., 1957.

Parrish, Charles J., Arpad von Lazar, and Jorge Tapia-Videla. *The Chilean Congressional Elections of March 7, 1965: An Analysis*. Washington, D.C., 1965.

Partido Socialista de Chile. *Cartilla sindical campesina*. Santiago, 1940.

______. *El Partido Socialista y su 6° Congreso Ordinario*. Santiago, 1940.

______. Comité Central Ejecutivo. *Tesis sindical presentada al V Congreso del Partido celebrado en Santiago en diciembre de 1938*. Santiago, 1939.

Pascal, Andrés. *Relaciones de poder en una localidad rural*. Santiago, 1968.

Petras, James. *Politics and Social Forces in Chilean Development*. Berkeley, Cal., 1970.

______, and Hugo Zemelman Merino. *Peasants in Revolt: A Chilean Case Study, 1965-1971*, tr. Thomas Flory. Austin, Tex., 1972.

Phelan, John L. *The Kingdom of Quito in the Seventeenth Century: Bureaucratic Politics in the Spanish Empire*. Madison, Wis., 1967.

Pike, Frederick B. "Aspects of Class Relations in Chile, 1850-1960." *Hispanic American Historical Review*, 43 (1963), 14-33.

______. *Chile and the United States, 1880-1962*. Notre Dame, Ind., 1965.

______, and Thomas Stritch, eds. *The New Corporatism: Socio-Political Structures in the Iberian World*. Notre Dame, Ind., 1974.

Pinochet LeBrun, Tancredo. *Inquilinos en el fundo de Su Excelencia*. Santiago, 1916.

Pinto Lagarrigue, Fernando. *Crónica política del siglo xx. Desde Errázuriz Echaurren hasta Alessandri Palma*. Santiago, 1972.

Pinto Santa Cruz, Aníbal. *Chile, un caso de desarrollo frustrado*. Santigao, 1962.

Poblete Troncoso, Moisés. *La organización sindical en Chile*. Santiago, 1926.

______. *El problema de la producción agrícola y la política agraria nacional*. Santiago, 1919.

Primer Congreso Nacional de Alimentación Popular. Antecedentes y trabajos. Valparaíso, 1932.

Primera semana social agrícola. Santiago, 1913.

Quiros-Varela, Luis. "Agrarian Policies in Chile: Stagnation, Reform and Counter-

Reform in the Countryside." Unpublished dissertation in political science, University of North Carolina, Chapel Hill, 1979.

Ramírez Necochea, Hernán. *Historia del movimiento obrero en Chile. Antecedentes, siglo xix*. Santiago, 1956.

Reinsch, Paul S. "Parliamentary Government in Chile." *American Political Science Review*, 3 (1909), 507-38.

Remmer, Karen L. "The Timing, Pace and Sequence of Political Change in Chile: 1891-1925." *Hispanic American Historical Review*, 57 (1977), 205-30.

Representación del pueblo de Santiago al Congreso de la República con motivo del proyecto de impuesto al ganado arjentino. Santiago, 1888.

Resúmen de la hacienda pública de Chile desde 1833 hasta 1914. London, 1914.

Ringlien, Wayne. "Economic Effects of Chilean National Expropriation Policy on the Private Commercial Farm Sector, 1964-69." Unpublished dissertation in economics, University of Maryland, 1971.

Rivas Vicuña, Manuel. *Historia política y parlamentaria de Chile*. 3 vols. Santiago, 1964.

Ross Edwards, Agustín. *Chile, 1851-1910: sesenta años de cuestiones monetarias y financieras y de problemas bancarios*. Valparaíso, 1910.

______. *El impuesto al ganado arjentino: folleto de actualidad*. Valparaíso, 1888.

Rowe, Leo Stanton. *The Early Effects of the European War on Chile*. New York, 1918.

Roxborough, Ian, Philip O'Brien, and Jackie Roddick. *Chile: The State and Revolution*. New York, 1977.

Ruiz Tagle, Jaime. "El nuevo plan laboral: ¿libertad o liberalismo?" *Mensaje*, 28, no. 281 (Aug. 1979), 433-37.

Rumbold, Horace. *Reports by Her Majesty's Secretaries . . . on the Manufactures, Commerce, etc*. London, 1876.

Sánchez C., Elías. "Plan laboral y reacciones." *Mensaje*, 28, no. 277 (Mar.-Apr. 1979), 101-4, 172.

Sarfatti, Magali. *Spanish Bureaucratic-Patrimonialism in America*. Berkeley, Cal., 1966.

Sater, William F. "Economic Nationalism and Tax Reform in Late Nineteenth-Century Chile." *The Americas*, 33 (1976), 311-35.

Schneider, Teodoro. *La agricultura en Chile en los últimos cincuenta años*. Santiago, 1904.

Sepúlveda, Sergio. *El trigo chileno en el mercado mundial*. Santiago, 1956.

Shafer, R. J. *The Economic Societies in the Spanish World (1763-1821)*. Syracuse, N.Y., 1958.

Sigmund, Paul E. *The Overthrow of Allende and the Politics of Chile, 1964-1976*. Pittsburgh, 1977.

Smith, Henry Nash. *Virgin Land: The American West as Symbol and Myth*. New York, 1950.

Snow, Peter. "The Radical Parties of Chile and Argentina." Unpublished dissertation in political science, University of Virginia, 1964.

______. *El radicalismo chileno: historia y doctrina del Partido Radical*. Buenos Aires, 1972.

Sotomayor, A. "La vida que pasa." *Sucesos: Semanario de Actualidades*, año XX, no. 1023 (May 4, 1922), unpaginated.

Stallings, Barbara. *Class Conflict and Economic Development in Chile, 1958-1973*. Stanford, Cal., 1978.

Stanfield, David. "The Chilean Agrarian Reform, 1975." University of Wisconsin, Land Tenure Center, *Newsletter*, no. 52 (Apr.-June 1976), 1-13.

Stavenhagen, Rodolfo. "Seven Fallacies about Latin America." In James Petras and Maurice Zeitlin, eds. *Latin America: Reform or Revolution*? Greenwich, Conn., 1968.

Steenland, Kyle. *Agrarian Reform under Allende: Peasant Revolt in the South*. Albuquerque, N.M., 1977.

Stein, Stanley J. "The Tasks Ahead for Latin American Historians." *Hispanic American Historical Review*, 41 (1961), 424-33.

______, and Barbara H. Stein. *The Colonial Heritage of Latin America*. New York, 1970.

Sternberg, Marvin J. "Chilean Land Tenure and Land Reform." Unpublished dissertation in economics, University of California, Berkeley, 1962.

Stevenson, John Reese. *The Chilean Popular Front*. Philadelphia, 1942.

Stewart, Watt. *El trabajador chileno y los ferrocarriles del Perú*. Santiago, 1939.

Subercaseaux Browne, Julio. *Reminiscencias*. Santiago, 1976.

Super, Richard R. "The Chilean Popular Front Presidency of Pedro Aguirre, 1938-1941." Unpublished dissertation in history, Arizona State University, 1975.

Swift, Jeanine. *Agrarian Reform in Chile: An Economic Study*. Lexington, Mass., 1971.

Tapia-Videla, Jorge. "The Chilean Presidency in a Developmental Perspective." *Journal of Inter-American Studies and World Affairs*, 19 (1977), 451-81.

Tarr, Terence S. "Military Intervention and Civilian Reaction in Chile, 1924-1936." Unpublished dissertation in history, University of Florida, 1960.

Thiesenhusen, William C. *Chile's Experiments in Agrarian Reform*. Madison, Wis., 1966.

Thomas, Jack Ray. "Marmaduke Grove: A Political Biography." Unpublished dissertation in history, Ohio State University, 1962.

______. "The Socialist Republic of Chile." *Journal of Inter-American Studies*, 6 (1964), 203-20.

Torres Orrego, Guillermo. *El Comisariato General de Subsistencias y Precios de la República*. Santiago, 1947.

Touraine, Alain. *Vida y muerte del Chile popular*, tr. Aurelio Garzón del Camino. Mexico City, 1974.

Ulrich B., Kurt. *Algunos aspectos del control del comercio en la agricultura chilena, 1950-58*. Santiago, 1964.

Universidad de Chile, Instituto de Economía. *Family Income and Expenditures in Greater Santiago: Experimental Survey*. Santiago, 1966.

______. *Subdivisión de la propiedad agrícola en una región de la zona central de Chile*. Santiago, 1960.

______. *La tributación agrícola en Chile, 1940-1958. Algunas implicaciones económicas del sistema tributario chileno*. Santiago, 1960.

Urzúa Valenzuela, Germán. *Los partidos políticos chilenos*. Santiago, 1968.

———, and Anamaría García Barzelatto. *Diagnóstico de la burocracia chilena (1818-1969)*. Santiago, 1971.

Valenzuela, Arturo. *The Breakdown of Democratic Regimes: Chile*. Baltimore, 1978.

———. *Political Brokers in Chile: Local Government in a Centralized Polity*. Durham, N.C., 1977.

———, and J. Samuel Valenzuela, eds. *Chile: Politics and Society*. New Brunswick, N.J., 1976.

———, and J. Samuel Valenzuela. "Visions of Chile." *Latin American Research Review*, 10, no. 3 (Fall 1975), 155-75.

Valenzuela, O. "Condiciones de vida de los campesinos." *Mensaje*, 26, no. 260 (July 1977), 354-58.

Varas, José Miguel. *Chacón*. Santiago, 1968.

Vargas Cariola, Juan Eduardo. "La Sociedad de Fomento Fabril, 1883-1928." *Historia*, 13 (1976), 5-53.

Véliz, Claudio. "La mesa de tres patas." *Desarrollo Económico*, 3 (1963), 231-48.

———, ed. *Obstacles to Change in Latin America*. London, 1965.

———. "Obstacles to Reform in Latin America Today." *The World Today*, 19, no. 1 (Jan. 1963), 18-29.

———, ed. *The Politics of Conformity in Latin America*. New York, 1967.

Venegas, Alejandro (pseud., Dr. Julio Valdés Cange). *Sinceridad: Chile íntimo en 1910*. Santiago, 1910.

Villanueva, Víctor. *Modelo contrarrevolucionario chileno*. Lima, 1976.

Villela, Hugo. "Autoritarismo y tenencia de la tierra: Chile 1973-1976." *Revista Mexicana de Sociología*, 41, no. 1 (Jan.-Mar. 1979), 205-41.

Viviani Contreras, Guillermo. *Sociología chilena*. Santiago, 1926.

Vuskovic, Pedro, *et al*. "La política económica en Chile de 1970 a 1977." *Investigación Económica*, 36, no. 2 (Apr.-June 1977), 9-181.

Walker Linares, Francisco. *Panorama del derecho social chileno*. Santiago, 1950.

Wright, Thomas C. "Agriculture and Protectionism in Chile, 1880-1930." *Journal of Latin American Studies*, 7, no. 1 (May 1975), 45-58.

———. "Origins of the Politics of Inflation in Chile, 1888-1918." *Hispanic American Historical Review*, 53 (1973), 239-59.

———. "The Politics of Agrarian Reform in Chile, 1919-1940." Pacific Coast Council on Latin American Studies, *Proceedings*, 6 (1977-79), 59-71.

Yeager, Gertrude M. "The Club de la Unión and Kinship: Social Aspects of Political Obstructionism in the Chilean Senate, 1920-1924." *The Americas*, 35 (1979) 539-72.

Young, Jordan M. "Chilean Parliamentary Government, 1891-1924." Unpublished dissertation in political science, Princeton University, 1953.

Zeitlin, Maurice, and Richard Earl Ratcliff. "Research Methods for the Analysis of the Internal Structure of Dominant Classes: The Case of Landlords and Capitalists in Chile." *Latin American Research Review*, 10 (1975), 5-61.

Index

A Note on the Author

THOMAS WRIGHT received his Bachelor of Arts degree in 1963 from Pomona College and his master's and doctorate in Latin American history from the University of California at Berkeley. He is currently associate professor and chairman of the Department of History at the University of Nevada, Las Vegas. Professor Wright has lived in Chile and Peru for four years, and has published several scholarly articles on modern Chilean history.